LITERATURE, POLITICS, AND THE ENGLISH AVANT-GARDE

Accounts of the "historical avant-garde" and of "high modernism" often celebrate the former for its revolutionary aesthetics or denigrate the latter for its "proto-fascist" politics. In *Literature, Politics, and the English Avant-Garde*, Paul Peppis shows how neither interpretation explains the writings of avant-gardists in early twentieth-century England. Peppis reads texts by writers like Ford Madox Ford, Wyndham Lewis, Dora Marsden, and Ezra Pound alongside English political discourse between the death of Victoria and the end of the Great War. He traces the impact of nation and empire on the avant-garde, arguing that Vorticism, England's foremost avant-garde movement, used nationalism to advance literature and avant-garde literature to advance empire. Peppis's study demonstrates that these ambitions were enabled by the period's conception of nationality as an essence and construct. By recovering these neglected aspects of avant-garde politics, Peppis's book opens important new avenues for assessing modernist politics after the war.

PAUL PEPPIS is Assistant Professor of English at the University of Oregon. He has written a range of articles and reviews on modernist authors, modernist theories of race, and modernism and the Great War, in journals such as *Modernism/Modernity*, *Modern Philology*, *Twentieth-Century Literature*, and the *Yale Journal of Criticism*.

LITERATURE, POLITICS, AND THE ENGLISH AVANT-GARDE

Nation and Empire, 1901–1918

PAUL PEPPIS

CAMBRIDGE
UNIVERSITY PRESS

PUBLISHED BY THE PRESS SYNDICATE OF THE UNIVERSITY OF CAMBRIDGE
The Pitt Building, Trumpington Street, Cambridge, United Kingdom

CAMBRIDGE UNIVERSITY PRESS
The Edinburgh Building, Cambridge, CB2 2RU, UK http://www.cup.cam.ac.uk
40 West 20th Street, New York, NY 10011–4211, USA http://www.cup.org
10 Stamford Road, Oakleigh, Melbourne 3166, Australia

First published 2000

Printed in the United Kingdom at the University Press, Cambridge

Typeset in Baskerville 11/12.5pt [VN]

A catalogue record for this book is available from the British Library

Library of Congress Cataloguing in Publication data

Peppis, Paul, 1962–
Literature, politics, and the English avant garde: nation and empire, 1901–1918 / Paul Peppis.
p. cm.
Based on the author's thesis (University of Chicago)
Includes bibliographical references and index.
ISBN 0 521 66238 9 (hardback)
1. English literature – 20th century – History and criticism. 2. Politics and literature – Great Britain – History – 20th century. 3. Literature, Experimental – Great Britain – History and criticism. 4. Lewis, Wyndham, 1882–1957 – Criticism and interpretation. 5. National characteristics, English, in literature. 6. Great Britain – Politics and government – 1901–1936. 7. Modernism (Literature) – England. 8. Nationalism in literature. 9. Imperialism in literature. 10. Vorticism – England. I. Title.
PR478.P64P46 2000
82009'358–dc21 99–22648
CIP

ISBN 0 521 66238 9 hardback

For Tess, Cole, and Libby

Contents

Illustrations

Acknowledgments

In writing this book my thoughts and words have benefited from the wisdom and support of many. I wish first to thank my advisors at the University of Chicago, Robert von Hallberg and Loren Kruger, for their rigorous criticism, thoughtful advice, and generous encouragement in the early stages of the project. Other colleagues at the University of Chicago aided the evolution of my argument in myriad ways, especially Wayne Booth, Jessica Burstein, Lee Garver, David Kadlec, Mark Morrisson, and members of the Avant-Garde Workshop. At the University of Oregon, Ian Duncan, Karen Ford, John Gage, Dick Stein, and Richard Stevenson provided invaluable commentary and advice as I reconceived and revised the manuscript into its current form. For assistance with research, I am grateful to the Andrew W. Mellon Foundation for a dissertation fellowship, which assisted early on; to the librarians at the Division of Rare and Manuscripts Collections of the Carl A. Kroch Library at Cornell University for guidance and aid in the Ford Madox Ford and Wyndham Lewis Collections; and to the University of Oregon for a New Faculty Research Award, which helped bring the research to completion. My thanks to my anonymous readers at Cambridge University Press, and to my editor Ray Ryan, copy-editor Rachel Coldicutt, and publishing assistant, Jenny Landor, for their consistent aid, good humor, and hard work during the process to publication. I am especially indebted to Omar S. Pound, the Estate of Wyndham Lewis, the Estate of Mrs. G. A. Wyndham Lewis, and the Wyndham Lewis Memorial Trust for their generous permission to quote from the texts of Wyndham Lewis, (c) The Wyndham Lewis Memorial Trust, a registered Trust in the United Kingdom and to reproduce graphics featured in *BLAST*, (c) the Estate of Mrs. G. A. Wyndham Lewis, by permission. Earlier versions of two chapters have been published previously. Chapter 4 is an expanded version of "'Surrounded by a Multitude of other Blasts': Vorticism and the Great War," which originally appeared in *Modernism / Modernity* 4.2 (April 1997): 39–66, (c) 1997, The Johns Hopkins University Press. Chapter 5 is an expanded version of "Anti-Individualism and the Fictions of National Character in Wyndham Lewis's *Tarr*," which originally appeared in *Twentieth Century Literature* 40.2 (Summer 1994): 226–55. I am grateful to The Johns Hopkins University Press and to William McBrien, editor of *Twentieth Century Literature*, respectively, for permission to reproduce these essays.

To David Thompson, heartfelt thanks for incomparable hours of comment and debate. To Alex, Anne, and Phil, much love for years of faith and support. To Susy and Jack, love and thanks for interest, openness, and generosity. My deepest gratitude and love to Tess, Cole, and, above all, my wife, Libby Wadsworth, who has, throughout this long and often arduous process, shown her characteristic good humor, common sense, and commitment. Without her faith and friendship this book would never have been conceived, much less completed.

INTRODUCTION

Nations, empires, and the historical avant-garde

> I came to the conclusion that, however good a "Pole," a stray German, Lapp, Esquimau or other dim and hyperborean personage who had found his way to these parts might become, it took an authentic Slav to make a real "Pole."
>
> Wyndham Lewis, "The 'Pole'" (1909), 218

> Once this consciousness towards the new possibilities of expression in present life has come . . . it will be more the legitimate property of Englishmen than of any other people in Europe.
>
> "Manifesto," *BLAST* (1914): 41

Literature, Politics, and the English Avant-Garde concerns the persistent and thorny problem of modernist politics. Not only did a number of (mostly male) modernist writers from Britain and America produce literary and polemical works in which readers have identified "reactionary" or "protofascist" tendencies (aggression, elitism, racism, anti-Semitism, misogyny, homophobia);[1] not only were some attracted to, or even collaborators with, mid-century Europe's various radical right-wing political movements; but evidence of such attitudes in the works and lives of these writers – T. S. Eliot, Wyndham Lewis, and Ezra Pound in particular – has spawned one of the longest-lived and most contentious arguments in the history of the study of modernism in Britain and America. For over sixty years it has raged, at least since the publication of Lewis's somewhat enthralled study of Hitler and "Hitlerism" in 1931.[2] The intensity has ebbed and flowed, heating up in the face of Pound's wartime radio broadcasts from Italy and his subsequent receipt of the Bollingen Prize for the *Pisan Cantos* in 1949, dying down with the academic ascension of Eliot, New Criticism, and the autotelic aesthetic object in the fifties and sixties. Through the seventies, eighties, and nineties, it has flared again, fueled by demographic changes in the academy and the rise of critical and theoretical methodologies responsive to questions of context, psychology, and power. Throughout partisans and opponents have wrangled over what should be done about these politics; how their presence should affect our judgments of these writers and their works; what they should tell us more generally about modernism as a cultural and political movement.[3]

These problems invite interest in part because they remain unsettled, still nagging, regularly provoking new passion and anger. But some rather puzzling rhetorical tendencies recurring in the debate command particular attention. On one side, arguments motivated to expose and condemn modernist elitism, racism, and totalitarianism sometimes become totalizing and reductive, showing excessive indignation and contempt. On the other, arguments motivated to justify and praise modernist artistic innovations sometimes become aestheticizing, showing excessive disregard for questions of context and politics, while those aiming to explain the modernists' later politics sometimes become defensive and apologetic, tending toward special pleading and denial. This study begins with the assumption that the perseverance and the peculiarity of these debates has as much to do with us, our politics, and the way we construe the politics of modernism, as it has to do with what "reactionary" modernists originally thought and wrote.[4]

To avoid as far as possible the snares of condemnation and apology, this study takes as its field of inquiry a body of modernist politics that does not clearly fit the reigning terms of discussion. Its topic is not modernist anti-Semitism or fascist modernism. Nor is its tack to focus on those works in which reactionary politics and anti-Semitic animus are most often identified (Lewis's political tracts of the thirties, Pound's radio broadcasts or middle *Cantos*, Eliot's passing references to Jews or oblique comments on *L'Action française*, the French royalist movement led by Charles Maurras). I'm interested in the politics of modernism *before* any of these works were produced, before the Great War, when these writers were actively participating in that unprecedented international movement of artistic, social, and political experiment now known as the "historical avant-garde" and often celebrated for its more progressive art and political intentions.[5] I concur with an increasing number of analysts that credible accounting of modernist politics after the Great War must begin with an examination of those the avant-gardists supported before it.[6]

Literature, Politics, and the English Avant-Garde attempts to resist the temptation of anachronistically reading modernist statements about politics and aesthetics before the Great War through the lens of those made after it and thereby finding (not very surprisingly) that the early politics and aesthetics were, in effect, always already fascist.[7] By taking more seriously the avant-gardists' original claims about their political ambitions and the political significance of their works, and by contextualizing those claims in terms of the broad body of public discourse they originally engaged,[8] this study finds a politics and an aesthetics more complex and conflicted than many influential "political" analyses recognize.[9] I hope to show that these findings have significant implications for the way we understand the reputations of writers like Eliot, Lewis, and Pound, the politics of the avant-garde, modernist notions of race and gender, modernism's post-war politics, and the ways these authors and topics have been institutionalized in the academy.

The decade before the Great War witnessed an unprecedented surge of artistic activity across Europe. This phenomenon of the artistic avant-garde achieved a kind of cultural "critical mass" sometime between 1907, when Pablo Picasso painted *Les Demoiselles d'Avignon*, and 1909, when the French journal *Le Figaro* published F. T. Marinetti's first Futurist manifesto. Inspired by a Spanish painter and an Italian poet working in Paris, the avant-garde was cosmopolitan from inception. A generation of young artists and writers, sympathetic to aesthetic and social revolution and stimulated by the Cubists' experimental painting style and the Futurists' promotional and performative strategies, rapidly initiated their own rebellious art movements in nearly every European metropolis. In the next three or four years, self-consciously "modern" art and literature spread through Europe as avant-garde groups sprang up in London, Milan, Moscow, Munich, and Vienna.[10]

Since the early twentieth century, discussions of this international avant-garde have often focused on radical artists' efforts to alter the established relations between "art" and "life," in which the former is understood as detached from the latter. The Futurist painters insist in their first "Technical Manifesto" (1910) that they will "at any price re-enter into life."[11] The young Swiss writer Blaise Cendrars asserts in a 1913 manifesto that "[l]iterature is a part of life."[12] In a 1914 polemic, Lewis, then a leading spokesman for advanced English art, explains that "[i]t is necessary, in the profoundest sense, that humanity should live, and place their living above everything else, for Art to arrive at its goal."[13] Scholars like Peter Bürger, Terry Eagleton, Andreas Huyssen, and Marjorie Perloff have followed the avant-gardists' lead, emphasizing in various ways this desire to insert art into life and thereby transform both.[14] Perloff joins Raymond Williams in pointing out that the avant-garde's innovative literary form, the art manifesto, expresses that desire by appropriating a political genre and adapting it for revolutionary artistic purposes.[15] Bürger maintains that while the avant-gardists "failed" to achieve this revolutionary insertion of art into life, thwarted by the bourgeois institutionalization of aesthetic autonomy, they did succeed in revolutionizing art: by putting "life" into their art through the techniques of collage, often cited as the avant-garde's central artistic innovation, they challenged the status of the "aesthetic" as a category above and beyond "the praxis of life."[16] Bürger's account of failure notwithstanding, Perloff chooses to emphasize in the "formal ruptures" of the collage aesthetic the avant-gardists' most progressive political ambitions, "the larger desire . . . to break down existing economic and political structures and to transcend nationalist barriers."[17]

Perloff's conjunction of cultural internationalism and progressive reform of economic and political structures in her reading of avant-garde collage reveals an interpretive preference that helps explain a tendency common among previous interpretations of the historical avant-garde. While many accounts emphasize that the Europe in which the avant-gardists attempted their progressive transformations of art and life was the bourgeois, capitalist Europe of the late-nineteenth and early twentieth centuries, they often overlook or downplay the fact that the international nation-state system ruled that Europe.[18] Avant-gardist efforts to *épater la bourgeoisie* and undermine the bourgeois institution of art as well as the limits placed on those efforts by that institution have been usefully illuminated. But studies too often undervalue a fact that political historians insistently promote: the nation-state system and its attendant psychological category of nationality and collectivist sentiment of nationalism shaped late-nineteenth and early twentieth-century western history no less than class, democracy, socialism, even capitalism.[19] The age of the avant-garde was also, historians remind us, a moment when the imperial nation-state had become the prevailing category of international order and psychological community. It has been aptly dubbed the Age of Nationalism, the Age of Empire.

Given this historical context, it is unsurprising that the rebellious young artists and writers who were seeking to transform "art" and "life" in the early century deployed the rhetoric of imperialism and exploited the sentiments of nationalism in their polemics and performances. Even the most cursory reading of Italian Futurist and English Vorticist manifestos, for instance, cannot but reveal the centrality of these topics to the avant-gardists' artistic and social ambitions. "We wish to glorify War –

the only health giver of the world – militarism, patriotism," proclaims the "Initial Futurist Manifesto" (1909), "[i]t is in Italy that we launch this manifesto of violence, destructive and incendiary . . . we would deliver Italy from its canker of professors, archaeologists, cicerones and antiquaries."[20] The Futurist painters, their "Technical Manifesto" explains, joined the movement "to protect from certain death the genius of Italian Art."[21] The Vorticists countered the Futurists' formidable international popularity in their quarterly *BLAST* (July 1914) with their own brand of avant-garde patriotism: "BLESS ENGLAND"; the "Modern World is due almost entirely to Anglo-Saxon genius," thus the "consciousness towards the new possibilities of expression in present life" should "be more the legitimate property of Englishmen than of any other people in Europe."[22] These flamboyant proclamations confirm that the historical avant-garde, like western culture more generally during the period, was, as Edward Said puts it, "manifestly and unconcealedly a part" of the "imperial process."[23]

Coming to grips with such blunt nationalism, such bold-faced advocacy of empire in the writings of authors frequently cast as cosmopolitan, progressive, or revolutionary requires understanding the dynamics of cultural competition during the Age of Nationalism. Recovering those dynamics is one of this study's major aims. Tom Nairn's account of the role of "uneven development" in the history of modern nationalism provides a useful opening. During the nineteenth century, as Nairn explains, the spread of an acute consciousness of uneven development among nation-states compelled "under developed" states "to attempt radical, competitive short-cuts in order to avoid being trampled over or left behind" by the extreme economic and technological transformations being brought about by the world's "developed" nations.[24] Driven by the competitive dynamics of this disproportionate system, "under developed" states used nationalism to help "propel themselves forward." Nairn contends that this use of nationalism was typically motivated by a sense of uneven economic and industrial development.[25] My analysis complements Nairn's by showing that many of the young artists and writers who constituted Europe's avant-garde movements, especially those from Italy and England (for reasons this study will elucidate), shared an acute sensitivity to evidence of uneven development in the cultural sphere.[26] The avant-gardists responded to their perceptions of cultural inequality in much the same way that European governments responded to perceived economic, industrial, and military inequalities: they would bring nationalism to the aid of advanced art.[27]

Benedict Anderson has established the crucial role that print capitalism played in the rise of modern nationalism, especially in producing the "imagined community" of the nation and in fostering sentiments of national loyalty.[28] He argues that the nineteenth century's imperial monarchies used technologies of print capitalism to promote nationalism and thereby legitimate their imperial dynasties in the eyes of their domestic and colonial publics, in his words, "stretching the short, tight skin of the nation over the gigantic body of the empire."[29] Anderson terms this state strategy "official nationalism." I argue that avant-garde movements followed the lead of Europe's governments, appropriating the techniques of print capitalism and exploiting popular nationalist sentiments to advance the cause of new literature and art.[30]

During the Age of Empire, moreover, Europe's self consciously oppositional art movements worked to support, even lead, the official nationalist strategy that their governments were pursuing: the promotion of national prestige, a prestige that advanced artists and writers conceived as being not only military, imperial, and economic in nature, but cultural as well. Despite their commitments to transform established art and political institutions, despite their cosmopolitan interest in participating in an international effort of aesthetic and social revolution, Europe's avant-garde art groups were particularly motivated to elevate their own nation's prestige. Ernest Gellner has emphasized the central role that modern educational institutions played in producing national consciousness and loyalty.[31] Anderson and Said have studied the role of the novel in the process.[32] I show that avant-garde arts and polemics also contributed. Opposed in principle to state-controlled institutions of education and conventional forms of literature and art, however, the avant-gardists offered their artistic products as an alternative mode for defining, transforming, and promoting national culture.

Given the avant-gardists' historical context and the content of their polemics then, it is surprising that literary scholars have only recently begun paying serious attention to the significance for the history of the avant-garde of the nation-state system, the dynamics of cultural competition under that system, the institutions of empire, and the cult of the nation.[33] In the case of Vorticism, the group Lewis and Pound led, the defining roles of Vorticist aesthetics and interpersonal and artistic politics in the emergence of modern Anglo-American art and literature have been thoroughly examined. The effects of nationalist politics and international affairs on English avant-garde aesthetics and politics have not. So while studies correctly argue that the founding of Vorticism should be understood as a reaction against Futurist successes in England, they almost wholly neglect the fact that the reaction was comparably conditioned by period conceptions of Britain's (failing) international status and Italy's (expansionistic) imperial activities, and above all, by a commitment among both English and Italian avant-gardists to use modern writing and art to advance empire.[34] And while subsequent studies aim at ever more subtle understandings of the interactions between the Futurists and Vorticists, they view those relations almost exclusively through the lens of aesthetics, finding the basis of English modernist literary practice in Marinetti's *Parole in libertà* and *L'arte di far manifesti* or in the Vorticist theories and literary works of Lewis and Pound.[35] As this study shows, however, English avant-garde theory and aesthetic practice before the "high" modernist years *entre deux guerres* were structured at least as strongly by avant-gardist desires to achieve international success and defend national prestige.

Indeed, historians of twentieth-century Britain remind us that in prewar England, where Vorticism was born, political and cultural circumstances intensified both international ambition and national identification.[36] During the Edwardian and Georgian periods profound changes were occurring in the British empire's international status and in the way the English perceived it. In the political realm, English women and men were coming to recognize that their nation had moved from its nineteenth-century position as the world's supreme imperial and economic power to its early twentieth-century position as one among a number of competing powers. Looking toward the Continent, they confronted a German-backed annexation by Austria-Hungary of the Balkan provinces Bosnia and Herzegovina, a naval build-up and increasing population in Germany, and Italian and German moves to expand their imperial possessions;[37] while at home, they were witnessing the "strange death" of Liberal England, with all its indications of internal instability and decline: the Suffragette movement, trade union activism, parliamentary crises, working-class agitation, Irish rebellion, unemployment, rising poverty.[38]

And, if in the political realm the English were confronted with increasing evidence of national decline, in the cultural realm they were encountering formidable evidence of defeat: a proliferation of new European artistic and philosophical movements, a marked increase in Paris's influence on Europe's cultural activities, a domestic artistic community seemingly unable to compete with its European counterparts, and a generation of young English artists, writers, and critics who flocked to the Continent or embraced new European cultural movements rather than the literature, art, and philosophy of their own country. Combined with the prevailing intellectual view, codified by Matthew Arnold nearly half a century earlier, that the English "spirit" was essentially practical, provincial, even philistine, these indications of cultural imbalance magnified concerns over national decline and aspirations to international success, especially among ambitious writers, artists, and intellectuals. I read the works of England's avant-gardists as very specific responses to these anxieties and ambitions and to the authority of the Arnoldian account of English culture. Accordingly, this study takes as its principal evidence avant-gardist expressions of nationalism, analyses of nationality, and assertions of imperial ambition. Its contextualization of that evidence in terms of general Edwardian and Georgian discourse on the topics, especially concerning the interests and activities of Britain and its primary competitors (Germany in the imperial realm, the "Latin" nations of France and Italy in the cultural) sheds important light on the evolution of modernism in Britain and its complex relations to the evolution of modern nationalism in Britain and Europe generally.

This study treats the political engagements of numerous players (well known and not) active in the English cultural sphere during the years leading up (and in) to the Great War. Some, like Huntly Carter, Ford Madox Ford, Henri Gaudier-Brzeska, R. B. Cunninghame Graham, W. H. Hudson, James Joyce, J. M. Kennedy, Dora Marsden, Ezra Pound, George Bernard Shaw, and Helen Saunders receive sustained attention. Others, like Clive Bell, Arnold Bennett, Robert Bridges, Rupert Brooke, G. K. Chesterton, T. E. Hulme, F. T. Marinetti, John Middleton Murry, Alfred Orage, and H. G. Wells appear more briefly. Playing a particularly dominant role, though, is Wyndham Lewis. He bulks large in this reconsideration of avant-garde politics and modern nationalism not simply because of his alleged centrality in the phenomenon of "fascist" or "reactionary" modernism after the Great War. Of all the artists and writers who participated in England's avant-garde scene and in the development of modernist doctrine and practice before the war, he engaged most consistently the relations between nation and avant-garde, the competing claims of nationalism and internationalism in the activities of advanced art movements, and the role of national avant-gardes in the promotion of imperial prestige. Moreover, his typically Edwardian fascination with the phenomenon of "national character" – its complicated role enabling *and* constraining the activities of nations and national art movements – illuminates the complex of assumptions and expectations that underlay and structured the ways Edwardians and Georgians – even aggressive skeptics like Lewis – understood the world in which they lived and experienced national ambitions and anxieties.[39]

These views on national character also encourage some reconsideration of the familiar picture of Lewis and his closest comrades as essentially essentialists.[40] The first three chapters together argue that in the years before and during the Great War, numerous writers, especially Lewis and others nearest to him, wrestled with the notion that persons and nations have a fixed core identity. Even as their works reveal investments in conventional notions of racial and national hierarchy and determinism, they fitfully articulate a vision of national identity as a cultural construct, susceptible to modification by cultural training and individual will. This conception of nationality as (alternately) essence and construct underwrote the greatest (and for us perhaps paradoxical) ambition of England's self-consciously "advanced" writers and artists before the war: to create in England an imperialist avant-garde art group. The arrival of that group was boisterously proclaimed in the Vorticist movement's celebrated and patriotic journal, *BLAST* (Summer 1914).

As central to this study as any particular writer or artist, indeed, are the avant-garde magazines and movements so active and influential during the period. Numerous works and debates of early modernism originally appeared in these periodicals, contributing to and conditioned by their particular cultural and political policies. Because these reviews played such a crucial role in the promotion of avant-garde movements and in the early institutionalization of modernism, they serve as primary subjects and textual sources here. Each chapter focuses on and draws its principal evidence from a single modernist magazine at the moment of its greatest cultural influence, and the group or movement most closely associated with it. Chapter 1 examines *The English Review* of 1908–10 and the "Impressionist" writers affiliated with its editor, Ford Madox Ford. Chapter 2 studies Alfred Orage's "Independent" socialist organ *The New Age* during 1910–12 and its loose federation of radical left-wing intellectuals. Chapters 3 and 4 treat the Vorticist movement of 1914–15, and the two issues of its official periodical *BLAST*. Chapter 5 considers the radical "Individualists" associated with *The Egoist* of 1914–16, the celebrated anarcho-libertarian political and cultural review edited by the dissident feminist-turned-anarchist philosopher, Dora Marsden. When early modernist works are read in this journalistic context, with special attention paid to the political debates featured in the magazines and the avant-gardists' participation in them, it becomes clear that nation, nationality, and empire were the subjects of continuous, often heated, debate among self-consciously "advanced" writers and artists. And as I hope to show, these debates tell us things about the political history of modernism in Britain, its institutions, and institutionalization that complicate and enrich prevailing accounts.

By setting avant-gardist treatments of nationality, nationalism, and empire in the context of the public arguments they originally engaged (both intellectual and popular), *Literature, Politics, and the English Avant-Garde* makes two broader arguments. First, the conception of nationality as essence and construct was widespread among English intellectuals[41] and had significant repercussions for avant-garde aesthetics and politics. Second, the Vorticists' articulation of an explicitly nationalistic cultural doctrine in *BLAST* brought to the surface the hidden ambition of numerous (perhaps most) English intellectuals before the war: despite lingering commitments to the Arnoldian tradition of cultural internationalism and assertions of political disinterestedness or avant-garde critique, these artists and writers supported the aims of British imperialism, offering their works as a means of helping to consolidate or "revitalize" British power and prestige against rising foreign competition and domestic "degeneration" – a goal roughly consistent with popular patriotism and government policy.[42]

The background of this argument is developed in chapters 1 and 2. The first demonstrates that Ford Madox Ford's illustrious and insistently internationalistic and "disinterested" little magazine, *The English Review*, where the early works of Lawrence, Lewis, and Pound among others first appeared, betrays a nationalistic investment in British imperialism common among Edwardian intellectuals, including *les Jeunes* (as Ford dubbed them).[43] The second chapter shows that popular anxieties of national decline and ambitions for international success conditioned the responses of both older, more self-consciously "patriotic" intellectuals (who opposed increasing international contacts), and those younger and more self-consciously "cosmopolitan" (who advocated increasing such contacts) to evidence of foreign competition, whether in the imperial-military realm or the cultural. That conditioning, chapter 3 demonstrates, shaped the consolidation of Vorticism in 1914 as an explicitly nationalistic and imperialist avant-garde movement.

Yet while *BLAST* identifies Vorticism as an imperialist art movement, it also displays political commitments and national affiliations that oppose such a definition. On one hand, *BLAST*'s manifestos ally Vorticism with the anti-statist "Individualist" movement around Dora Marsden and *The Egoist*. Marsden's movement followed the lead of the German nominalist, Max Stirner, whose anti-liberal tract, *Der Einzige und sein Eigentum* (1844), became a touchstone for Anglo-American anarchists and libertarians soon after its translation into English as *The Ego and His Own* in 1907.[44] The Egoists celebrated the vital and autonomous individual, advocated an anarcho-libertarian politics, and promoted artists, writers, and art movements that manifested an appropriately "individualistic" temper. *The Egoist* implacably assailed the British state and its institutions as unnecessary restrictions on individuality, publishing positive analyses of art exhibits in which Vorticist artists were featured as well as critical and literary works by Pound, Lewis, and other contributors to *BLAST*. The Vorticists repaid the compliment. *BLAST* describes Vorticism as "an art of individuals" that will help "make individuals," and attacks, *à la* Marsden, those British persons and institutions the Vorticists deemed to be obstructing individual vitality and creativity.[45] Yet on the other hand, despite *BLAST*'s nationalistic assertions that the artworks it features display the "most fundamentally English" characteristics, and are thus England's "necessary native art," the majority of its polemical and literary pieces, as well as a number of the visual, were contributed by the movement's three most-celebrated figures, Lewis, Pound, and the sculptor Gaudier-Brzeska, all of whom lacked the pure "English blood" presumably necessary to establish credibility for such a project. By parental lineage, Lewis was Anglo-American (his father born in New York), Pound an American, and Gaudier French. I focus attention on these and other related contradictions, recovering and analyzing their entanglement with period notions of nationality and national competition, their various consequences, as well as what the Vorticists and their contemporaries made of them. For as we will see, the Vorticists were by no means oblivious to the complexity of their position. On the contrary, *BLAST* insists on it, loudly proclaiming Vorticism an anarcho-imperialist movement of vital individuals who have transcended the limits of nationality, even while affirming that Vorticist art is "fundamentally English" and will facilitate the pressing project of revitalizing the ailing empire.[46]

Accounts of modernist politics become unpersuasive, I would argue, when they underestimate or fail to acknowledge that modernism's early politics were not simply "protofascist," displaying certain anticipations of later "reactionary" or "fascist" tendencies (an elitist distance from the masses, a fascination with the charismatic individual, a distrust of parliamentary democracy), but were also, in a sense, anti-fascist, committed to the radical anti-statist politics of anarcho-libertarianism, which opposed in principle the sort of centralized, authoritarian state that would later develop in Hitler's Germany and – to a lesser extent – in Mussolini's Italy.[47] The coexistence of these competing, at times contradictory, political commitments helps explain Raymond Williams's productive observation that "the politics of the avant-garde, from the beginning, could go either way."[48] Mitigating or denying the presence of the radical streak in the early politics of modernism contributes to an appealing though ultimately unsubstantiated view that underwrites the posture of certain analyses that attack (reactionary) modernism as confidently and contemptuously as Pound attacked the world conspiracy of "kike" bankers and arms merchants: namely, that modern left-wing politics are categorically different from those of the right, immune to the temptations of intolerance to which a number of modern right-wing movements and thinkers have succumbed.[49] As this study emphasizes, the political trajectory of modernism had as much to do with its "progressive" commitments to anarchism, individualism, and artistic, social, and political change, as with its "reactionary" commitments to empire, nationalism, and "racial" renewal. To adapt Williams's formulation, in the beginning, the politics of the avant-garde (in England at least), went both ways at once. The failure to acknowledge this uncomfortable fact encourages reducing a deeply conflicted body of political beliefs and utterances to some monolithic and comfortably alien form of fascist reaction.

Once we acknowledge Vorticism's concatenation of seemingly incompatible political aims, in which a nationalistic conviction that empire must be revitalized vies with an anarcho-libertarian belief in the vital individual as the enemy of the (liberal) parliamentary state, we are confronted no longer with the problem of recovering modernism's protofascism, but rather with the need to account for its early anarcho-imperialism. And as this study shows, the Vorticists did not see these political aims as incompatible. Their conjunction was justified in part, we will see, by the period conception of nationality as construct and essence. It was further authorized by the cult of masculine vitality so dominant in prewar Britain, underwriting a vast range of political agendas and movements, including the government's official nationalist doctrine of imperial consolidation and domestic renewal, the Fabian-Socialists' advocacy of gradualist social and political reform led by an elite of "brain workers" and "efficiency men," the Tories' assault on Liberal government policies (especially the effort to implement Irish home rule), the popular press's promotion of worries about national "degeneration" and foreign (primarily German) invasion, as well as the avant-gardists' critique of calcified institutions and worship of the strong individual.[50] As others have demonstrated, the changes racking English society before the war – the rise of movements for working-class, colonial, and women's political rights; the growth of foreign economic, military, and imperial competition; the attendant sense of embattlement on the part of the largely upper-class, male, and English ruling elite and intelligentsia – provoked a masculinist backlash, in which perceived threats to British prestige were gendered female and denigrated, as the traditional upholders and bastions of such prestige were gendered male and celebrated.[51]

One of the histories recovered here is the English avant-garde's difficult effort to position itself as a vital and manly movement for cultural, social, and political renovation, militantly opposed to outdated, decrepit, and unmanly traditions and institutions, while at the same time, countering the accusation "patriotic" guardians of those same institutions kept leveling: that the avant-garde was basically just another effeminate, degenerate rabble (tainted by foreign origin and contact) threatening national "hygiene." This problematic negotiation illuminates both the extent and the limits of avant-gardist complicity in the prevailing politics of the Edwardian and Georgian moments. The Vorticists' embrace of masculine vitality facilitated their program of anarcho-imperialism, at least theoretically. In their eyes the anarchistic opposition to tradition and statist institutions, as well as the nationalist desire to revitalize the ailing empire by reforming English culture (making it "harder" and "colder"), were motivated by the same underlying desire: to defeat the effeminate forces of degeneration and decline (whether of domestic or alien origin), and reinject manly vitality into English art and life. To the extent that they supported the goal of imperial consolidation and bought into the masculinist system of values that underwrote that goal, the Vorticists collaborated, despite noisy rhetoric to the contrary, with the overriding ambitions of the British government and popular press.

But while this subscription to the cult of masculine vitality facilitated the Vorticists' political aims of anarchist revolution and imperial reform on the level of theory, on the level of practice, those aims were more difficult to reconcile. Not only were the avant-garde's experimentalist aesthetics, social non-conformity, and anti-statist politics practically incompatible with state mechanisms of imperial power. In addition, the empire's rulers and their allies in the intelligentsia and press believed that their interests would be better served by promoting a picture of the avant-garde not as part of the solution, but as part of the problem, yet another source or symptom of the alarming national decline the government and its supporters opposed. In the context of prewar England, *BLAST* was therefore unlikely to achieve either of its principal aims: to put English art at the forefront of European culture and to "Vorticize" the British empire.

This predicament instantiates the internal contradiction Renato Poggioli found, over thirty years ago, at the heart of the theory of the avant-garde: the ultimate incompatibility of its simultaneous effort to become, on one hand, the nation's anti-culture, the outsider society of artistic and political antagonism, non-conformity, and critique, and on the other, *the* culture of modernity and/or the future. If the avant-garde succeeds in the former aim how can it achieve the latter? If it succeeds in the latter how can it achieve the former?[52] My analysis confirms that this theoretical doublebind obtained before the Great War in England, when the most rebellious artists like the Vorticists could hope for, as Marinetti's Futurists had demonstrated, was to create a new aesthetic and promotional style, provoke controversy about that style in the press, and achieve a faddish level of public attention (by no means insignificant achievements). But as the Futurist case indicated, no such movement could, practically speaking, either significantly affect the imperial status of its home nation or create a truly populist politico-artistic movement. Try as the avant-gardists might, their achievements, their "conquests," remained primarily in the realms of discourse, performance, and art, enacted on pages of little magazines, in bohemian auditoriums, and on gallery walls.[53] During the *avant guerre*, to borrow Bürger's familiar formulation, the avant-garde's revolutionary effort to insert aesthetics into the "praxis of life" and thereby transform both was only partially successful: it could only "revolutionize" art.[54] In this context, the avant-gardists' fascination with violence, and especially their proclivity to fisticuffs, indicates a physical effort to overcome or deny this limitation.

Still, this study finds at least two ways in which the prewar effort on the part of avant-garde groups like the Vorticists in England and the Futurists in Italy to serve as their respective nations' leading modernist art movements had significant practical effects. First, their self-representations as imperial avant-gardes struggling against each other in the Darwinian realm of international competition actually structured that competition. Chapter 3 traces that structuring both in the Futurists' unprecedentedly successful "conquest" of the European art world and the consolidation of Vorticism in response to the extension of that project into England. Second, in the case of England, where a traditional commitment to cultural internationalism and an investment in the notion of "disinterestedness" had long restrained intellectual embraces of any baldly "partisan" political position, the Vorticists' noisy public promotion of an explicitly nationalist cultural policy helped to legitimate patriotism among an (at least overtly) hesitant intelligentsia. Vorticism thus played a real role in encouraging English intellectuals to greet the advent of European war in August of 1914 by rushing to their nation's cause, in Rupert Brooke's famous phrase (of which he became the national embodiment), "as swimmers into cleanness leaping."[55]

Chapter 4's analysis of the second issue of *BLAST*, the so-called *War Number*, published nearly a year into the Great War (July 1915) and still neglected in favor of its flashier predecessor, finds that during the earliest months of the conflict, in England at least, circumstances changed in such a way as to alleviate significantly the avant-garde's prewar inability to realize its most grandiose political ambitions (other formidable problems arose). In a context where the government was expanding control of public discourse, clamping down on dissent, and promoting an anti-modernist cultural policy,[56] the Vorticists' paradoxical project became considerably more appropriate. By reorienting the foreign target of their opposition from Italian Futurism to Prussian imperialism, the Vorticists could assert that their project was allied with the war effort against Germany. So while in the *avant guerre*, the wars, conquests, and battles the avant-gardists undertook remained metaphorical, always bracketed by quotation marks, the Great War allowed them to participate in an actual military conflict (not simply spectate on one, as Marinetti had at Tripoli and Adrianapolis). Suddenly the war the avant-gardists had so long fantasized was *real*. All they needed to do was convince themselves and their supporters that it was also a war for modernism – not an insignificant task, but one which, we will see, circumstances conspired to advance.

Chapter 4 argues that the dynamic whereby Vorticist doctrine dovetailed with wartime events in such a manner as to newly validate that doctrine, achieves its most intense and revealing expression in

"Vortex Gaudier-Brzeska," the central contribution to the *War Number* of the young French sculptor who was killed in action, June 1915. The "Vortex" is the culminating document of the *War Number*: it extends Vorticism's paradoxical program to its theoretical telos, recording and enacting the glorification of Gaudier-Brzeska in death. By sacrificing his life in the Vorticists' two-front war against Germany and *passéism*, Gaudier provides the ultimate authorization of Vorticist collaboration *and* resistance.

The Vortex's celebration of annihilation as the fullest proof of manly life anticipates, perhaps more than any other evidence one could cite from the early writings of Lewis, Pound, and their comrades, what has come to be called fascist modernism. Klaus Theweleit and others have argued that the German *Freikorps* novels and memoirs of the twenties, for example, similarly fetishize the moment of manly self-sacrifice in the national cause as the ultimate proof of personal and national vitality, a moment that epitomizes the masculinist psychosis of the so-called fascist unconscious.[57] In the context of this study, however, the striking resemblance reinforces two other points. First, the ideology of masculinist vitalism that would come to play such a critical part in the formation of Fascism in Italy, Nazism in Germany, and similarly oriented, if finally less popular, movements in England and France, was as much an inheritance from Europe's prewar political culture and cultural politics as it was a product of the Great War.[58] The death and idealization of "fallen soldiers" like Gaudier and Brooke suggests, indeed, that the Great War itself was the ultimate manifestation of that prewar ideology's internal logic, wherein ideology is relegitimated through the sacrifice of its most heroic agents. Second, avant-gardist investments in the imperial politics and nationalistic psychology of the *avant guerre* played at least as important a role in determining the modernists' post-war political ideals, as did their prewar aesthetics, racial attitudes, or intellectual elitism. Among other things, this study tracks the complicated ways in which the avant-gardists' commitments to nation and empire conditioned their conceptions of art, race, and social hierarchy.

Thus the fifth and final chapter develops the implications of these points for current understandings of modernist aesthetics and theories of group identity by bringing its revisionist analysis to bear on a major modernist novel, Lewis's *Tarr*, completed in November 1915, shortly before his departure for the front. By rereading *Tarr* in the context of *The Egoist*, where it originally appeared, chapter 5 finds, somewhat surprisingly, that Lewis's ungainly, satiric novel carries out a keen fictive critique of Marsden's individualist anarcho-libertarianism, a critique which importantly anticipates Lewis's later role as literary satirist and "enemy" of canonical modernism. Recovering this fictional assault on Egoism also makes clear that *Tarr* marks the point in Lewis's career as avant-gardist when his commitment to aesthetic and political opposition began to outstrip both his idealism about individual creativity and his patriotic investment in British imperialism. This intensification of skepticism regarding individualism and nationalism, the chapter demonstrates, encourages Lewis in *Tarr* to articulate a conception of national character that modifies and complicates the prewar moment's (double) vision of the category as essence and construct. At the heart of *Tarr* is a dark portrayal of human identity as a site of irreducible chaos, a picture that undermines the period's two competing and entangled conceptions of national character, both of which Lewis and numerous of his contemporaries often – sometimes simultaneously – embraced: the racialist view of nationality as an internal and essential category, the result of an "heredity" that fundamentally defines the character of individuals of a particular "race" or nation; and the individualist view of nationality as an external, non-essential category, the result of a restrictive regime of cultural training that persons of sufficient energy, insight, and will can and should overcome. What replaces – or rather supplements – this conception of nationality as essence and construct is a kind of "racial" determinism, if by race we understand not the different and competing (sub)species nineteenth-century racialists believed inhabited the nationalized, Darwinian world, but rather the race *in toto*.

This understanding of race urges further reconsideration of the problem of racism or racial determinism often identified as central to the development of fascist modernism. In certain accounts of modernist "protofascism," Lewis, Pound, Eliot, or others can seem to subscribe, relatively unambiguously, to the hierarchical, polygenic, racialist model of humanity popular among nineteenth-century anthropologists, viewing Jews (or blacks, or women) as permanent members of an alien "race," essentially different from, and lower on the bio-cultural scale than, the manly Aryan (or Nordic, or Anglo-Saxon) race to which Lewis (or Pound, or Eliot) believes he belongs. The first four chapters of this study demonstrate that even as avant-garde writers partake of that view, they also assail it. Chapter 5's analysis of *Tarr* further complicates the picture, indicating that by the early months of the Great War (if not before), English avant-gardist writers were also entertaining a more explicitly universalist brand of "racial" determinism – itself a paradoxical idea if you believe, as some do, that universalism ("all men are created equal") is in some sense antithetical to differential determinism. This study as a whole provides significant evidence, I believe, that at least part of the reason why early century modernists could think in ways that may seem to us deeply incoherent is because these three modes of thought are not nearly as incompatible with or separable from each other as we might like to suppose. Part of what enables their conjunction is the masculinist ideology that underwrites, in one way or another, all three conceptions (even *Tarr*'s universalist racism idealizes the manly courage of an author brave enough to confront humankind's essential ugliness). Part of what enables it is the three conceptions' complex and parasitic entanglement with each other. Thus, for example, all three accounts depend on some form of (masculinist) bio-cultural determinism: that all men are essentially chaotic; that all men are members of distinct "races," each of which has a particular and permanent character; or that all great men are inherently capable of escaping the biological or cultural forces that essentially define all other men.

As this chapter summary indicates, *Literature, Politics, and the English Avant-Garde* is less a work of literary or art criticism or of politico-aesthetic theory than of cultural history. My intention is not to argue for (or against) the aesthetic or political value of English avant-garde writing and art (tasks already performed by others), but to provide a fuller and more historically fine-grained accounting of the ways in which engaged writers and artists participated in and responded to the dynamic politics and political debates occurring in England between the death of Queen Victoria in 1901 and the end of the Great War in 1918. Adopting a methodology suited to its project of recovery and revision, this study employs documentary approaches to history, practicing a historicism that locates avant-garde political texts within the dense and lively public discourse of their period. Numerous such documents – many, now forgotten or neglected by canonical or familiar authors; many, by figures now forgotten or neglected – are examined in the context of the issues and events they originally engaged. I consider not only "literary" texts, like the travel tales of W. H. Hudson, R. B. Cunninghame Graham, and Norman Douglas (discussed in chapter 1) or novels like Joyce's *A Portrait of the Artist as a Young Man* or Lewis's *Tarr* (treated in chapter 5), but also political journalism, newspaper cartoons, art polemics, wartime propaganda, cultural criticism, anthropological studies, and magazine editorials published in avant-garde journals like *The English Review*, *The New Age*, *BLAST*, and *The Egoist* and in popular and mass-market periodicals like *Punch*, the *Times*, and the *Morning Post*. England's avant-garde writers and movements treated these texts and the political positions they articulate as central to their ambitions and achievements; I have taken them at their word, an approach that is also in line with current practices of cultural studies and historicism in modernist studies.

These methods are not intended to access "scientifically" early modernism's "objective existence," however. Needless to say, the sort of archival research and contextual reconstruction carried out here cannot provide unmediated access to the original intentions of the Vorticists, their contemporaries, or to the milieu in which they lived. No brand of historicism can eliminate fully the mediation of current concepts and analytical paradigms. Any late twentieth-century effort to use historicist procedures to question established accounts of the literature and politics of the early century will be shaped by today's academic politics, discourses on modernism, debates on historiography, not to mention such professional requirements as the need to distinguish an individual rhetorical position or establish an academic reputation. I am convinced, nonetheless, that the project of historical recovery *Literature, Politics, and the English Avant-Garde* attempts – limited and provisional though all such efforts must be – not only enriches established accounts of the English avant-garde, Edwardian and Georgian culture, the development of modernist politics, and the involvement of modern literature and art in nationalism and empire, but also helps unsettle the primacy of scholarly constructions ill-suited to register the complexity of literature and politics during the first two decades of the twentieth century.

My overriding effort to reassess the political commitments and gyrations of avant-gardists in early century England is ultimately intended as a means of continuing to open up the study of modernism and modernist politics to new possibilities. I finally hope to make persuasive the claim that once we more fully acknowledge the presence and articulate the significance of the myriad contradictions in modernism's early politics, we will both want and be in a better position to reconsider prevailing assessments of the "reactionary" modernists, especially the development of their political ideas and commitments. Such a reconsideration should also prompt a fuller analysis of the political investments we late twentieth-century academics bring to the study of writers and artists whose politics we do not much like (or like too much), and the ways those investments have over the years conditioned our evaluations.

CHAPTER 1:

Conjuring new character: The English Review, *Wyndham Lewis, and the reconstruction of Englishness*

> He was extraordinary in appearance . . . He seemed to be Russian. He was very dark in the shadows of the staircase. He wore an immense steeple-crowned hat. Long black locks fell from it. His coat was one of those Russian looking coats that have no revers. He had also an ample black cape of the type that villains in transpontine melodrama throw over their shoulders when they say "Ha-ha!" He said not a word.
>
> I exclaimed:
>
> "I don't want any Tzar's diaries. I don't want any Russian revelations. I don't want to see, hear or smell any Slavs." All the while I was pushing him down the stairs. He said nothing. His dark eyes rolled. He established himself immovably against the banisters and began fumbling in the pockets of his cape. He produced crumpled papers in rolls. He fumbled in the pockets of his strange coat. He produced crumpled papers in rolls. He produced them from all over his person – from inside his waistcoat, from against his skin beneath his brown jersey . . . All the time he said no word. I have never known any one else whose silence was a positive rather than a negative quality. At last he went slowly down those stairs. I had the impression that he was not any more Russian. He must be Guy Fawkes.
>
> He had thrust all those rolls into my arms. I went up again into the dining-room and dropped the rolls before Marwood. He looked at one of them for no more than a second and said:
>
> "We are saved."
>
> Ford Madox Ford, *Return to Yesterday* (1932), 389–90

Ford Madox Ford's story of Wyndham Lewis's theatrical arrival in 1909 at the offices of Ford's illustrious literary magazine, *The English Review*, is one of the great origin legends of British modernism. Reading today any of the numerous published versions of Lewis's sudden appearance on the Edwardian stage as a fully realized "avantgardiste," we are meant to recognize a number of portentous beginnings: of a single career, a literary movement, even a cultural epoch. In Ford's most elaborate retelling, this chapter's epigraph, the shocked Edwardian editor recognizes in the arrival of the alien and anarchistic personage on the stairway, the start of literary revolution in England.[1]

I begin with this tale of arrival not only because my book is concerned with the cultural events it announces – the careers of Ford and Lewis, the English avant-garde, British modernism – but also because this chapter examines the stories Lewis gave Ford on that apocryphal day and their role in fashioning the figure of the revolutionary, foreign-seeming avantgardiste who heralds the arrival of modernism in Britain. Since the book as a whole carries out a project of reconstruction and revision, the chapter works to excavate the myth, retrieve its sources, and to re-examine the event it narrates, the characters it portrays, the moment it reports. Because I am especially concerned to chart the (neglected) influences of nation, empire, and nationalism on the formulation of modernist politics, I will pay particular attention to the significance of Ford's representation of Lewis as a figure who appears a Russian anarchist but turns out to be a revolutionary English writer. As we will discover, the reasons behind that writer's particular appearance in the origin myth cast new – and distinctly nationalistic – light on the early formation of the avant-garde and modernism in England.

This chapter starts seeking those reasons by evoking the literary context where Lewis's earliest literary works originally appeared and found their meaning. Beginning with an analysis of Ford's *English Review*, it argues that the journal's voice, aesthetic ideals, and political commitments articulate the paradoxes of Edwardian liberalism. The *Review*'s editorials reveal Ford advocating an ideal of critical "disinterestedness" that draws on Matthew Arnold's universalist conception of "culture" as a category transcending nationality and the practical sphere, but which Ford instead bases on the practical, nationalistic ambition of bolstering Britain's flagging international status.[2] The *Review*'s travel literature is given particular attention because it makes especially clear the journal's participation in patriotic efforts to fix Englishness and better secure empire, because it is the genre in which Lewis first began fashioning his "modern" style and persona, and because it clarifies early avant-gardist involvements with Edwardian nationalism.

This chapter then turns to Lewis's *English Review* stories, the three travel tales that appear in the discovery myth on all those rolls of paper: "The 'Pole'" (May, 1909), "Some Innkeepers and Bestre" (June, 1909), and "Les Saltimbanques" (August, 1909). Reading these stories in the context of the *Review* helps clarify Lewis's early cultural interests and the ways they conditioned his initial literary efforts, as well as how those interests and efforts contributed to the early formulation of English modernism. Lewis's travel stories fitfully imitate, attack, affirm, and revise the literary modes and political ideals being celebrated in Ford's journal as cosmopolitan, civilized, and modern. They are also important literary origins for the general avant-garde project to reform English culture and character that is this book's central concern, a project which would lead Lewis and his collaborators alternately to question and affirm period constructions of national character.

To track the development of Lewis's cultural and political ambitions as his generation of artists and writers gained cultural stature, the chapter concludes by considering his neglected but illuminating comic polemic on sport and English character, "Our Wild Body," published nine months after the *Review* tales in the more programmatically radical *New Age*. This (national) character sketch-cum-cultural manifesto confirms that by 1910 Lewis had begun extending the agenda latent in his travel stories into a broader project to revitalize English character. "Our Wild Body" spurs the over-civilized and repressed English to imitate the more spontaneous, more bodily "Latins" as a means of re(dis)covering their own primitive passions and attachments to the body, violence, and irrationality. While this vital-irrationalist scheme to untame Englishness opposes *The English Review*'s cosmopolitan imperialism in a number of ways, its implied aim of untaming English character, making it healthier, more bodily, more wild, is as patriotic as Ford's, an affinity that reveals a common (Edwardian) politics which, we will see, will have a defining influence on modernist doctrine in England before the Great War.[3]

THE ENGLISH REVIEW AND THE PARADOXES OF EDWARDIAN LIBERALISM

[W]e need a national army, simply because we stand in a different plane of civilisation from almost all our neighbours, and, since we are more peace-loving, since we are more civilised, we must be prepared, for the sake of humanity to be able, not only to maintain ourselves but to maintain the integrity of the nations most allied to us in the love for peace and civilisation. That is . . . the duty of an Imperial race. (editorial, *The English Review* (April 1909): 144)

Ford's self-portrait in the origin myth as the prescient discoverer of the new English writer and the epochal shift he initiates conforms to expectations. We have come to think of him, to borrow Michael Levenson's phrase, as a crucial "link between two generations."[4] He appears most often as the author of an important Edwardian novel whose significance for the history of modernism derives more from his role in facilitating younger writers. After all, he discovered Lawrence, Lewis, and Pound, publishing their first works in *The English Review.* As a literary innovator, Ford seems to have been superseded by his protégés. Ford himself was the progenitor of the portrait. His autobiographical writings evoke the familiar figure. In a 1921 volume of memoirs, Ford describes *The English Review* as "an *aube de siècle* Yellow Book," a "movement-producer" aimed at promoting the art movements of the early twentieth century, just as Arthur Symons's late-Victorian *Yellow Book*, had promoted the Decadent and Symbolist movements of the closing nineteenth.[5] In a 1932 autobiography, Ford justifies his overthrow by *les Jeunes* as a natural and necessary step in a Darwinian struggle of artistic evolution. "That is Nature asserting itself," he writes, "[i]n the end the young cockerels must bring down the father of their barnyard. Without that the arts must stand still."[6] There is certainly truth in this portrait. But it is keyed more to a sense of the position Ford has come to occupy in the history of modernism, than to his position during the Edwardian moment. In mid-1909, however, when Lewis submitted the manuscripts of three comic travel stories for publication in *The English Review*, the journal and its editor *did* occupy, if but for a brief moment, a position at the apex of English intellectual culture, and articulated the paradoxical political, social, and literary standards of liberal England under Edward VII.[7]

Ford's cultural ideals, as expressed in his *Review* editorials, are largely derived from Matthew Arnold's mid-Victorian model of literary liberalism. When Ford writes in an 1909 piece that "The English Review stands for peace, for . . . it is only in times of peace that the arts flourish,"[8] he places British "culture" above its politics and thus returns to an argument Arnold had made over forty years earlier. In the 1860s, Arnold had positioned himself as a moderate but skeptical liberal intellectual. He criticized the Liberal right, which supported imperialism and leaned toward the Tories, by attacking nationalism as provincialism and comparing English culture unfavorably to its classical precursors and continental (especially French) contemporaries; he criticized the Liberal left, which assailed imperialism and advocated social and political reforms to improve the lot of the working classes, by attacking its efforts to inject criticism and art into the "practical" sphere, insisting on culture's position above practical life.

Ford presents *The English Review* as an effort to resuscitate Arnold's dream of an international literary culture detached from what the Victorian had called "the world of catchwords and party habits."[9] "The English Review," Ford's opening editorial puts it, "sets boldly upon its front the words 'No party bias' . . . [W]e are here not to cry out 'Go in this direction,' but simply to point out where we stand."[10] And by describing the *Review* as a literary "meeting-place" in England something like the "Academy . . . of the Immortal Forty" in France,[11] Ford implies that his journal will fill a cultural lacuna Arnold identified nearly half a century earlier. According to the Victorian, the "essential characteristics" of the English "spirit" have always impeded the formation in England of an institution like the French Academy.[12] He identified the English spirit's chief characteristics as "energy and honesty" as opposed to the French spirit's more "Athenian" characteristics of "[o]penness of mind and flexibility of intelligence."[13] Because "[g]enius is mainly an affair of energy," he explained, the energetic and honest English excel in "poetry and science," two fields requiring the "free activity of genius."[14] The French, on the other hand, excel in prose and support an academy because their "national bent" is "towards the things of the mind, towards culture, towards clearness, correctness, and propriety in thinking and speaking."[15] The English spirit's characteristic energy, in Arnold's view, thwarts the development of such Athenian fruits of intelligence: "energy . . . above everything demands and insists upon . . . freedom; entire independence of all authority, prescription, and routine . . . [A] nation whose chief spiritual characteristic is energy, will not be very apt to set up, in intellectual matters, a fixed standard, an authority, like an academy."[16]

Ford characterizes *The English Review* as the sort of elite literary institution his Victorian precursor claimed England could not maintain. Since the "English man of letters . . . has no Academy like that of the Immortal Forty," Ford explains, "[i]t is with the attempt to form some such meeting-place that *The English Review* has set out upon its career."[17] And when he asserts that the *Review* "set out to enjoin upon the Englishman a Critical Attitude,"[18] Ford resurrects Arnold's ideal of the "critical spirit." Defining criticism as "*a disinterested endeavour to learn and propagate the best that is known and thought in the world*,"[19] the Victorian insisted that the English are temperamentally ill-suited to satisfy the ideal. The "spirit" of England's "practical race" deters England's critics from achieving sufficient disinterestedness to "see . . . things as they are" and identify the best that is known and thought in the world.[20] Indeed, it is because English criticism has "so little kept in the pure intellectual sphere, has so little detached itself from practice, has been so directly polemical and controversial, that it has so ill accomplished . . . its best spiritual work."[21] The resulting "provinciality" leads England's critics to mistake their nation for the world, studying only the best that had been known and thought at home, ignoring the rest of the best.[22] Nationalistic fervor, under this view, inhibits cultural progress: "all mere glorification by ourselves of ourselves or our literature . . . is both vulgar, and besides being vulgar, retarding."[23] In response, the Victorian critic recommends a more internationalistic attitude: "[b]y the very nature of things, as England is not all the world, much of the best that is known and thought in the world cannot be of English growth, must be foreign . . . The English critic of literature, therefore, must dwell much on foreign thought."[24] While taking care to note the improbability of realizing the ideal, Ford fashions his journal as the sort of disinterested and internationalistic literary institution Arnold had called for; as its editorials affirm, *The English Review* seeks to speak "from a standpoint . . . as aloof and impartial as is practicable to mortal man"[25] and to promote "a greater comprehension of international characteristics."[26]

The English Review does not exactly fulfill Arnold's critical and cultural ideals, however.[27] For although the *Review* advocated an ideal of cultural cosmopolitanism, publishing texts by a number of European authors, Ford also featured literature particularly motivated to advance English interests; and although Ford cast the *Review* as a politically disinterested journal, with "No party bias," its non-literary second section, "The Month," served primarily as a forum for discussion among the liberal intelligentsia of the moment – Fabians, social imperialists, moderate Labourites, New Liberals. Much of the opening issue (December 1908), for example, is devoted to "the problem of the poor": Ford's own editorial on "The Unemployed," former Scottish Labour Party MP, socialist activist, and colonial adventurer, R. B. Cunninghame Graham's "Aspects of the Social Question," and Georgian poet W. H. Davies's "How It Feels to Be Out of Work." Even Ford's Tory co-editor Arthur Marwood contributed a rather socialistic polemic on how to better the lot of the poor, entitled "A Complete Actuarial Scheme for Insuring John Doe against All the Vicissitudes of Life." And during Ford's thirteen-month stint as editor, the *Review* featured works by a number of celebrated left-wing intellectuals: former Fabian H. G. Wells's *Tono-Bungay*, a satiric novel assailing modern capitalism; Graham's travel tales and essay on social unrest in Spain (September 1909); Fabian leader Sydney Webb's article on "The Economic Aspects of Poor Law Reform" (October 1909); radical Liberal elder Sir Charles Dilke's "Foreign Affairs" piece on Anglo-Russian relations (October 1909); radical journalist Henry W. Nevinson's article in support of militant suffragettes (November 1909); and essays by the New Liberal economist and analyst of imperialism J. A. Hobson, including one on "The Extension of Liberalism" (November 1909).

The *Review*'s appearance in 1908 as a politically liberal periodical reflects a resurgence of English liberalism following the Anglo-Boer war that swept the Liberal Party, after eleven years as the opposition, into governmental control in the victory of 1906. Under the leadership of the so-called New Liberals, men like H. H. Asquith and R. B. Haldane who favored a strong state and a strong empire, the Liberal government worked to defend the imperialist mission of the English nation, while extending the institutions of a progressive English state: they established a school meal program (1906) and a school medical service (1907), guaranteed miners an eight-hour day (1908), instituted an old-age pension system (1908), reformed the structure of the welfare bureaucracy (1909), and improved working conditions in factories (1909).[28] And because the Tory members of the House of Commons held only 157 seats to the Liberals' 377, Liberal control went relatively unchallenged, at least at first.

Frustrated by the Liberals' zeal yet unable to restrain their reforms in the House of Commons, the Tory leadership began encouraging the land-owning aristocrats in the House of Lords to thwart Liberal legislation. The Lords thus defeated an education bill and a plural voting bill (1906), a series of land reform bills (1907), and a new licensing bill (1908). The tension between Liberals and Lords intensified, coming to a head over Lloyd George's controversial budget bill of 1909. The Liberals' ensuing struggle to eliminate the Lords' veto power, mythologized in George Dangerfield's *Strange Death of Liberal England* (1935), provoked a constitutional crisis, led to two elections (in January and December, 1910), and lessened Liberal control of the Commons. But after two years of political strife, and in spite of greater constraints on their control of government, the Liberals managed to outmaneuver the Lords and restrict their veto power definitively.[29]

Historians have debated the significance of the Liberals' success in limiting Tory influence. R. K. Webb, a liberal himself, interprets the achievement as the culminating event in England's "great Liberal reforms."[30] Though he explains that Liberals had begun "destroying" the "traditional political power of the landed aristocracy" as early as the Third Reform Act of 1884, Webb suggests that the defeat of the Lords' veto completed the process, which he describes admiringly as the "break with the assumptions and theory of English politics" since the seventeenth century.[31] Under the account of the Marxist Tom Nairn, in contrast, the Liberals' defeat of the Lords' veto is part of a less overt, more sinister, process. He contends that by the nineteenth century, England's ruling elites – the urban bourgeoisie and the land-owning aristocracy – had formed a "joint front . . . against the proletariat which arose in the industrial revolution."[32] This "patrician class" responded to the mounting demands of the increasingly politicized lower classes with a "social strategy of containment" in which superficial reforms were implemented to improve the lot of the poor and the workers.[33] But these reforms did not, in fact, substantially threaten the hidden alliance between agrarian aristocrats and urban elites that insured upper-class control of the state, and ultimately "prevented the 'second bourgeois revolution' in the British Isles."[34] "Patrician liberalism" had thus "defeated radical liberalism."[35] The Edwardian Liberal party's defeat of the Lords' veto, under Nairn's sort of account, only shifts power slightly between different segments of the "patrician elites," leaving the plight of the working class essentially unaffected.

Ford initiated *The English Review* at a moment when, in Webb's terms, the Liberal Party was striving to reshape the English state from an aristocratic oligarchy to a modern social democracy, but when, in Nairn's terms, the ruling classes were making political concessions to contain the working classes yet were concerned about the effects of those concessions. Politically, the *Review* reflects the paradox: it endorses many New Liberal reforms, but worries about their consequences. So while Ford devotes much of the opening issue to addressing "the problem of the poor," recommending in his editorial on unemployment a new book by the little-known provincial writer Stephen Reynolds because it makes a "serious" attempt to render the realities of "the life of the poor man,"[36] the editorial also warns ominously: "[T]he poor are breaking in on us everywhere. They break in on us as we drive through the streets. We see them in their knots, in their bands, at street corners; the parks are full of them, the public squares. We drive past these broken knots with a touch of fear. If the winter is very hard – they may crowd together. They may sack West London."[37] This nightmare of English elites overthrown by a politicized poor seems excessively alarmist at a moment when the

Liberal government was actively engaged in extending state institutions to improve the lot of the lower classes. The intensity of the concern animating Ford's vision suggests that the editorial expresses not just a commitment to improve the lot of the poor, but also anxiety about lower-class empowerment.

This ambivalence on the part of liberal intellectuals like Ford and his collaborators at *The English Review* helps illuminate the modernist discovery myth, in which an urbane cultural guardian attempts to repel an unexpected, inscrutable, and threatening Russian revolutionary. The fictionalized editor's rejection of the Lewis figure on national and racial grounds – "'I don't want any Russian revelations [revolutions?]. I don't want to see, hear or smell any Slavs'" – presents in fictive form the Edwardian elite's worry that a violent political revolution, like that which had transpired in Russia in 1905 and 1906, might be pending in England. Along with many of his intellectual contemporaries, Ford knew and had supported Kropotkin, the exiled Russian prince-turned-anarchist who wrote and traveled widely to win support for the 1905 revolt among Europe's elites. But our reading of the discovery tale indicates that while Ford may have been willing to support a revolution in Russia, he was considerably less enthusiastic about the prospect of such a rebellion occurring at home.[38]

Indeed, *The English Review* portrayed Britain as threatened by the political radicalization not only of the English masses but also of its colonial subjects. Since the late-1800s westernized, educated colonial elites, inspired by European socialist movements, had been encouraging nationalistic resistance to European rule among their native masses. Upheavals in India, for example, provoked from Marwood a worried reconsideration of the English "endeavour" to "serve" India's "interests."[39] "Our position in India concerns us seriously," he explains, "because it is a great national responsibility, second only to our responsibility to England herself" (569). But despite a century of efforts, "sincere and intelligent we have always thought," to fulfill that national responsibility, "we are compelled to ask ourselves whether India repudiates us" (569). This worry about possible Indian "repudiation" prompts a defensive expression of the enlightened liberal "intentions" animating British imperium: "[s]urely our intentions are good. Every Englishman, who thinks about India, wishes that the native may be well fed, cared for in sickness, and protected from oppression either of the private enemy or the public official" (570).

The *Review*'s apprehensions about the politically organized subjects at home and in the colonies were augmented by those concerning the "European Powers," especially Germany. Though Ford chastises the government for a too-panicky reaction to Germany's efforts to expand its navy, he concurs that increasing German militarization threatened Britain's national security and naval supremacy: "attempting . . . to attain to an absolutely impartial standpoint, to an attitude that is absolutely critical, we seem to see Great Britain drifting inevitably towards a war with Germany. There are a hundred factors that make for it; we can observe none which makes for peace."[40] The same editor who favors a program of domestic reform more radical than any Tory would advocate, responds to the perceived German threat in a manner similar to that of the Tories and liberal imperialists in the face of Boer resistance a decade earlier. He asserts defensively Britain's imperial superiority and the need to maintain its international dominance:

> [A] strong, an invulnerable Great Britain is essential to the peace of the world and to the future of civilisation. We must be strong; we must be immensely strong; we must be invulnerable, so that we may be tranquilly confident. We must be tranquilly confident, so that we may have time to think of other things than war.[41]

The English Review's politics mirror the attitudes of the (New) Liberal government during this period of perceived internal unrest and external competition: domestically the *Review*'s policies are more progressive and socialistic; internationally its policies are closer to those of the Tories, more conservative, patriotic, and imperialist. Most important in our context is not that Ford's allegedly non-partisan journal would so candidly defend British imperium, however, but that it would go on to use that defense to underwrite an Arnoldian doctrine of "culture" and critical "disinterestedness." The *Review*'s ideal England is culturally urbane because it is imperially supreme: cultural excellence depends on and assists imperial dominion.

So while Ford presents *The English Review* as the sort of disinterested and internationalistic literary institution Arnold advocated, he "modernizes" the Victorian's universalist conception of "culture" as a category transcending nationality and the practical sphere. The *Review*'s ideal of critical disinterestedness is based on considerably more nationalistic and practical concerns: Ford's notion of "culture" requires and, in his account, will preserve Britain's increasingly contested international supremacy. Arnold's program reflected Britain's situation in the

1860s, a time when the empire's status as world leader was generally perceived as uncontested, but when the English state was gripped by a series of violent political actions by the poor and working classes. The most celebrated of these were the so-called Sheffield Outrages of 1865–66, in which unionized cutlery workers in the North harassed non-union workers (sometimes violently), and the "Hyde Park Riots" of 1866, in which government efforts to block a mass demonstration in favor of expanded male suffrage provoked working-class and trade-unionist members of the Reform League to "riot" through Hyde Park and some of the surrounding upper-class neighborhoods.[42] The violent tactics of the Sheffield strikers and the London rioters were reported widely and provoked a strong backlash among the upper classes. Arnold, whose *Culture and Anarchy* (1869) was prompted in part by these protests, reacted primarily to the domestic threats he recognized around him: an anarchic lower class, a philistine and provincial middle class, the Church's decline and the loss of a moral center it provided. The liberal Victorian critic would combat such evidence of domestic "decay" by substituting culture for religion, locating order and morality in the cultural sphere, advocating educational reforms to elevate the masses, and placing criticism firmly above and beyond the practical realm from where it could best help improve English art and society.

In contrast, the (new) liberal Edwardian editor, perceiving his nation as threatened both internally and externally, responds in the paradoxical manner we have come to expect from a leader of the prewar intelligentsia: like a member of the intellectual elite concerned with cultural decline, Ford resists provincialism and disdains the practical realm; but like a member of the ruling elite concerned with imperial decline, he advocates military build-up and imagines victory over foreign competition.[43] *The English Review* articulates the paradoxes of Edwardian liberalism because it displays at once the ruling classes' ambivalent commitment to internal social reform, in which progressive ideals are restrained by elitist fears, and the intelligentsia's conflicted commitment to cultural disinterestedness, in which universalist ideals are put in the service of a nationalistic desire for international supremacy.[44]

The unexpected appearance of a revolutionary English writer in Ford's legend reflects both period anxieties about domestic unrest and foreign competition and period ambitions for national success. The figure who arrives in the nick of time, at a moment of crisis, bearing revolutionary writing that "saves" Ford, English culture, even the empire, incarnates Ford's Edwardian hope that the young modernists he "discovered" would once more put English culture and Britain at the forefront of Europe. The legend expresses in its way the predicament of the Edwardian intelligentsia: the mythic modernist appears at once a dangerous foreign political revolutionary, who signals the intelligentsia's anxiety about domestic and colonial social revolt and foreign competition and contamination, and a revolutionary English writer, who heralds a needed cultural renaissance, embodying the intelligentsia's nationalistic hopes that English culture might be brinking on an epoch of unprecedented excellence.

RETRIEVING ENGLISHNESS; REVIVING EMPIRE

Ford's Arnoldian editorials on "The Functions of the Arts in the Republic" and "The Critical Attitude" cast the literary works featured in *The English Review* as products of a "certain school of Literature."[45] The writers composing this "school" practice in their own ways the brand of subjective realism Ford theorized in the *Review* and elsewhere termed "Impressionism."[46] Just as Flaubert had for the French, this "sober, sincere, conscientious, and scientific body of artists" will "crystallis[e] . . . modern life" for English readers.[47] Like the French novelist, the *Review*'s writers are "intent merely to register – to *constater*."[48] Yet even as Ford evokes a "scientific" ideal of disinterested observation, he locates the value of the practice in the personality of the author. "The functions . . . of imaginative literature" are, he explains, "to record life in terms of the author."[49] The "actual and first desire" of the *constateur* of modern life "must always be the expression of himself [and] . . . of his view of life as it is."[50] Ford commends Henry James as such a disinterested, interesting writer. Most important for us, he grants this new school a *national* interest. Ford's writers register "the true characteristic of modern life" in order to (re)locate "England," to show it "where it stands" and "to what it tends."[51]

That Ford's new aesthetic reveals commitments to competing trends within Edwardian liberalism is consistent with *The English Review*'s paradoxical construction of a cosmopolitan ideal of cultural disinterestedness on the grounds of an "immensely strong" empire. His stress on the centrality to the aesthetic of the individual author's personality resonates with old Liberal individualism, while his view that the aesthetic's goal is to orient England and the English resonates with New Liberal efforts to reconstruct Englishness and expand the state to meet the competitive realities of twentieth-century life.[52] A consideration of the impressionistic travel stories Ford featured in *The English Review* during his tenure as editor clarifies the ways in which the literature of the *Review* participated in period efforts to construct a new Englishness based in the rural English past and use it to justify (an ailing) empire.[53]

The travel literature Ford featured in *The English Review* abides by his doctrine of subjective realism and the ideal of the *constateur* by rendering the subjectivity of a cosmopolitan tourist-naturalist/ethnographer who recounts his impressions as he travels to the margins of "civilization" – on the British Isles or the Continent – seeking places and peoples "primitive and undisturbed."[54] Because the *Review*'s travel tales "express" their authors' personalities and "view[s] of life," they expose ambivalences common among liberal intellectuals. The *Review*'s typical tourist-narrator displays, in his idealizing descriptions of unsullied nature and his negative representations of modern life, what A. M. Quinton terms "a hostility to the style of life in an urban mass" of "industrial society."[55] Yet when this narrator travels to the unsullied places of rural England (as in the stories of W. H. Hudson and J. W. Allen), his idealizing naturalism serves patriotically to locate an essential English place, the locus for a new Englishness. And when this narrator travels to the margins of civilization on the Continent (as in the stories of R. B. Cunninghame Graham and Norman Douglas), he responds equivocally to the foreign people he observes: even as he idealizes their innocence, lamenting the costs and complexities of modernity, he casts them as superstitious primitives, reaffirming (quietly) the nationalist type of the (liberal) Briton who, obeying what Ford terms "the duty . . . of an Imperial race," presides benevolently over an enlightened empire, an empire of the Spirit. Consistent with the *Review*'s lurking nationalism, indeed, its travel tales finally use such encounters with the primitive as a kind of literary therapy to purge the narrator's feelings of guilt and regret, re-enlivening commitment to British civilization.[56]

We can begin to chart the ideological work of the travel literature Ford selected for *The English Review* by considering *Review* stories by the celebrated naturalist W. H. Hudson. In a *Review* profile on Hudson, Ford portrays the writer as a naturalist version of the cosmopolitan *constateur* evoked in his "Functions of the Arts" editorials; a writer "who, having galloped with young gallantry through the thistle-down of early life on the pampas, comes with the fresh eyes of a stranger and the keen love of an exile into green and ancient lands, there to spend long hours in the delight of lying still, of gazing at common things, of giving himself up utterly to the spirit of the place."[57] But while Ford's description works to portray Hudson as a naturalist devoted to delighting in "the Green Mansions of the world" (158), its eager allusion to the "green and ancient lands" where Hudson journeys in the pages of *The English Review*, quietly links naturalism to nationalism. Hudson's pieces further articulate that conjunction. In these stories, "Stonehenge" (December 1908) and "Goldfinches at Ryme Intrinsica" (May 1909), Hudson's narrator travels to the peripheries and primitive places of England seeking a purifying experience of the natural through the act of reflective observing. But by locating his celebratory encounters with nature in England, specifically the rural south or "South Country," Hudson turns his naturalist *constateur* into cultural patriot, agent of the broader period project to fix Englishness. Alun Howkins has shown that Hudson contributed to the "discovery of Rural England," helping to "create . . . the world of the South Country and fix . . . it as part of national ideology";[58] our account establishes the part Ford's *English Review* played in the project and elucidates the particular contribution of Hudson's *Review* stories.

Early in "Stonehenge," Hudson's narrator recounts his responses as he first approaches the ancient stones on Salisbury plain. He is overwhelmed not by a sense of wonder at the monument as we might expect from Hudson's title, but by the power of what lies beneath it – the English landscape:

> Was *this* Stonehenge – this cluster of poor little grey stones, looking in the distance like a small flock of sheep or goats grazing on that immense down! How incredibly insignificant it appeared to me, dwarfed by its surroundings – woods and groves and farm-houses – and by that vast extent of rolling down country visible at that point.[59]

Here stretching out before him is an ideal England, a "construction" of "populated and cultivated landscapes";[60] natural, orderly, simple. Here lives a hardworking people who still reverence ancient customs; for them "The Stones" still compel obeisance:

> I gather from natives in the district that it is an old custom for people to go and watch for sunrise on the morning of June 21. A dozen or a score of natives, mostly old shepherds and labourers who lived near, would go and sit there for a few hours and after sunrise would trudge home . . . "How long has the custom existed?" I asked a field labourer. "From the time of the old people – the Druids," he answered. (63)

Hudson's narrator is strongly attracted to this image of dignified natives assembling to pay respect at the altar of a druidic Sun-cult. He finds in it a kind of spiritual belief nearly displaced by industrial modernity.

But when he attempts to participate in the ancient custom (curious act for a naturalist), he is disgusted by the spectacle of "The Stones" overrun by the crass inhabitants of Victorian modernity:

> Altogether about five to six hundred persons gathered at "The Stones," mostly young men on bicycles who came from all the Wiltshire towns within easy distance from Salisbury to Bath. I had a few good minutes at the ancient temple when the sight of the rude, upright stones looking black against the moonlit and star-sprinkled sky produced an expected feeling in me: but the mood could not last; the crowd was too big and noisy and the noises they made too suggestive of a Bank Holiday crowd at the Crystal Palace. (67)

This picture of an ancient and faithful Englishness under siege in the south country issues a quiet call to patriotic countrymen to return to this place, these ways, to come and reverse this defilement. Hudson's disillusioned evocation of a Bank Holiday crowd at the Crystal Palace on Salisbury plain underscores the ironic fact that this reverence for traditional rural England helps advance the interests of the modern British empire.

If Hudson's *Review* stories play a particularly important role in establishing the south country as a basis for modern English ideology, J. W. Allen's "The Back of Beyond" (March 1909), makes particularly clear the paradoxical configuration of the temporal narrative at the heart of that ideology.[61] Allen's story of a trip into the Black Mountains on the border between south Wales and the English counties of Hereford and Worcester, charts a course for Britain's future by way of a return to England's past. As Allen's narrator describes his journey through an unnamed "colliery village" we get a nearly official picture of the terrible effects of industrial modernity:

> On each side was a row of houses of grey sandstone, of a dismal natural colour, begrimed and neglected. Broken windows, heaps of rubbish in filthy little yards, not a green thing growing, not a flower-pot . . . The people were as dirty as their dwellings. Clothes, hands and faces, no less than the houses, were begrimed with coal-dust . . . Now and again we caught the reek of smoke or of oil. And between the houses we had glimpses of scarred mountain-sides, blackened and desolate, heaped with coal-tips and dotted with smoking chimneys. (620)

Allen's narrator shares with Edwardian sociologists a sense that living and working conditions in industrial England are dehumanizing and intolerable;[62] he does not advocate social or economic reform to remedy those conditions, however. Instead, Allen's narrator ascends to an older rural England; after "a long pull uphill . . . out of the city of furnaces" (622), he is transported ahead to the English past:

> It was as though I had entered a new world, an older world. The road narrowed as my wheels advanced. It became a rough lane between low hedges. On my left were swift visions of land-locked, rock-guarded bays, of rugged limestone cliffs, of cove within cove, of delicate, lonely, curved stretches of sand, of glittering, tumbled water. On my right a heathery saddle-black, green with bracken and grey with great stones. I began to think of those squalid streets and that forest of chimneys as of something already clean passed away from the earth. (623)

He experiences this ancient English landscape as a spiritual cleansing: liberal guilt is purged as the dirty squalor of modern England and concerns about the industrial working-class and the urban poor "pass away." No liberal hand wringing is expressed in response to the squalor, no expansion of the liberal state advocated to eliminate it. Allen's narrator discovers an unsullied rural England:

> Every half-mile deepened my sense of something primitive and undisturbed. I had entered a region as remote from the life of cities as the Happy Isles . . . The scattered farm-houses had an air of aloofness and self-sufficiency. All of stone, whitewashed, heavily thatched and gabled, they had been renewed from generation to generation and had never become modern. Ancestral dwellings, they vied in antiquity with our historic mansions but were more perfect in dignity, untouched by the vulgarity of conscious wealth. (632)

This "new world," this new England, is not, our narrator indicates, some utopian scheme of the liberal state, beyond reach. It is "an older world," an older England, that survives in secluded villages across a still "green and pleasant land." We have only to journey to these villages to find an ancient race of clean and self-sufficient men and women, paradigms for a new, older English race:

> Go about among these people and you will soon learn to admire. You will admire the specklessness of their homes, with the old dressers and ancestral china that is not for sale. You will take pleasure in their old-world appliances, their cupboard-beds, their brass sugar-cutters, the pack-saddles that their grandfathers used. You will respect their independence, their plain simplicity, the excellence of their manners. You will see old men and women among them with blue eyes as lucid and clear as the eyes of a child. In time you may come to envy the laborious and frugal dignity of their lives. (622–23)

The narrator's journey the "back of beyond" mimics the paradoxical trajectory of new liberal imperialism: the future of the empire can be insured by a return to England's past, to a new "older" Englishness grounded in rural places and "traditions." The independent, hardworking, clean, dignified Englishmen and women Allen's narrator discovers appear fit citizens for a world empire.

The terms of the *Review* travel narrative shift somewhat when the narrator goes to an idyllic place on the periphery of Europe. Here the idealization of (non-English) nature and natives is in tension with patriotic naturalism or the recovery of a rural population of "traditional" Englishmen. The remote places celebrated by R. B. Cunninghame Graham and Norman Douglas are not offered as the locus of a (nearly) lost but still retrievable English essence; the natives are not presented as paradigms of an ancient and industrious English race inviting emulation. But these continental outlands still prompt the narrator's disgust at industrial modernity, these natives still provoke his envy at the simplicity of their customs and lifestyles, these encounters still serve to purge disgust and envy. The stories are most important for us, however, because they present most clearly, through their representation of the relationship between the advanced traveler from the imperial center and the childlike natives of the periphery, how the travel stories Ford featured in *The English Review* use the primitive other to reaffirm British imperial privilege.

Philip Dodd reminds us that "the definition of the English is inseparable from that of the non-English," that "Englishness is not so much a category as a relationship."[63] The travel stories of Graham and Douglas show how *The English Review* represents Englishness as a conflicted relationship with primitive Europeans. Graham's story about a journey to an isolated republic in the Pyrenees, "Andorra" (January 1909), articulates this set of representational strategies and makes clear their role in underwriting British claims to empire.[64] Throughout the story, Graham's tourist-narrator swings between nostalgic yearning for intimacy with primitive Europe and a sense of imperial superiority to the people and customs he encounters. As he approaches the hidden republic from the mountains above, a sense of its mystical isolation overwhelms him: "Andorra yet survives and flourishes, one of the last of the innumerable small States that once were set as thick upon the map of Europe as stars in heaven on a clear winter's night."[65] His idealizing evocation of a lost Europe of liberty both confirms his anti-modernism and quietly conjures a vision of modern Europe as big and oppressive, consistent with the sometimes menacing Europe of the *Review*'s editorials. An unpleasant encounter with the locals raises the narrator's defenses, however, as he reasserts his status as a being more advanced and active, amused by the primitive and animalistic Andorrans: "the people have a look as of a Puritan bull-terrier, uncouth and awkward, but not encouraging, should any person happen to tread upon its tail" (206). The image of a British tourist attending an "uncouth and awkward" dog not only works to contain anxieties about Europe by representing Europeans as animals, but also exposes the racism at the heart of many Edwardian defenses of empire. Despite his candid assertion of (race) superiority, the narrator cannot shake feelings of wonder and desire in the face of this state of pre-modern peace:

> A priest assured me that there is no written law in the community, but that in spite of this the folk are honest and God-fearing, and as there are no laws to break, they never break them, which piece of reasoning upon his part seemed to me quite conclusive, and taken into consideration with the fact that public functionaries have no fixed salaries, but serve their valley all for the honour and the glory of the thing, makes up a state of things almost ideal in this transitory world, that is if transitory can be applied to places like Andorra, which never can have suffered any change since God was God or the sun first commenced to shine upon the hills. (222)

The Edenic scene – an enduring world of perfect order, where the folk live harmoniously abiding by ancient codes of "honour and glory" – predictably provokes from the narrator regret about the costs of tourism and modernization: "[t]he greatest piece of fortune that has happened to this happy valley lost in the hills, is that up to the present time it has had no roads. Want of communication has kept out the tourist, under whose foot all ancient customs wither, as certainly as did the grass under the horse's hoof of Attila" (206). In this overblown picture (penned by a tourist), tourists and travel writers are barbaric Huns, brutally overrunning the innocents' ancient customs. Here Graham turns Andorra into a receptacle for his jaded tourist's yearnings and regrets, his disillusionment about modernity.

Douglas's "The Island of Typhoëus" (February 1909) articulates further the privilege that authorizes a damning analysis of modern tourism even as it exempts the tourist-author from participation in the trampling of "ancient customs." Douglas's narrator concludes his account of a trip to Ischia, an island off the coast of Naples, with an analysis of the "native" character that delineates the cultural gulf separating the citizen of the British empire from the native of the European periphery. In the voice of a worldly and intellectually advanced modern, Douglas describes the Ischians as pre-modern innocents animated by "the simple desire for sunshine and family life, and a pantheism vague and charming, the impress of nature in her mildest moods upon the responsive human phantasy."[66] Yet despite his tone of charmed yearning, the narrator pictures Ischian people as less evolved beings, subject to instinct, indulging pagan religious urges. This narrator may be disillusioned with aspects of industrial modernity, but he still embodies English qualities of intellectual and cultural advancement – sympathy for the less fortunate, critical detachment, an active will, a skeptical attitude toward religion – that are central to Ford's editorial assertions that the English "stand in a different plane of civilisation" from their neighbors and thus have a "duty" to "maintain" their empire of "peace and civilisation."

Accordingly, the *Review*'s tourist-narrator at the margins of Europe does not take the radical option of "going primitive"; he recognizes its dangers – the loss of moral compass and connection to civilization embodied by Conrad's Kurtz – but also cannot evade his obligations as a member of an "Imperial race." Thus, he uses a confrontation with the primitive other to re-establish equilibrium, reaffirm connection to imperial civilization, and reconstruct the figure of the enlightened Briton fit to preside over the world's most advanced empire. These *Review* tales, like those of Hudson and Allen, are therapeutic: by encountering "primitive and undisturbed" places and peoples at the margins of Europe, the disillusioned (liberal) narrator from the imperial metropolis is not only able to vent doubts and regrets regarding modern civilization, but also ends up having relocated a sense of imperial entitlement through a relationship of sympathy for and superiority to the primitive European. Thus Graham's "Andorra" ends with a moment of reverie in which the world-trotting British narrator rejoices as much in his voyeuristic visit to this outpost of pre-modern Europe as in his impending departure from it:

> Next morning saw me early on the road, riding along and smoking, musing contentedly on this thing and on that, upon the fall of nations and of kings, creeds, principalities and powers, and why it is that fate had spared Andorra when it had eaten up Greece, Rome and Babylon, and also on the various ways in which men pass their lives struggling to do things quite impossible to do, when, after all, nothing is better than to jog along the road and to shout "Arre" loudly now and then when a mule lags behind. (222)

Despite expressing regrets about modernity's complexities and costs, the travel tales in Ford's *English Review* in the end reject neither empire nor "civilization." Like Ford's ambivalent editorials, they perform a strained negotiation between Edwardian liberalism's moral distaste for the violence and complexity of modernity and its defensive advocacy of Englishness, state expansion, and imperial consolidation. The narrators' encounters with rural England and with innocents at empire's margins expose regrets about modernity and imperialism, even as they use the primitive to purge guilt and reaffirm ideals of Englishness and empire.

INTO THE WILD

In the decidedly urbane context of *The English Review*, Lewis's three comic travel tales – "The 'Pole,'" "Some Innkeepers and Bestre," and "Les Saltimbanques" – present themselves as rather impolite interlopers.[67] While they share with *Review* travel stories a rough plot – all follow a cosmopolitan tourist-narrator as he impressionistically describes the locals and locales he observes at the margins of European civilization – Lewis's tales depart from the genre's conventions in particular ways.[68] First, unlike the typical tale, which has the tourist-narrator observing pre-modern natives, Lewis's narrator scrutinizes in addition a plethora of other types: not only Bretons, who basically fit the stereotype of superstitious innocents living a primitive life, but also Eastern European refugees, would-be-artists, and various other cosmopolitan eccentrics, who together compose a kind of traveling circus of exiles, émigrés, and vagabonds.[69] If most *Review* tales are concerned with the ambivalent modern's confrontation with the primitive other, Lewis's tales are more interested in cosmopolitan life and its most marginal participants. His narrator contemplates with fascination the complicated – and comic – tensions produced when persons from different races, nations, and social positions with different habits and behaviors come together in unfamiliar places.[70]

A reading of Lewis's stories in the context of other *Review* travel literature clarifies his efforts to manipulate the conventions of the genre in order to fashion himself a cosmopolitan *Review* writer, but one whose aims and techniques were more vital, more aggressive, more modern than those of the *Review*'s older, established authors. But even as Lewis's stories work to subvert the *Review*'s agenda by presenting themselves and their author as embodying aggressively *new* cultural ideals, they ultimately complement that agenda: while rejecting certain conventions of typical *Review* travel tales as expressing an overly repressed and traditional notion of Englishness, Lewis's stories likewise articulate a paradoxical ideal of cultural cosmopolitanism as the best means to strengthen English character; they too use the "primitive" other as a catalyst in that nationalistic project.

Like other *Review* travel stories, Lewis's tales condescendingly traffic in period stereotypes concerning foreigners ("primitives," Russians, Poles, Bretons, Jews, and Germans). But they differ in their paradoxical insistence on the particularity and uniqueness of the marginal individuals under observation. The first-published story, "The 'Pole'" presents itself as a comic study of a particular type of cosmopolitan refugee common in Brittany, a type the narrator terms a "Pole":

> A young Polish or Russian student, come to the end of his resources, knows two or three alternatives. One is to hang himself – a course generally adopted. But those who have no ties, who take a peaceful pleasure in life, are of a certain piety and mild disposition, borrow ten pounds from a friend and leave their country for ever – they take a ticket to Brest. They do this dreamily enough, and of late years almost instinctively. Once arrived there, they make the best of their way to some one of the many *pensions* that are to be found on the Breton coast . . . They pay two or three months' board and lodging, until the ten pounds is finished, and then, with a simple dignity all their own, stop paying. Their hosts take this quite as a matter of course. They henceforth become the regular, unobtrusive, respected inhabitants of the house.[71]

The characteristics the narrator attributes to these characters conform to stereotypes about (at least) two specific groups: Russians as psychologically unbalanced and suicidal, popularized in England through the contemporaneous translation of Dostoyevsky, Tolstoy, and Turgenev;[72] and Jews as rootless and parasitic refugees, periodically revived during the period whenever Eastern European immigration increased, as after the Russian revolution of 1905–06. Despite this dependence on stereotypes and the narrator's condescending tone, the story's agenda is not just that of ridiculing Jews, Poles, Russians, and Bretons. Lewis also plays against those types, injecting humor into the genre, sometimes calling into question the validity of the totalizing descriptions of primitive character he elsewhere perpetuates.

This more comic and interrogative approach is evidenced in the narrator's shifting use of the designation "Pole" in the opening of the story. In these paragraphs, a sociological analysis of the "Pole" phenomenon, the narrator's use of the term is elastic, as he shifts swiftly from one period signification to another. When the narrator first identifies a Pole as a "young Polish or Russian student," he uses the term to designate Slavic racial identity, a handling consistent with the contemporary view of Poles and Russians as members of a single race.[73] That use is confirmed when he explains that the "Slav cares little what his material environment may be, so wrapt is he in his thoughts" (209). But once the narrator has identified the "Poles" racially as Slavs, he uses the term to signify nationality, referring to the many "young Polish student[s]" who travel to Brittany. This sliding across competing accounts continues in an editorializing footnote, which claims to clarify things but only confuses them further by contradicting understandings of "Pole" as racial *and* national; now we are told that "'Polonais' or 'Pole,' means to a Breton peasant the member of no particular nation, but merely the kind of being leading the life" the story portrays (209). Is a "Pole," the story prompts readers to ask, a Slav, a Pole, or someone living a Pole-ish lifestyle?

While this sort of terminological flexibility reflects popular Edwardian usage – as George Stocking has demonstrated, the resilience of a Lamarckian conception of heredity led to a blending of forces of biology and culture in period accounts of personal and group identity[74] – Lewis's aims are somewhat more parodic. That the cumulative effect of the narrator's discussion of the "Pole" phenomenon is to confuse the differences between competing uses of the term is part of the story's comic point. By blurring the distinctions between race, nationality, and lifestyle – implying in short that the term "Pole" always be bracketed by inverted commas – the story questions deterministic accounts of group identity. And because these anarchical characters act out of a multitude of competing and confused motives and impulses, the tales undermine as often as they affirm determinism.

"The 'Pole'" continues calling into question the stereotypes it also perpetuates when the tourist-narrator offers, as evidence for his opening generalizations, a series of portraits or case studies of specific "Poles." But none of these quite fits the narrator's categorical parameters. There's Isoblitsky, "imbued with several passions more common and proper to men *dans le siècle* than to a 'Pole'" (212); his greatest preoccupation is not mooching off innkeepers, but compulsively demonstrating that he is "tremendously independent" (212–13). Another, "a great *farceur*," has as his distinguishing trait not a "simple dignity" in avoiding paying, but a desire to entertain his friends with outlandish comic antics, like "introduc[ing] . . . his forefinger" into the open mouths of sleeping strangers (215). And the German "Pole" is no "unobtrusive, respected inhabitant" of the pension, but the violent lover of its proprietress, who beats her nightly (216). By insisting on the uniqueness of the "Poles" even while portraying them as chaotic and inscrutable outcasts, Lewis's stories toy with the contemporaneous anthropological dilemma of how to reconcile evidence of individual human variation with the "scientifically" validated stereotypes of race and nationality.[75]

Lewis's travel tales also deviate from convention because their narrators do not filter observations exactly as other *English Review* narrators do. Their "egos," to borrow Ford's later terminology, are rather different.[76] Lewis's narrators act the civilized imperial observer like their counterparts, but they do not envy the innocence, purity, and simplicity of the natives. While Graham and Douglas nostalgically present the inhabitants of their tales in a state of pre-modern innocence, of intimate harmony with nature, the subjects of Lewis's narrators' attention – whether Breton peasants, exiled pseudo-artists, or refugees from European metropoli – exist in a state of psycho-physical compulsion, by turns violent, comic, pitiful; Ian Duncan has aptly called Lewis's Bretons "studies in atavism."[77]

Lewis's characters appear calculated to jostle *The English Review*'s ideal travel writer and alarm its ideal reader. Graham mourns for the lost victims of imperial aggression; Lewis's "Poles" and Bretons aggressively victimize each other. The portrait of the German "Pole" establishes the pattern. "Another of my fellow boarders last summer, a 'Pole' in the Breton sense, though a German by birth," the narrator explains, "used to throw Mademoiselle Batz down in the kitchen and stamp on her" (216). By making this brutish boarder a German who beats women, Lewis maximizes his original readers' confrontation with brutality: he exploits contemporary English views of Germans as especially violent and uncivilized people and of Germany as England's most threatening competitor and Europe's most aggressive state,[78] and violates the bourgeois liberal ideal – if not practice – of respectful admiration for women. Flaunting disagreement with the *Review*'s civilized and pacifistic ideals, Lewis's narrator studies the German precisely because of his misogynistic violence. He enjoys watching the German abuse Mademoiselle Batz nearly as much as she seems to enjoy being abused:

> She now gave herself up frankly for a few weeks to the pleasure of quarrelling with him, being hurled down on the floor – her Breton nature thoroughly appreciating this side of his character . . . Then the making it up, with its glows and titillations.
>
> After one of their quarrels, they organised a dance to celebrate its completion; their two gaunt and violent forms whirling round the narrow room, quite indifferent to the other dancers, giving them terrible blows with their driving elbows, their hair sweeping on the ceiling. (217)

Lewis's narrator is not interested in happy innocents; he finds these strange and brutal compulsives far more exciting: vital, bracing, dangerous. If Ford agreed with Arnold that "civilization" defined the "modern," then by assailing Ford's conception as too repressed, dispassionate, and rational, Lewis's stories propose an anti-civilized modernism that celebrates the vitalizing power of irrationality and aggression.[79] Yet the narrator's fascination with this spectacle of irrational violence – specifically violence against a woman – not only contests the Fordian cult of civilization; it also exposes, briefly but strikingly, the masculinist overtones of Lewis's prewar literary project and developing avant-garde politics.[80]

The final evidence of Lewis's break with *Review* convention is the way his tales conclude. They do not climax with a departure from civilization's margins that catharts imperial guilt or bolsters Edwardian ideals, but with some bizarre spectacle that leaves the tourist-narrator in a state of blank incomprehension, short-circuiting the ideals of rationality, civility, and order on which Ford's doctrine depends. The pattern is taken to its furthest extension at the end of Lewis's third-published piece, "Les Saltimbanques" (August 1909), the serio-comic story of a ramshackle Breton circus troupe, which culminates with a chaotic performance by the motley carnies. As the ringmaster, a man deeply depressed and dissatisfied by his work, performs an increasingly ridiculous set of antics to squeeze some modicum of appreciation from a surly audience, the narrator tells us that "a strange thing happened. A little boy in the front row began jeering at the proprietor. It was apparently a spontaneous and personal action, and very sudden" (246). In response

> [T]he showman prowled about the enclosure, grinning, and casting sidelong glances at his poet. His vanity was in some very profound and strange way tickled. But his face would suddenly darken and he would make a rush at the inexplicable boy. This latter, however, was strong in his inspiration. He would no doubt have met death with the exultation of a martyr, rather than renounce this transfigured image of an old and despondent mountebank – like some stubborn prophet that would not forego the splendour of his vision – always of the gloom of famine, of cracked and empty places, and the elements taking new and extremely destructive forms for the rapid extermination of man. (247)

This finale presents Lewis's assault on Fordian civilization in its most grandiose form: the enthralled narrator finds in this boy's antic laughter a modern apocalypse. Not all of Lewis's tales go this far. But in the refined and earnest context of *The English Review*, the stories and the persona they fashion of a new writer "behave," in effect, like anarchistic insurgents, subverting aesthetic conventions, questioning cultural stereotypes, disrupting political consensus.

The description of Lewis's travel stories and their attendant persona in terms similar to Ford's description of the avantgardiste in the legend is of course intentional. Following James Clifford's lead, we can think of the stories as a kind of field work from which Lewis "ethnographically" fashioned the avant-garde persona that inspired Ford's portrait.[81] The stories suggest that an ethnographic consciousness of cultural difference – in particular the differences between (over)civilized narrators from imperial metropoli and violent, atavistic outcasts and primitives at empire's margins – alerted Lewis to the possibility that identity was not rigidly determined by national training or racial imperatives, but might be subject to willed modification. This possibility was compelling, we will see, because it helped Lewis justify two of his early cultural-political ambitions: to fashion a new artistic persona, more vital and violent than the urbane *constateurs* of Ford's *Review*, and to refashion, along similar lines, a depleted English national character.

Lewis's tales roughly sketch two methods of personal transformation that depend on an understanding of identity as not rigidly determined by racial and cultural forces: one which uses modes of imitation, the other employing shock tactics. The first approach is evidenced in the portrayal of Isoblitsky, where Lewis casts this "Pole's" characteristic role-playing as a technique for personal change. In this description, Lewis's narrator speculates on the role of will and nationality in individual identity. Questioning a radical determinist account of personality, he initially presents Isoblitsky attempting to regulate his character through conscious effort: "He wanted one to believe . . . that he was tremendously independent. He put himself to great pains to prove it. He must have possessed some such simple axiom as: One is much more apt to bestow things upon a person who dislikes accepting anything, than upon one who would take all you offered him" (212–13). Despite the suggestion that Isoblitsky might be able to change himself by following the independence axiom, the narrator's explanation of Isoblitsky's aim in adopting an independent persona – to get as many "things" as possible – undermines the power of will in identity by asserting that Isoblitsky is ultimately defined by his parasitism, a trait the narrator has already identified as "racial," one which "young Polish or Russian student[s]" follow "almost instinctively" (209). Yet the narrator's analysis of Isoblitsky's other strategies for regulating behavior not only reiterates the importance of will in defining individual identity, but also extends the range of ways in which persons may modify themselves. Isoblitsky's case suggests to the narrator that individual character can be altered by repeated imitation of another person:

> He constantly spoke of a friend of his, a "Pole" also – not because he was rich, or famous or aristocratic, but because he was apparently a fellow who showed a great and startling independence of spirit, and who was prodigiously strong; far stronger than he, Isoblitsky. He looked upon this person's qualities as his own, and used them as such. This shadowy figure of the friend seemed indeed superimposed on Isoblitsky's own form and spirit. (214)

The process by which Isoblitsky changes his behavior depends on a regimen of willed imitation: he repeatedly mimics his friend's "qualities" until they become his "own," part of himself.[82]

Yet even as the narrator raises the possibility that individual agency has priority over national and racial categories, his description of Isoblitsky posits a divided notion of identity that circumscribes the possibilities of self-definition, reaffirming the stereotype of the irrational primitive. While Isoblitsky actively strives to act independently, his character is passively subject to another part of himself that will not conform to the axiom, a part he only half-recognizes and observes with incomprehension:

> His preoccupation to appear independent and strong-minded did not permit of any other conscious sentiment: but he had the suavity and natural coquetry of a pretty brute, that – as he was not aware of it – was constantly baffling him and relaxing his stern purposeful independent expression, sometimes at a crucial moment. His nature was the darkest of mysteries for him, and this enemy in the camp, this something that was constantly corrupting his implacable self under its very nose, perplexed him somewhat, and he mused about it. (213)

The narrator's paradoxical representation of Isoblitsky as, on one hand, self-aware and self-defining, and on the other, passively subject to forces beyond his ken or control, manifests an ambivalence at the center of Lewis's stories. They are animated by an avant-gardist desire to flaunt the conventions of the typical *English Review* travel tale, especially its binary opposition between peaceful primitive threatened by encroaching modernity and guilty modern in need of emotional catharsis, and the radically determinist account of (national) identity that freezes both types in a hierarchy of development. But the stories construct their own characterological binary – of the violent and irrational outcast performing incomprehensible acts for the enthralled and repressed modern needing revitalization – and never push the critique of determinism to the breaking point, where the hierarchy of modern over primitive would collapse. Despite their bracing and comic vitality, despite their flashes of characterological plasticity, Lewis's outcasts, émigrés, and vagabonds remain essentially underdeveloped: more passive, less rational than the narrators who describe them with rapt attention.

Reflecting this paradox, Lewis's tales propose another method of personal transformation that contests determinism, even as the agent of that contestation is a primitive type: the *farceur* – a "lonely hero" – who is, unlike the urbane English imagined by Ford's *Review*, in touch with his "primitive soul," and whose unexpected antics shock people into change. While Isoblitsky wants to change himself, the *farceur* changes others:

> The practical joker is a degenerate, who is exasperated by the uniformity of life. Or he is one who mystifies people, because only when suddenly perplexed or surprised do they become wildly and startlingly natural. He is a primitive soul, trying to get back to his element. Or it is the sign of a tremendous joy in people, and delight in seeing them put forth their vitality, and in practical joking of a physical nature a joy in the grotesqueness of the human form. (216)

The *farceur* taunts uniformity; this "primitive soul" is propelled by his primitive soul to assail social conventions with jokes and horseplay. These comic attacks mystify, perplex, and surprise people, shocking them back to nature, to their primitive souls, reawakening inherent vitality. Unlike Isoblitsky's self-transformation, which progresses incrementally as he consciously follows the independence maxim and repeatedly imitates his independent friend, the *farceur*'s transformation of others occurs in a startling moment of assault as his unexpected shenanigans break down and shake up their calcified characters.

Interestingly, we can find resonances of both these models for character change in Ford's arrival legend. The imitation approach to personality change is reflected in Ford's representation of the young English writer appearing in the guise of a Russian anarchist. The legend dramatizes an application of transformative shock tactics as the revolutionary writer startles, dumbfounds, and converts the Edwardian sage. The mythic modernist looks and acts very like the strange and inscrutable Slavs and Bretons of Lewis's stories, his passive–aggressive behavior a *farceur*-like attack on the Edwardian and the cultural ideals the latter embodies.[83] Indeed, the artistic interloper in the myth resembles closely the tales' favorite French innkeeper, the violently silent star of Lewis's second published story, "Some Innkeepers and Bestre." Like Ford's new writer, Bestre deploys a physical rhetoric of silent hostility, in which inexplicability becomes a mode of aggression:

> Bestre conducts long and bitter campaigns with some neighbour, that will consist almost entirely of dumb show, a few words only being exchanged – antagonisms that will become more and more acute through several weeks, burst forth and wear themselves out with their own violence – all without words, or even actions that could be remarked as distinctively hostile by an uninitiated observer. (229)

Because Ford had positioned his journal at the apex of English literary culture and himself as the epitome of urbanity and imperial civilization, he was an appropriate candidate for this sort of modernizing assault. The arrival myth reflects the benefits of these shocking tactics when the arriviste's strange appearance, inexplicable silence, and revolutionary writing jolt the muddled Edwardians into modern consciousness: once recovered from confusion, they recognize this strange figure as the great English writer who heralds the vital new cultural movement that will save them, their nation, even the empire.

Lewis's *English Review* travel tales indicate that he first became fascinated with the relations between individuals and categories of group identity as he worked to articulate an alternative literary style that celebrated violent irrationality as vitalism and to fashion a persona consistent with that style.[84] The stories fitfully ridicule a radically deterministic conception of identity, in which personality is seen as absolutely defined by racial essence or national character, occasionally raising the possibility of a more anti-determinist view, in which identity is seen as learned and transformable through will. But the tales do not dispense with determinism. Their aggressive humor depends on a hierarchy of "racial" development nearly as rigid as that on which other *Review* travel tales rely. The comic conclusion of "The 'Pole'" playfully pits anti-determinism against determinism, mocking the desire that animates such analyses, even as it reaffirms the foundational role of nationality and race in structuring identity: "I came to the conclusion that, however good a 'Pole', a stray German, Lapp, Esquimau [*sic*] or other dim and hyperborean personage who had found his way to these parts might become, it took an authentic Slav to make a real 'Pole'" (218).

This comic and conflicted moment helps clarify the stories' overall approach to the fictions of national character: they playfully question the determining influence of nationality and toy with the possibility of its cultural construction, yet just as often, they assert nationality's defining force, along with the racialist hierarchy of development used to justify both imperial conquest and British supremacy. The narrator's habitual tendency to conflate determinist and anti-determinist accounts may attest to a developing sense on Lewis's part that personal identity is defined through a struggle between individual prerogatives on one hand, and cultural and biological forces on the other. Yet, as we will see in our reading of Lewis's 1910 essay on sport and English character, his fascination with irrational foreigners and period constructions of nationality was also (perhaps primarily) driven by his embrace of Edwardian concerns about England and the English and ambitions for international success, concerns and ambitions also animating Ford's cosmopolitan imperialism.

UNTAMING ENGLISHNESS

> No one would be so indignant as the Englishman if you told him he ignored his body – outraged and amused, he would conduct you grimly to his bathroom. It has a room all to itself merely to be cleaned in! He would stride over to his bedroom, show you india-rubber implements dangling on the wall, Indian clubs, and a large coloured chart to direct his morning's exercises. But these things are only part of a vast Anglo-Saxon conspiracy against the body. The bath is, figuratively, to drown it in, the instruments on the wall to indebt it to science and tame it. With characteristic cunning, as in dealing with a native chief, the Anglo-Saxon pretends that he is working entirely in its interests. But he has reduced it at last to be the most practical symbol of the Anglo-Saxon world. Of all the triumphs of the English in substituting for imaginative vision a barren formula . . . this triumph is the greatest, the masterpiece of the modern Anglo-Saxon genius. (Wyndham Lewis, "Our Wild Body" (1910), 251)

The possibility of radical character change is vexed in Lewis's *English Review* stories and they never suggest altering more than an individual personality. Lewis's neglected national character sketch-cum-cultural polemic, "Our Wild Body" (*New Age*, 5 May 1910), confirms that in the nine months after his travel tales appeared, this vacillating attitude on the relations between individual identity and group character had solidified into a more radical anti-determinism. Lewis entertained a conception of character as changeable not only because of his interest in creating a new kind of artist. A brief analysis of "Our Wild Body" concludes this first chapter because Lewis's text turns his travel tales' vitalist urge to fashion an avant-garde persona toward the larger project of revitalizing an ailing nation.

Lewis created this proto-avant-garde manifesto by elaborating and repackaging concepts only tentatively formulated in his *English Review* travel tales; if the stories are interrogative and enthralled, "Our Wild Body" is declarative and hortatory. The piece may not, like F. T. Marinetti's Initial Futurist Manifesto of 1909, announce or promote a specific radical art group (Lewis was not yet associated with one), but it does, like many such texts, diagnose a national disease, suggest a cure, and project a renewed nation.[85] "Our Wild Body" deviates from the conventions of avant-garde polemic, however, by advocating a change not in aesthetic practice, or political and cultural institutions, but in national character: it urges England's repressed, over-civilized natives to overthrow the "vast Anglo-Saxon conspiracy against the body" and rediscover their own primitive passions and attachments to the "Wild Body," its violence and irrationality. To untame Englishness, Lewis's vitalist essay advises the English to behave more like the inhabitants of his travel tales.[86]

These modifications in ambition and rhetoric are reflected in a shift in journalistic venue. Lewis's first stories were published in Ford's liberal-imperialist *English Review*, the title of which alone indicates its commitment to the civilized evaluation of thought, literature, and culture. "Our Wild Body" appeared in a more programmatically radical journal edited by one of London's best-known intellectual rebels. As its title suggests, Alfred Orage's *New Age: an Independent Socialist Review of Politics, Literature, and Art* was committed editorially to the revolutionary political and cultural agenda of initiating a vital future. In the context of Orage's insurgent socialist periodical, which succeeded *The English Review* as the home of cutting-edge literature and theory, "Our Wild Body" became part of a developing movement of national reformation more radical than any articulated by Ford and his comrades. By recasting his project in "Our Wild Body" as an effort to reform both literature and national character, Lewis begins positioning himself explicitly as an avant-gardist. If his *Review* stories are the field work toward fashioning a new writer, *The New Age* essay is that writer's first revolutionary proclamation, an avant-garde effort at base nationalistic.

To promote its fantasy of national revitalization, "Our Wild Body" prods the English to imitate "Latins" because they are more physical people, who do not, like their counterparts across the channel, alienate their minds from their bodies. Because "Englishmen and women, essentially of much the same stuff as other men and women, have become proverbial for their virtuosity in withstanding temptation or pretending it is not there,"[87] the piece advises them to release their primitive souls. It analyzes the English obsession with sports as evidence of their alienation from the vitality of the Wild Body and mocks them for repressively channeling their natural instincts for sex and aggression into such foolish, "civilized" antics. Re-embrace physicality, reacknowledge the pleasures of violence, rediscover the "warlike spirit of the race" the essay urges:

> We perpetuate in our games the primitive art of war – the triumph that, relying on mere skill, and physical strength and courage, one man or company of men may gain over another. But it is artificial and no longer a vital and fundamental part of life, this exercise of our strength. So we have wiped out the old sentiment for the body and its eternal significance that still exists in France, for instance, by renewing and perpetuating our interest in it, but in connection only with a travesty of life, a game instead of war. Even when two Englishmen fall out and fight they are bound by certain rules, as though they were playing a game . . . "[T]he famous warlike spirit of the race" is diminished by these score of substitutes for war. It need not be, but it is. (253)

By asserting that this diminution of English bellicosity "need not be," the piece implies that the English should reverse the process by rediscovering their inherent vitality, aggression, and irrationality. "Our Wild Body" thus makes explicit what is only implicit in Lewis's *English Review* tales: that transforming identity is not only possible but also desirable, a necessary strategy, in fact, for national reform. While Lewis began his literary career opposing the "civilized" cultural ideals of Ford's *Review* and the liberal intelligentsia, "Our Wild Body" shows that he shared with his elders a nationalistic desire to reconstruct Englishness and restore English culture. Like other *Review* writers, Lewis thought his nation to be in decline and sought to use writing to revive it; but while Ford's *constateurs* believed that industrial modernity had left the English in a state of disillusioned alienation from the simplicity and dignity of an older, more innocent Englishness, Lewis believed that the values of Victorian civilization had, in effect, colonized the English, leaving them in a state of repressed alienation from the vital and unpredictable drives of the Wild Body. Lewis's remedy consisted therefore not in making the English more cultured and civilized, but more instinctual and unconscious.

Thus while Lewis's early stories and proto-polemic together question racial and national determinism, this plan to untame the English depends on a more general, biological essentialism. "Our Wild Body" claims that all men and women, regardless of race or nation, are "essentially of much the same stuff" (251), deploying a totalizing notion of human "instinct" that casts vitality as everything opposed to "civilization," in short, the very "primitive" qualities – desire, violence, pain – that Lewis's tourist narrators find compelling in his Slavs and Bretons.[88] In so doing, Lewis's earliest literary maneuvers toward avant-garde reform participate in the broad "reorientation in European social thought" occurring at that moment among young European artists and writers. Having discovered Nietzsche, Bergson, and Sorel, this generation rejects the nineteenth century's bourgeois ideals of rationalist evolution, arguing instead that the future of culture depends on re-accessing the destructive and vitalizing energies of human irrationality.[89] But even as Lewis's vision for national revitalization depends on a generalized biological essentialism, and partakes of a European wide cult of irrationality, it puts that vital essence of irrationality in the service of projects exclusively English. This dynamic is an important early instance of a recurrent – and neglected – configuration this book will track throughout the prewar period, in which avant-garde commitments to opposition, individuality, and revolution compete against and cohabit with patriotic commitments to national health, military potency, and imperial supremacy, a configuration that will, we will see, structure the trajectory of modernist doctrine and politics in *avant guerre* England.

Questioning somewhat the high-drama of Ford's arrival legend, this chapter has argued that Lewis's career as avant-garde provocateur and dissident modernist began somewhat more quietly in a series of comic travel stories that engaged and questioned the cultural ideals of Edwardian England as articulated in *The English Review*. Central to those efforts, we have seen, was a fascination with categories of group identity and an ambivalent literary investigation of their influence on persons. As Lewis's earliest works played with the competing claims of individuality and nationality, of hierarchy and movement, of determinism and transformation, they began to articulate a (for us perhaps contradictory) vision of nationality as at once an essence and a construct. Recovering this conception helps to specify Lewis's own agency in creating the mythic figure of the epoch-announcing avantgardiste who appears as a foreign revolutionary. He encouraged such a portrayal at the start of his career first, by fashioning tentatively an avant-garde persona through a number of travel tales focused on a motley crew of eccentric and inexplicable European outcasts, and second, by advocating in an early polemic that national reformation should begin with a revitalization of English character achieved through the imitation of such foreigners. So while Lewis may have rejected the anxious liberalism and urbane imperialism of Ford's *English Review*, he shared with his elders a sense that the "health" of England was at risk, and agreed with them that foreigners – albeit of a somewhat different type – could be used – albeit in a somewhat different way – to help inject new life into an enervated national culture. The following chapter's analysis of English views of Europe in *The New Age* will show that the intellectuals associated with *The English Review*, whether urbane *constateurs* like Ford or insurgent interlopers like Lewis, were not alone in holding such cosmopolitan–nationalist agendas. As we will see, a significant number of self-styled "cosmopolitan" intellectuals shared a sense that England and English culture were depleted, declining, on the defensive, and advocated in response the international exchange of art and ideas, a program hotly opposed by England's more programmatically "patriotic" intellectuals, who rejected such policies as threatening English cultural purity and national health, advocating instead heightened support for "native" cultural traditions and movements. The intensity of these debates only increased with the death of King Edward in May 1910 and the contemporaneous increase in evidence of European challenges to English cultural prestige and British imperial power. Chapter 2 examines the implications of these challenges and the debates they provoked among radical intellectuals for the development of modernist cultural and political doctrine between 1910 and 1912.

CHAPTER 2

Narratives of ambition and anxiety: confronting Europe in The New Age

> This country has been extremely prosperous, and prosperity unfortunately carries in itself the germ of decay. The son seldom rises to the energy and ability of his father, if the latter has been a very prominent man. Born with a silver spoon in his mouth, the son does not exert himself as much as the father, who was, perhaps, a self-made man. Necessity is the great teacher, and to feel the pinch is not unwholesome; being pushed by its rivals, England will learn a good lesson.
>
> Supplement, *The New Age* (20 January 1910): 3

This chapter considers a period of spirited public controversy in which English intellectuals argued vociferously over artistic and imperial developments occurring on the Continent between May 1910, when King Edward VII died, and March 1912, when the Italian Futurists' first international exhibition opened in London to a storm of controversy. In our context, this period appears a pre- or proto-avant-garde moment. Bounded by a death signaling the end of the brief but heady Edwardian moment with its reserved, urbane, and imperial modernism, and a modern art exhibition signaling the beginning of the brief but heady avant-garde moment with its aggressive, anarchic, and imperializing modernism, these two years find English intellectuals confronting a succession of conspicuously new continental cultural movements and imperial activities. They react to this evidence of rising European competition, we will see, in ways that make English culture and cultural doctrine both more cosmopolitan and more nationalistic, preparing the ground for the consolidation of a self-consciously English avant-garde movement that would occur in the summer of 1914. As self-styled cosmopolitan intellectuals advocate increasing Anglo-European contacts to advance England's art, literature, and cultural status, work to promote peaceful international exchange and introduce new continental movements into the English cultural sphere, programmatically patriotic critics oppose such contact as a source of danger, strive to prevent the assimilation of "alien" culture, and urge English cultural purity and British military supremacy. These antagonistic camps come into conflict over a series of events in Anglo-European relations between 1910 and 1912, two of which will be considered here: the arrival of "new" French cultural movements in England beginning with Roger Fry's controversial Post-Impressionist exhibition of 1910; and the "German Threat," culminating in the Agadir Crisis of 1911, when a Franco-German territorial dispute in northern Africa nearly precipitated a European war in which Britain would side with France against Germany.

To clarify the range of views of Europe and European cultural and imperial competition among "advanced" English intellectuals between 1910 and 1912, I examine responses to new French culture and the German Threat primarily from one literary context, Alfred Orage's "Independent Socialist Review of Politics, Literature, and Art," *The New Age*. *The New Age* is an appropriate source for examining intellectual attitudes during 1910–12 not only because it featured works by many of the period's advanced intellectuals: it also succeeded Ford's *English Review* as England's leading journal for "modern" cultural and political discussion after 1910,[1] and had an eclectic editorial policy, featuring articles by authors of varied political commitments, generations, nationalities, and aesthetic beliefs.[2] Overall, *The New Age* served as a forum for wide-ranging and lively discussion of the remarkable political events and cultural movements that engaged English attention before the Great War. Many of those events and movements took place on the Continent or were originated by continental writers and artists, many impacted Anglo-European relations, many deeply exercised engaged writers and artists in England.

Debates over Anglo-French cultural and Anglo-German political relations in *The New Age* reveal the ambitions and anxieties that governed English perceptions of Europe more generally. (Post-) Edwardian responses to Britain's continental competitors sprang out of a common world view that held England and the empire to be in decline and their European competitors – especially France (England's major cultural rival) and Germany (Britain's principal military and imperial rival) – to be in ascent.[3] While *New Age* debates over new French culture clarify the ways in which this world view conditioned intellectual perceptions of European art and literature, debates over German military and imperial maneuvers elucidate the structural dynamics of the world view, exposing the limits of the cosmopolitan intelligentsia's internationalistic cultural doctrine. Although cosmopolitans believed England "fit" enough to benefit from contact with European nations and culture without being contaminated, co-opted, or consumed, subscribing to the (post-) Edwardian world view entailed the possibility that if this conviction were to change, if a sense of Britain's position relative to its continental competitors were to shift and European contact came to seem a threat, cosmopolitans would become chauvinists. This potential should come as little surprise in our context because the cosmopolitan intelligentsia's doctrine of cultural internationalism was at base, as chapter 1 argues, patriotic and imperialist. It aimed to boost England's flagging cultural status and bolster Britain's flagging imperial status.

ENCOUNTERING FRENCH CULTURE

Sometime in late 1909 or early 1910, the increasing notoriety of a series of modern cultural movements in France – especially Post-Impressionism, Cubism, and "Bergsonism" – began inspiring England's self-styled "cosmopolitan" curators, translators, editors, and critics to defend, explain, and promote the French movements at home. These efforts provoked heated critical debate on the value and effects of exposure to French culture. Orage's *New Age*, with its editorial commitment to "new" culture and "independent" discussion, became a leading forum for the debate, which manifested the contradictory hopes and fears of England's intellectual elite in the wake of Edward's death.

The treatment of France and its artistic and philosophical movements in *The New Age* epitomizes the poles of the English controversy over French modernism. While "cosmopolitan" enthusiasts like Arnold Bennett, Huntly Carter, T. E. Hulme, and John Middleton Murry praise the French movements as "advanced," casting their absorption as necessary to revitalize a native culture in arrest or decline, "patriotic" antagonists like Ernest Belfort Bax, G. K. Chesterton, and Vincent O'Sullivan assail France and French culture as "decadent," figuring cultural assimilation at best a misguided project, at worst a contaminating one. Carter, *The New Age*'s regular art and theater critic and its most enthusiastic Francophile, celebrates the "intuitional philosophy" of Henri Bergson for its vital modernizing effects: "the intuitional idea of the assertion of personality, and the death of dogmatism, is . . . marvellously . . . changing the trend of thought, and affecting the artistic aims and methods in Paris . . . rapidly bringing new and vital men to the front, while placing others on a receding horizon."[4] He praises one exhibition of new French paintings for its vigorous authenticity, calling it "the manifestation of a movement tremendously big, tremendously vital; not the mere outcome of trickery and charlatanism, but of intensity of vision carried to the highest pitch, almost to madness."[5] He deems the works of the French "Rhythmist" painters as "the starting point of a new movement in painting, perhaps the most remarkable in modern times."[6] Carter's enthusiasm for French culture extends to his vision of Paris itself, as he articulates the Francophilic view of the City of Lights as the world's most exciting and creative metropolis, literally "vibrating" with vitality and creativity: "[i]n this city of sex, at this shrine of the satisfaction of senses, with its fretwork of open-air cafés carving vibrating pathways of fine gold . . . men are everywhere busy, consciously or unconsciously, lifting the jewel of human vision out of the mire of logic."[7] Indeed, the Francophilic picture of Paris and French culture was contrasted with one of London and English culture as lacking in vitality, behind the times, provincial. In the first installment of his series of "Notes on Bergson," T. E. Hulme, then at work on the "authorized" translation of the philosopher's *Introduction to Metaphysics*, portrays the potentially "explosive" effects of exposure to French cultural vitality on the depleted English critic. Casting himself as unsuited to provide a "compte rendu" of Bergson's theories due to "a certain lack of vitality," Hulme instead "giv[es] simply a personal confession" of his liberating discovery of the Frenchman's work, which provoked "the exhilaration that comes with the sudden change from a cramped and contracted to a free and expanded state . . . an almost physical sense of exhilaration, a sudden expansion, a kind of mental explosion."[8] Another contributor calls "the Englishman . . . the least likely person in Europe to look with eyes of understanding upon a picture."[9] And Carter in the first article of his series on "The New Idea of Dramatic Action" (written each week from a different European metropolis), portrays the Continent as more culturally evolved than England: "the influence on artists themselves of the new ideas in painting is certain. On the Continent it is everywhere strongly marked. In England it occupies the position of . . . being the backbone . . . which is slowly coming to the front."[10]

The New Age's Francophiles seek to encourage the formation of cultural movements in England as advanced as those they admire on the Continent. But their view that English character is, at best, less evolved or behind the times, at worst, *essentially* provincial or philistine, calls into question the possibility of that translation project. In an approving letter on Carter's article on Bergsonism, Murry captures these conflicted feelings, excitedly exhorting his compatriots to join their French contemporaries:

> If every critic in England were sufficient of a philosopher to lay to heart the implications of the Bergsonian theories of time and change, creative art would receive a new lease of life. In France there can be no question that such a philosophy has had the most comprehensive and vital results, of which one alone, Post-impressionism, has sufficed at once to enrage and confound its critics here.[11]

Although Murry's use of the conditional tense to describe his desire that English critics should "lay to heart the implications" of Bergson's theories shows a hopeful sense of possibility, his sense of English provincialism raises doubts about his compatriots' ability to meet the challenge. Like Murry, other *New Age* Francophiles read as evidence of provincialism the rage and confusion provoked by Roger Fry's controversial art exhibition "Manet and the Post-Impressionists" (8 November 1910–15 January 1911). Arnold Bennett (writing under his *New Age* pseudonym Jacob Tonson) complains:

> The attitude of the culture of London toward [the exhibition] is of course merely humiliating to any Englishman who has made an effort to cure himself of insularity. It is one proof that the negligent disdain of continental artists for English artistic opinion is fairly well founded. The mild tragedy of the thing is that London is infinitely too self-complacent even to suspect that it is London and not the exhibition which is making itself ridiculous . . . London may be unaware that the value of the best work of this new school is permanently and definitely settled – outside London. So much the worse for London.[12]

Bennett exhibits an ambivalence many culturally ambitious intellectuals experienced in the face of French achievement and English incomprehension. An "Englishman" disappointed that London seems unable to "cure" itself of "insularity," Bennett casts himself at the same time as a European who, like the continental artists he admires, disdains English opinion and dismisses London's provincial complacency.

The tension in Bennett's hybrid self-representation as both English and European identifies a more general paradox central to the ideal of cosmopolitanism that he and his internationalistic compatriots advocate. In an approving letter on Carter's piece on Paris, Murry articulates the conception:

The atmosphere of Paris is not French; it is pre-eminently cosmopolitan. It is the students and artists of all European nationalities, whose meeting there makes Paris the very cross-roads of continental ideas. The advanced art, which has found a home in Paris, is not French: it is European. The political thought which has developed from Bergsonism is not Parisian; even the creative literature which has derived such philosophic inspiration from the new movement is cosmopolitan in character.[13]

Murry avoids identifying cultural advancement with any single nation, insisting instead that the ideal of cosmopolitanism requires the mixing of "all European nationalities." He thereby not only preserves the possibility that England's young intellectuals may join in the international project of advancing art, but also requires it as part of the definition of that advance. By thus ensuring English participation rhetorically, he works to make the dream of combining "all European nationalities" compatible with a commitment to Englishness. Recalling the arguments Ford Madox Ford had made in *The English Review*, *The New Age*'s internationalistic intellectuals do not seek a realm of "culture" above and beyond the provincializing effects of nationality as had Matthew Arnold before them. They seek to broaden England's cultural contacts in order to advance its culture. So Murry's conception of cosmopolitanism celebrates Europe as the locus of "advanced art" and advocates the Europeanization of English culture, even as it makes England an essential part of Europe and recommends a Europeanization of English culture that will preserve and strengthen England's international prestige.

While *New Age* cosmopolitans like Bennett, Carter, Hulme, and Murry idolize France as Europe's cultural hub and its mixing of nationalities as the key to cultural advance at home, more chauvinistic intellectuals like Bax, Chesterton, and O'Sullivan blast France's modern art and philosophy movements along with their English enthusiasts. *New Age* patriots invert the cosmopolitans' adoration of French creative vitality. Bax and O'Sullivan make Paris's delights the result of foreign creative dominance over France, evidence of French enervation. Bax, resident expert on philosophy, dons the guise of detached analyst and proceeds to demolish the Bergson cult. English philosophical genius rises from the rubble in the figure of Bax himself. "Reviewing Bergson objectively and impartially," he observes, "it is a little difficult to account for his sensational reputation at the present time by the intrinsic merit of his work alone."[14] Failing to find "what there is of newness or originality in the French thinker," he instructs instead that Bergson's treatment of the role of "purposive activity" in living beings, "approaches the lines of an hypothesis originally put forward by the present writer some twenty years ago and recurred to more than once since" (280). And as Bax dismisses a French philosopher for being out of date, aping the English, and plagiarizing his own theories, occasional contributor O'Sullivan, reviewing a book on "the Pleasures of Paris," turns the cosmopolitans' image of Paris as essentially European into evidence of French dullness, envy, and depletion. He dismisses as a "rather crude legend" the Francophilic idealization of Paris – in his words, "a perpetual carnival under the afternoon sun . . . a great capital existing and flourishing without work of any kind being done by its inhabitants"[15] – indulging and evoking anti-French sentiment along the way. O'Sullivan points out that the "gaiety" and "variety of energy" foreigners, "[e]specially that section of foreigners governed by artistic instincts . . . seek . . . in the Latin Quarter" is in fact the product of "the foreigners, not the natives": "If you hear a loud laughter in a Paris restaurant or theatre, it is probably English laughter; if you see people vigorously amusing themselves, they are probably Americans . . . Meanwhile the French look on with a smile of tolerance and pity, mingled perhaps with envy" (161). O'Sullivan overturns the Francophiles' vision of the Anglo-French cultural relationship in which insular English envy the vital French: his depleted Parisians are envious of their more vigorous and vital Anglo-American visitors. They realize, even if their English promoters do not, that the "Bohemia" of the Latin Quarter "has nothing French about it except that it exists in the heart of Paris" (162). Well-swollen with national pride, O'Sullivan tops off the analysis with a dash of English braggadocio: "we bring most of the entertainment with us: if we depended on the French for that kind of thing what a sodden time we should have of it!" (163).

G. K. Chesterton broadened the assault by targeting Cubism and Post-Impressionism. He perforates a Picasso study reproduced in *The New Age*:

> The eulogists of the latest artistic insanities (Cubism and Post-Impressionism and Mr Picasso) . . . circulate a piece of paper on which Mr Picasso has had the misfortune to upset the ink and tried to dry it with his boots, and they seek to terrify democracy by the good old anti-democratic muddlements; that "the public" does not understand these things.[16]

Chesterton's story of an English "public" immune to the appeal of Cubism and Post-Impressionism contrasts with his implication that the movements' English "eulogists" are anti-democratic elitists, duped by "artistic insanities." By casting Cubism and Post-Impressionism as a decadent French racket that elitist critics are trying to fob off on a sane and commonsensical English public, Chesterton re-presents the cosmopolitan ideal as a kind of crazy swindle, exploiting period stereotypes of French vice and corruption,[17] figuring himself an upstanding defender of a people wise and fit enough to resist such contaminating scams. Chesterton's piece typifies Edwardian attacks on the new French painting. England's self-styled patriotic critics, as Samuel Hynes puts it, "all saw Post-Impressionism as a foreign threat to native English art and essential English morality."[18] Accordingly, another *New Age* correspondent attacks the Picasso sketch along these lines with especial venom:

> While there are any deeper depths of degradation, inanity, or of sheer lunacy to be gone through the continental anarchists will drag the disheveled Goddess of Art through them . . . Post-Impressionism represented the art of the lunatic asylum fairly well; Picassoism represents a step lower; ingenuity will not stop there, and we may expect even worse things next year.[19]

The accusatory portrayal of Post-Impressionism and Cubism as aesthetically "anarchistic" movements and their European creators as political anarchists was contemporaneously being substantiated by increasing evidence of syndicalist violence in England and the reputed involvement of French artists in the Continent's anarchist movements.[20]

One of the most extravagant examples of the chauvinistic attack was supplied, as Hynes suggests, by Sir William Richmond, portrait painter and former Oxford professor of fine arts, in the pages of the *Morning Post.* Richmond rehearses the standard picture of the new French art as a threatening foreign contamination that the English are healthy enough to withstand. But Richmond's attack is notable in our context for its heated rhetoric, its gendering of the French–English opposition, and the defensive intensity of its distress. On first encountering Fry's exhibition, he recounts:

> For a moment there came a fierce feeling of terror lest the youth of England, young promising fellows, might be contaminated there. On reflection I was reassured that the youth of England, being healthy, mind and body, is far too virile to be moved save in resentment against the providers of this unmanly show.[21]

The appearance of a threatening and "unmanly" foreign art in England provokes from the male English viewer feelings of fear and disgust. He recovers by reasserting English health, virility, and inviolability. This pattern of xenophobic recoil succeeded by chauvinistic reassertion is evident, with varying degrees of intensity and flourish, in all the preceding examples of anti-French, pro-English criticism. Repetition of the pattern regardless of the example of French culture under consideration indicates that the criticisms reveal as much about the English critics as about the "character" of the movements they purport to evaluate. Consider the contrasting characteristics O'Sullivan, Bax, Chesterton, and Richmond attribute to the French and the English: the French are dull, envious, unmanly, derivative, insane, degraded, anarchistic; the English, vigorous, healthy, virile, advanced, original, sensible. The lists catalogue respectively the defensive accusations provoked by worries about French cultural competition and the idealizations called on to stave off those worries and the works that raise them.

Whether *New Age* intellectuals consider themselves cosmopolitan progressives sympathetic to continental advances or patriotic conservatives antagonistic to European decadence, however, they share a sense of English (cultural) weakness compared to France. *New Age* Francophiles exhibit this sense at moments of insecurity in their praise of French culture as Europe's most advanced, their view of English culture as provincial and behind the times, and their ambition to join in the Continent's cultural advances; they display it at moments of confidence by imagining England where France is, at the forefront of Europe's cultural life. *New Age* Francophobes – somewhat less secure than their internationalist compatriots – express it through moralistic attacks on the French movements, which ironically emphasize French cultural potency, and defensive idealizations of English culture and character, which ironically emphasize English insecurity and impotence. England's intellectuals, internationalist and patriot alike, cannot ignore evidence of increasing European political and cultural power and internal social instability, political unrest, and cultural inferiority. They share the belief that continental cultural movements are ahead or on the rise, worry that England and English art and literature are behind the times or in decline, and perceive their nation becoming increasingly entwined with the Continent's.

Indeed, subscribing to a world view in which British imperial power and English cultural prestige are flagging, even in decline, while continental nations and cultures, especially French and German, are strong and in ascent makes possible both the positive possibility that cosmopolitanism will advance English culture and the negative one that it will help continental movements contaminate, consume, even conquer that domestic culture. The crucial distinction between cosmopolitans and patriots is less intellectual than temperamental: the former are more optimistic than the latter. They believe that English intellectuals and culture are vital enough, despite evidence of current depletion, to absorb the lessons of French art without being co-opted or contaminated. But subscription to the (post-) Edwardian world view creates conceptual conditions which nearly guarantee that internationalists will become chauvinists: if their sense of England's position relative to continental nations were to change (and in the early teens how could it not?), if sufficient evidence was found that continental culture *did* threaten Englishness and English culture, then they too would embrace anti-continental attitudes. By examining English perceptions of changing German military and imperial power between 1910 and 1912, the following section confirms not only that such conceptual dynamics obtained as well in the realm of Anglo-European political relations, but also that threatening imperial maneuvers by Germany helped realize this theoretical potential for cultural realignment among cosmopolitan intellectuals of *The New Age*.

THE GERMAN THREAT AND THE POLITICS OF REALIGNMENT

Given the presence of a shared world-view figuring Britain in a (losing) competition with Europe, it is likely that the conflicted desires which underlay English arguments about new French culture would also characterize those concerning any continental nation perceived as challenging British power or prestige, whether the locus of power is construed as cultural, as in the French case, or military-imperial, as, we will see, in the German. Responses to Germany's changing military and imperial status in *The New Age* substantiate the possibility and provide an exemplary case of a specific occurrence of the radical realignment in cultural loyalty among internationalists that subscription to the (post-) Edwardian world-view made possible. If intellectual arguments over the new French culture expose underlying ambitions for success and anxieties of decline among English chauvinists and cosmopolitans alike, then the so-called Agadir Crisis of 1911 makes the threat of German military power appear so significant that even an emphatically cosmopolitan intellectual with especially strong ties to Germany and German culture is provoked to put aside internationalism in favor of nationalism: *The New Age*'s foreign affairs correspondent, J. M. Kennedy, aggressive publicist of Nietzsche, German culture, and aristocratic politics.[22] Kennedy's individual enactment of a realignment in cultural doctrine in response to European competition anticipates and illuminates the broader doctrinal shift that will occur among younger artists and writers with cosmopolitan sympathies in mid-1914 (the topic of chapter 3).

Invasion fantasies and internationalist rejoinders

The Edwardian years are marked, as others have established, by frequent and extreme expressions of national insecurity and international suspicion.[23] Politicians and popular writers, in particular those with a Tory affiliation or sympathy, publicly raise questions about the health and strength of their nation and empire and concerns about the activities and power of England's rivals, especially Germany, with its increasingly large navy and aggressive imperial policies. This literature of insecurity and suspicion finds a large and receptive popular audience, which the Tories and their allies exploit. The years 1900–14 witness a dramatic increase in the publication and the popularity of tales of decline and invasion. In these texts, Tory writers encourage popular anxieties about English decline and German aggression in part to advance their domestic and military policies, in part to cast the Liberals as morally suspect, soft on defense, and unpatriotic. The Tories ultimately dream of unseating the Liberal government. Unable to achieve that goal in a period of Liberal popularity, however, they settle for stirring up public fears to pressure their opponents into following a generally conservative military policy: to build up the fleet, consolidate Britain's imperial holdings, institute compulsory military service, and support the arms industry. General Baden-Powell, Tory military hero and former Inspector-General of the Cavalry, founds the Boy Scouts, as he puts it in the movement handbook, *Scouting for Boys* (1908), to counter "the deterioration of our race."[24] He figures this paramilitary organization, in Hynes words, "as a preparation for war and the defense of the empire."[25] "One cause which contributed to the downfall of the Roman empire," the handbook asserts, "was the fact that the soldiers fell away from the standard of their forefathers in bodily strength" (208). To avert the fate of Rome in Britain, Baden-Powell's scout masters will discipline the empire's youth into healthy and efficient soldiers – with Tory politics. The handbook implies – not particularly subtly – that no good scout would support the Liberals:

> There are always members of Parliament who try to make the Navy and Army smaller, so as to save money . . . These men are called "politicians." They do not look to the good of the country. Most of them know and care very little about our Colonies . . . [I]f they are allowed to have their way in the future we may as will learn German or Japanese, for we shall be conquered by these.
>
> But fortunately there are other better men in Parliament who are called "statesmen"; these are men who look out for the welfare of the country, and do not mind about being popular or not so long as they keep the country safe. (328)

Needless to say, Baden-Powell's "politicians" are Liberals, his "statesmen" Tories.

This anti-Liberal, pro-Tory argument is presented even more insistently in a typical scare novel of the period, *The Invasion of 1910* by popular author and amateur spy, William Le Queux. Like the novel's patriotic characters, Le Queux's narrator blames the imagined German invasion on the failings of Liberal government:

> The whole character of the nation and the Government had changed since the great days when, in the face of famine and immense peril, the country had fought Napoleon to the last and overthrown him. The strong aristocratic Government had been replaced by a weak administration, swayed by every breath of popular impulse.[26]

Le Queux's narrator articulates a paradox that characterizes many of these Tory propaganda texts. He appeals to patriotic sentiments and exploits anti-European anxieties in order to encourage his popular audience to support the Tories. But in scorning democracy and celebrating aristocratic government, he makes little effort to conceal loyalty to the ruling classes and antagonism to working-class social and political interests. Such Tory propaganda nevertheless strikes a popular nerve with its claim that Germany is an increasing, perhaps inevitable threat that Liberal England appears socially and militarily unprepared to meet.

Unsurprisingly, *The New Age*, with its cosmopolitan socialist bent and particular enthusiasm for German literature and philosophy (Orage and other regular contributors promoted Nietzsche with especial vigor), takes a strong stand against anti-German propaganda and popular literature. *New Age* internationalists consistently expose the ulterior motives and hidden agendas of the "scare-mongers," ridicule claims of inevitable war, dismiss the argument for military buildup, and criticize exploitation of "jingoism" for political gain. Anti-chauvinist arguments in *The New Age* tend to be of two sorts, which often overlap in individual accounts: some interpret the growth of anti-German suspicion and anxiety as part of a conspiracy on the part of Tories, Tory dupes, and industrialists to advance their militaristic interests and, as one contributor puts it, block the "growth of Socialism and of the Labour Party in this country";[27] others read it as the result of English chauvinism and attendant ignorance about Germany and the Germans. The conspiracy case is presented, for example, by C. H. Norman, *The New Age*'s former foreign affairs columnist who, it was rumored, had been such an outspoken critic of government policy that the Foreign Office pressured Orage to remove him from the post.[28] Norman prefaces an anti-scare piece titled "A Study in Jingoism" by asserting that:

> The following article summarises in parallel columns the arguments of the British and German Jingoes, by which they are driving the two countries into war. The similarity of the two cases as presented is very curious. The historical record of aggression by the two States is the same. The peoples of England and Germany were tools of their militarist and ruling oligarchies in the past; and only the greatest exertions will prevent them being tricked into war in the future.[29]

Although Norman assumes the familiar pose of (Arnoldian) disinterestedness, his account exposes the contradictory political and social commitments we have come to expect among (post-) Edwardian progressives. By characterizing England and Germany's rulers as "militarist . . . oligarchies," he reveals a pacifist, socialistic, anti-Tory bias. By describing the "peoples of England and Germany" as "tools" of those oligarchies, he exposes an upper-class sense of working-class inferiority. And by stating that "only the greatest exertions" will save those "peoples" from future war, he implies that only left-wing intellectuals – like him – can perform these heroic exertions, showing a sense of intellectual superiority to the masses.

Some *New Age* internationalists who interpret anti-German panic as the product of English insularity and chauvinism find in the Victorian tradition of Anglo-German racial relation a reason for optimism. C. R. Hennings, in a piece titled "Our German Cousins and the English Nation," argues that "[t]he prejudice of the English against the Germans" is due "a great deal to ignorance." He cites the fact that "few . . . in this country are masters of the German language," and asserts that "much remains to be done" to eliminate Anglo-German misunderstanding. He points to the hereditary links between the English and Germans as a source of hope: "England and Germany, coming from the same stock as they do, resemble one another more than any other nation. Differences there are many . . . Both, however, ought to love and esteem each other."[30] Hennings attempts to counter "the prejudice of the English against the Germans" and overcome English resistance to peaceful Anglo-German intercourse by reiterating the familiar Victorian claim that the English and the Germans are racially related.[31] Ironically, he strives to overcome anti-German prejudice, which depends on a negative stereotype of German character (as essentially expansionistic, militaristic, and untrustworthy), by recourse to the historical tradition of Anglo-German racial relation, which depends on a positive stereotype of German character (as essentially freedom loving and adventurous, linked by blood to their similarly constituted English "cousins").[32] This irony in Hennings's effort to counter anti-German prejudice by asserting an Anglo-German racial link, exposes friction between two pictures of German character competing for priority during the period; the first in historical decline, the second in ascent: while England's nineteenth-century historical tradition held the English and Germans to be racially related, most of its early twentieth-century political leaders, popular journalists, and imperialist intellectuals deemed Germans an essentially belligerent "race" and England's inevitable enemies.

These competing conceptions of Germany exert particular pressure on *New Age* internationalists because they advocate an ideal of cosmopolitan combination to advance English culture. The claim of Anglo-German racial relation is attractive because it counters the chauvinism that thwarts cosmopolitanism and encourages the international exchange of ideas and artworks. But because the internationalists' ideal also entails a risk to English cultural identity, they periodically worry about proliferating evidence of German expansion. One of the most interesting displays of the internationalists' paradoxical treatment of German character – in which a fair-minded tendency to defend Germans, competes with a defensive tendency to demonize them and aggrandize the English – occurs in a *New Age* piece by W. R. Titterton with the provocative title "Why Not Surrender to Germany?"[33] Titterton's article is a satiric attack on the "fervid flag-waving" and anti-Germanism of English chauvinists (562). It advocates the sort of Anglo-German cultural and political entente recommended by Norman and Hennings, though in rhetoric notably more extreme:

You keep on building "Dreadnoughts" and scrapping them. You keep on building soldiers and sailors and scrapping them. You keep on ranting and foaming and shouting and generally misconducting yourselves, and letting the government of the country and social reform go hang. The war scare, in fact, is a put-up job to keep the minds . . . of the people from the thought of oppressions nearer home . . . The union with Germany would stop all that. Jingo bulldogs of insular and continental breed could have a go at each other whenever they felt inclined, while the rest of us went on with our business of getting nearer and nearer to a mutual understanding. (563)

Titterton presents the pacifist–internationalist argument in satiric form: the hysterical tone of his attack against anti-German hysteria caricatures the attitudes he opposes, while his announced goal of English surrender to Germany ridicules the jingoists by recommending the very thing they most fear.

At the same time, however, Titterton's tactics complicate his criticism by partaking of the feelings he assails and indulging the fantasies he scorns. The traditional satiric technique of exaggerating the position under attack recurs throughout the piece, intensifying and undermining the force of its claims:

I am not much concerned with preserving the national boundaries, but I want very badly to preserve the national character, and I have been grieved to note that the English national character becomes year by year less clearly defined. This is an effect of our insularity that allows us to visit foreigners as tourists and prevents us from rubbing shoulders with them as neighbours. To be invaded and conquered is our only means of remedying this defect of nature, and invasion and conquest we have not enjoyed now for several centuries. I plead for a fresh conquest. (562)

Titterton mingles a chauvinist critique of English decadence and its underlying desire to "preserve" the national character with a radical version of the internationalist critique of English insularity, in which advocacy of international intercourse becomes advocacy of foreign conquest. He emphasizes and undercuts the arguments of both the Tory chauvinist and the internationalist anti-jingo. So his claim that, "we always have absorbed our conquerors" (562), stresses both English weakness, by flagging England's history of foreign invasion and conquest, and English strength, by re-presenting that history of domination *by* others as a history of assimilation *of* others.[34]

We have seen the simultaneous assertion of English weakness and strength around the topic of England "absorb[ing]" its foreign competitors before. Titterton's view recalls those of *The New Age*'s Francophiles and Francophobes concerning new French culture. As the former argue that cosmopolitan intercourse is the best means to achieve English cultural success, they worry that England is too weak to withstand the treatment; as the latter argue for English health and fortitude, they worry that England will not survive an influx of foreign culture. Like these examples of Edwardian anxieties of decline and fantasies of supremacy, Titterton's satiric strategy of intermingling and exaggerating internationalist and chauvinist arguments has the paradoxical effect of increasing the insecurities it aims to diffuse and undermining the confidence it seeks to bolster.

Thus Titterton's treatment of Germans and Germany shows an internationalistic desire to increase Anglo-German contacts competing with a chauvinistic distrust of "Prussia and Prussians" and an inclination to demonize German national character:

> The rigid and aggressive officialism of Prussia . . . grows more and more repugnant to the rest of the States . . . Prussia is a very powerful State, and the South German States, with Bavaria at their head, have difficulty in coping with . . . the Imperial Council. But say that England joined the Federation and took the side of South Germany! Where would Prussia be then? I want to save Germany from Prussia. (563)

Titterton resorts to the conventional – and fairly accurate – Edwardian argument, buttressed by the evidence of Prussia's role in the German wars of unification (1864–71), that the German empire is dominated by Prussia and its leaders.[35] Rhetorically, this separation of Prussians from Germans facilitates Titterton's satiric argument by allowing him to advocate entente with Germany at the same time that he accuses the "officialism of Prussia" of aggressiveness and rigidity. And Titterton's claim that England can "save Germany from Prussia" by "join[ing] the German federation," exhibits the period tendency to cover-up worries about national decline with assertions of English excellence. His exhortation aggrandizes England as embodiment and defender of freedom (a standard Victorian idealization)[36] and fantasizes a British victory over the nation the English were increasingly coming to believe they could not defeat.

Titterton's mixture of an internationalist's advocacy for Anglo-German intercourse and a chauvinist's defensive assertions of English excellence to counter worries about German strength parallels the Francophiles ambivalences toward French culture: their advocacy of cosmopolitan contact is finally motivated by a nationalist desire to supplant Paris as the capital of European art and France as the source of modern culture. Indeed, Titterton's announced aim parallels that of Francophiles like Bennett and Murry; he too recommends cosmopolitan combination to cure England's ills: "It is obvious, that *union with*

Germany is the only practical means of preserving and developing our national character" (563; italics original). By advocating Anglo-German union to "preserve and develop" English character, Titterton applies the cosmopolitan–nationalist program to the case of Anglo-German relations. That Francophilic and Germanophilic internationalists had the same overall aim adds weight to the argument that English responses to French culture and German politics exemplify English attitudes to the Continent more generally. The particular European nation with which the internationalists sought intercourse was less important than their nationalistic goal of "preserving or developing" English character, culture, and prestige.

Titterton's conclusion provides an exemplary case of the tendency of writings by cosmopolitan intellectuals to expose tensions between competing loyalties to internationalism and nationalism. He mingles cosmopolitan and chauvinist rhetoric in a paradoxical effort to support Anglo-German entente by exploiting the fear of German conquest:

> And let me warn you that if I have overestimated your intelligence, if in your blindness you do not surrender, a worse fate will befall you. You will be conquered piecemeal by alien ideas you do not understand. Wagner has conquered you, Ibsen (who was really German) has conquered you, Richard Strauss is conquering you, "The Merry Widow" has conquered you, State Socialism (a gross folly without the democratic spirit of the Germans) is conquering you, conscription is conquering you, German beer (a liquid insult in a stand-up bar) is conquering you . . . Surrender to the Germans! My dear fellow, you have surrendered long ago; it is only by a formal surrender you will get a quid pro quo for your humility. (563)

The intensity of Titterton's contempt for the English people and his evident glee in exploiting their fears of German invasion derives in part from his sense that they are essentially jingoistic. But by harping on all this alleged evidence of achieved German cultural conquest, he again fuels the attitude he ostensibly opposes. By now the pattern is familiar. Chauvinistic critics who attack Post-Impressionism as a foreign contamination and insist that the strong and vital people of England are immune to its infection emphasize both the foreign potency they seek to downplay and the national insecurity they seek to relieve. The recurrence of this pattern in responses of internationalists *and* chauvinists to Germany *and* France confirms two points central to this chapter's argument: English intellectuals regardless of cultural agenda share an anxiety about continental power and English weakness; they tend to expose national insecurities in response to evidence of continental potency regardless which European nation provides it or from what realm of prestige it comes. This chapter's concluding discussion traces the ways in which such concerns help provoke even an insistently internationalistic intellectual to a patriotic response when confronted with especially strong evidence of German imperial competition.

The Agadir Crisis and the realignment of the cosmopolitan intellectual

During the summer of 1911, in response to French and Spanish moves to protect their imperial interests during a revolt in Morocco, the Germans asserted their ambitions by sending the gunboat Panther to the south Moroccan port of Agadir. For a moment, Europe seemed poised on the brink of major war. If the Germans and the French were to declare war, treaty obligations would require Britain, Russia, Austria-Hungary, and Italy to join the conflict. By late September, however, French diplomacy and a warning that Britain would support France in the event of military conflict, convinced Germany to back down. Though the English public initially feared the conflict would precipitate the European conflagration that had haunted them for over a decade, they realized afterward that it had actually consolidated Britain's alliance with France in opposition to Germany. The crisis thus confirmed that Britain had moved from its Victorian position of independent international non-alliance to its post-Edwardian position as one member of the Triple Entente with France and Russia against the Triple Alliance of Germany, Austria-Hungary, and Italy.[37] War had been averted. But the decline of British power had not, a point not insignificant for the developments in English modernist doctrine considered here and in the following chapter.

For now, the treatment of the unfolding Agadir Crisis in *The New Age*'s "Foreign Affairs" column, written by the prolific cosmopolitan journalist and cultural critic, J. M. Kennedy, under the pseudonym "S. Verdad" (a play on the Portuguese for "it is true"), confirms two crucial points. It shows that changing Anglo-German political relations impacted negatively on the opinion of Germany held by one of England's most insistently pro-German intellectuals. Moreover, it instantiates the potential for realignment in cultural loyalties entailed by subscribing to the (post-) Edwardian world-view theorized above: when proclaimed internationalists become convinced that foreign competitors pose a serious threat to English interests or identity, they too will embrace nationalism and policies of cultural purity and military defense. Kennedy's columns on Agadir enact this re-alignment on an individual level in response to an international political event. A pro-German intellectual faced with sufficient evidence of German military aggression places his commitment to England before his commitment to Anglo-German entente and German culture. As the Crisis intensifies, Kennedy's discussion of German military aims and activities becomes increasingly negative as he more openly echoes the anti-German claims of the "scare-mongers," while his discussion of French military aims and activities becomes increasingly positive as he more openly praises France and embraces the emerging Anglo-French alliance.

Kennedy is particularly well suited to study on an individual level the effects of the Agadir Crisis because he came to it disinclined either to object to Germany and German culture or to celebrate France and French culture. As *The New Age*'s resident foreign affairs expert, he was at the center of the journal's political and cultural discussions. Besides the foreign affairs column, he contributed articles of cultural criticism under his own name and, as one of the most active members of the English Nietzsche movement, was sympathetic in particular to German philosophy and literature.[38] Most important, Kennedy's political bent was aristocratic and conservative; he was neither Liberal, Fabian, nor Francophile. He contributed the radical right-wing tract *Tory Democracy* to *The New Age* (May–September 1911). There and in his work of "Nietzschean" literary history, *English Literature, 1880–1905* (1912), he characterized the French revolution and nineteenth-century French literature and philosophy as key sources for the political liberalism and cultural romanticism he reviled.[39]

Like many of his intellectual colleagues, Kennedy disdains and distinguishes himself from the "scare-mongering" tactics of the popular press. He assumes in his foreign affairs column the posture of a level-headed realist, unswayed by popular emotions or prejudices:

> Whatever may be said about this page and its Editor, I think that even the worst enemies of its writer will admit that it has never degenerated into a mere scare-page. Any warnings which I have felt compelled to give from time to time, or complaints which I have felt it incumbent upon me to make, have invariably been supported by facts.[40]

In addition, and again like other "advanced" intellectuals, Kennedy positions himself ahead of the pack of analysts in the popular press. His formidable linguistic abilities (he was reputed to have mastered all European tongues) and his habit of reading European newspapers doubtless helped him beat popular journalists on some international scoops.[41] By his account, he had anticipated most press analyses of Germany's ambitions in Morocco, even before its gunship set sail for Agadir in early July. In the *New Age* of 13 July, he writes:

> It is often necessary for writers on this paper to slow down and let the ordinary daily Press catch up. It was so . . . in the case of Morocco . . . Germany's position and her various plans were referred to on this page weeks ago, and nothing has since been added to the information I have already given. Some authorities hold that Germany wants a coaling station on the Atlantic; others that she wants her African boundary lines better defined; others that she simply wants to drive as good a bargain as she can; others, again, that, in view of the approaching Reichstag elections and the Socialistic propaganda, she wants a little diversion abroad. These different points of view, I repeat, were all discussed in this paper weeks ago.[42]

Kennedy's catalogue is of general interest because it gives a sense of the range of competing readings of Germany's action being offered in English periodicals and intellectual circles. The catalogue is of particular interest because it indicates the existence among English students of foreign affairs, regardless of political affiliation, of a general consensus regarding Germany early in the Crisis. Though Kennedy positions himself as an especially informed and realistic analyst, who records only "facts," avoids "scare-mongering," and disdains popular negative readings of German national character, the picture of Germany he evokes is not so very different from that promoted by anti-German propagandists. Kennedy's Germany too is greedy ("Germany wants . . . she wants . . . she simply wants . . . she wants"), materialistic ("Germany wants a coaling station . . . to drive as good a bargain as she can"), expansionistic ("she wants her African boundary lines better defined"), and dominated by opportunistic imperialists ("in view of the . . . Reichstag elections and the Socialist propaganda, she wants a little diversion abroad").

But in the first days of the Crisis, before it was clear how France would respond to Germany's action, how Germany would react, and what position Britain would take, the aristocratically minded Kennedy differentiates himself from Germanophobes and Francophiles in the parliament, press, and intelligentsia. Applauding the Kaiser's government for aristocratic consistency, he criticizes France for democratic variability:

> What has undoubtedly strengthened Germany's power in her international dealings is the weakness of government in France. Democracy . . . does not suit a Latin country, particularly France. The people are too individualistic, and the struggle for power and "la gloire" is particularly bitter and continuous; hence the fifty or sixty Ministries in France since the formation of the Republic and

the consequent changes in policy . . . The ideal administration is that of Germany, where, no matter how many Foreign Secretaries may be in power, the Kaiser exercises full control.[43]

Yet Kennedy's distrust of "Latin" democracy and admiration for German autocracy are not as principled and absolute as his rhetoric of didactic certainty implies. Changing events at Agadir confirm that Kennedy's views of Britain's European competitors actually depend on the ways in which he conceives England and the empire in relation to these competitors.

Three weeks into the Crisis, antagonism between France and Germany had increased considerably; neither government seemed willing to compromise its claims, the possibility of a war which might involve Britain appeared more likely. In this atmosphere of heightened tension, Kennedy, who had praised the Germans for their resolve and criticized the French for their variability, now directs his ire against "certain Liberal" newspapers for accusing France of provoking the crisis. He counters such claims by modifying his earlier account; now France is the admirable, law-abiding, and consistent power, Germany the unworthy, treaty-violating, and unpredictable one. Kennedy dismisses efforts to "blame France" as the "solemn nonsense" of "leader-writers" ignorant of or oblivious to the "essential facts" of the situation, which the "real student of foreign affairs" carries "in his head." "France has really tried to abide by the spirit of the act of Algeciras," he continues, "the same cannot be said of her neighbours across the Rhine."[44] Kennedy, who had recently distinguished his account from anti-German reports in the popular press, now accuses an "expanding" Germany of having "no particular respect" for "treaties, diplomatic traditions, and international compacts," an accusation often used in the popular press to discourage Anglo-German entente.[45]

When the German government backed down in late September, Kennedy enthusiastically praised the French for their diplomatic victory, even expressing satisfaction at Germany's defeat. Refuting arguments in the popular press that the resolution of the crisis confirms France's status as the world's most peace-loving nation, he interprets it as evidence of a French return to warlike courage:

The German Government's gigantic bluff has collapsed. A settlement of the Moroccan question is now in sight, and that settlement will be favourable, more than favourable, to France . . . [T]he French people have recovered from their fright of Germany, a state of mind which has haunted them for years. The French are once again ready to fight, and it is all nonsense to try to make out –

as, of course, our old friends the "Daily News," the "Star," and "Reynolds's" attempt to do – that the French, above all nations, have come to look upon war as barbarous and inhuman.[46]

The particular emphasis Kennedy places on this French recovery from "fright of Germany" not only confirms a level of admiration for France and distrust of Germany inconsistent with his earlier comments about these nations, but also hints at a level of commitment to English nationalism inconsistent with his posture of cosmopolitan disinterestedness. For part of what animates Kennedy's admiration for the French is a patriotic wish that the English too will recover from *their* "fright of Germany."

Kennedy's political realignment in response to the Agadir Crisis shows that the period's increasingly antagonistic Anglo-German political relations impacted negatively even on the view of Germany of an especially pro-German intellectual. Before the crisis, Kennedy had publicly embraced a political and cultural doctrine that celebrated many of the values conventionally attributed in England to Germany and the Germans (aristocracy, aggressiveness, modernity) and had criticized many of the values conventionally attributed to France and the French (democracy, pacifism, romanticism). Indeed, he had defined his public identity largely through opposition to and aristocratic difference from the "masses," whether popular journalists, political liberals, cultural romanticists, philosophical anti-Nietzscheans, or even old-style Tories. Yet when faced with a credible threat of German imperial aggression and Anglo-German conflict, Kennedy put Englishness before elitism, before Germanophilia, before cosmopolitanism, and got into line with what he had referred to only months before in *The New Age* as "the stupid . . . greed[y] . . . masses."[47]

This is not to suggest that Kennedy's increasing conviction in the German threat leads him to embrace wholeheartedly the deterministic stereotype of German national character that so appealed to the English public during the period. Rather, Kennedy's view that the German threat at Agadir to English interests is sufficiently serious causes him to adopt a more explicitly anti-German, pro-French posture than he had publicly embraced before. That he occasionally reiterates anti-German arguments of the moment is not surprising. Our reading shows that both English chauvinists, who promulgate a determinist analysis of German character, and internationalists, who favor a pragmatic one, roughly agree on what Germany's national characteristics are (aggressiveness, autocracy, expansionism, militarism, and materialism). They disagree on the source of those characteristics: while chauvinists tend to view them as the result of the Germans' racial heritage, internationalists tend to interpret them as the result of the German empire's social, political, and historical circumstances. It is because Kennedy shares not only this view of Germany, but also the period concern with British decline that when faced with sufficient evidence of a German threat, he exchanges cosmopolitanism for patriotism.

The foregoing analysis of the (post-) Edwardian intelligentsia's ambivalent perceptions of Britain's European competitors as played out in the pages of *The New Age* confirms that the cosmopolitan intellectuals' strategy to modernize English culture and establish an English avant-garde – importing the Continent's new art, translating its new literature, imitating its new behaviors – succeeds in inspiring young artists and writers to emulate their continental counterparts and in internationalizing England's cultural sphere, but at the same time, that success intensifies English anxieties of vulnerability. These developments make possible the crucial shift in cultural doctrine among England's advanced intellectuals that will occur in 1914: when confronted with evidence of European competition – from, in this case, an Italian avant-garde art movement – the "advanced" intelligentsia, predominantly internationalistic since before the century's turn, organizes one of Europe's most insistently nationalistic avant-garde groups, the Vorticists, and embraces a cultural doctrine "fundamentally English." By identifying and anatomizing the anxieties and ambitions that governed English perceptions of England's continental competitors between the death of Edward and the "Futurist Invasion," this chapter has articulated the political and attitudinal dynamics that paved the way for that doctrinal realignment, the topic of chapter 3.

CHAPTER 3

Advancing art and empire: Futurism in England, Italy in Libya, and the founding of Vorticism

> Proud to feel that the war-like fervor which animates the whole country equals our own, we incite the Italian government, finally become Futurist, to magnify all national ambitions, scorning the stupid accusations of piracy and proclaiming the birth of PANITALIANISM.
>
> F. T. Marinetti, "Italian Tripoli" (October 1911), I: 32

> "Futurism" is largely Anglo-Saxon civilisation. It should not rest with others to be the Artists of this revolution and new possibilities in life. As modern life is the invention of the English, they should have something profounder to say on it than anybody else.
>
> Wyndham Lewis, "A Man of the Week: Marinetti" (May 1914), 32

In response to the opening of the Italian Futurists' first international exhibition at London's Sackville Gallery in March of 1912, Walter Sickert, English Impressionist painter, founder of the New English Art Club, and critic of Picasso and Matisse, wrote a surprisingly positive review. Like many English commentators, he condemned the Futurists' tendency to over-explain their paintings in print. But he did not resort to the other accusations most often leveled at the Italian painters. In the first month of the exhibition, critics writing in intellectual and popular publications had attacked the Futurists and their art on ethical grounds for being "anarchistic," "nihilistic," "morbid," "destructive," and "degenerate."[1] Sickert disagreed. "One thing the Futurist movement certainly is not," he wrote, "and that is, immoral." Instead, he found it "[a]ustere, bracing, patriotic, nationalist, positive, anti-archaistic, anti-sentimental, anti-feminist."[2] Sickert was following the lead of the movement's impresario, F. T. Marinetti. In the "Initial Manifesto of Futurism," translated in the exhibition catalogue, the Italian poet-propagandist had celebrated "militarism, patriotism" and attacked "museums," "libraries" and "feminism."[3] But of all the Futurists' official values, Sickert emphasized one in particular: "The Futurist movement is essentially a movement of Italian patriotism."[4] English press accounts of Italy's international activities at the moment of the exhibition indicate that Sickert had precise – and rather political – reasons for stressing above all the Futurists' patriotism.

When the Futurists stormed London in the spring of 1912, what the English were hearing and reading about Italy concerned its imperialist war with Turkey in North Africa. Initiated by Italy, the Turko-Italian War was an effort to wrest from Ottoman control the disputed North African regions of Tripolitania and Cyrenaica. Patriotic Italians had dreamed of restoring their nation's reputation ever since its humiliating defeat in Ethiopia of 1896. Nationalists had long argued that "Libya" was Italy's "fourth shore." So when domestic pressure for military action reached fever-pitch in late-September of 1911, Giolliti's government dispatched troops against the Turks.[5] The conflict was another in a series of imperial disputes that brought the "Powers" increasingly close to a European-wide conflagration in the years leading up to August 1914.[6] It was bloody (the Turks, their Arab allies, and the Italians were all accused of brutality), short (lasting just over a year), and inconclusive (victors on paper, the Italians succeeded in securing only a small portion of disputed territory, and the war's close was brought about primarily through European pressure and the Turks' need to respond to the more threatening aggression of Bulgaria, Serbia, and Greece).[7] English commentaries on the Libyan war confirm that English understandings of Futurism were entangled with perceptions of Italy and that those were importantly conditioned by the war. English avant-garde polemics, especially those in *BLAST* (July 1914), the periodical of the Vorticist movement, articulate both the ways this conditioning structured the founding of Vorticism as a programmatically anti-Futurist and nationalistic art group, and more generally, the lines of complicity and resistance between the historical avant-garde and early century imperialism.[8]

ITALIAN OCCUPATIONS

Two examples of the English literature prompted by the Turko-Italian conflict, Charles Lapworth's *Tripoli and Young Italy* (March 1912) and Francis McCullagh's *Italy's War for a Desert* (May 1912), plot the range of response and demonstrate the entwinement in English thinking of Futurism and Italian imperialism.[9] Both works give an extended analysis of the conflict and its significance, but from diametrically opposed positions. Lapworth's idealistic, pro-Italian account, written with the sanction of Italy's government, effectively translates the official Italian explanation of the war. In Lapworth's picture, "Young Italy" is a nation animated by a "new spirit" (5), determined "to count for something in international affairs, and to prevent herself from being hemmed in and stifled by other contending powers" (6). His Italy is driven to initiate the "Tripoli campaign" by Turkish "persecution of her subjects and the studied boycott of her business interests" in Tripoli (18), a region Italy's "right to" had "been acknowledged for many years by England and France" (41). This military action manifests Italy's "new-found strength" (32), "compel[s] . . . other nations to respect her," and proves that "she is in a fair way to becoming a World Power" (315). In contrast, McCullagh's "realistic," anti-Italian account, based on his first-hand observations as foreign correspondent for the *Westminster Gazette*, articulates the pacifist, anti-imperialist condemnation of the war. In McCullagh's picture, Italy, "the weakest of the Powers," has been misled by "jingoists" (4), who have stirred up an "intolerant Chauvinist spirit" (xx) and a "craze for militarism" (xxxiii). Combined with a "sentimental claim" (3) on "an enormous waste of bare rock and sand" (38), the craze had driven Italy and her people to attack Turkish Tripoli, breaking "diplomatic, international, hygienic, and strategical laws" (xxix).

Despite considerable differences in opinion, Lapworth and McCullagh concur that Italian nationalism and the so-called Young Nationalist movement are behind the conflict. Lapworth takes the positive view. "Nationalism, as a broad principle and not a narrow, political creed," he reports enthusiastically, "has come to be recognised as a driving force in Italy to-day, and it has played no small part in the recent stirring events" (285).[10] He describes the rise of nationalism before the war, as a group of "young men" grew increasingly alarmed by the "wave of Pan-Germanism, which threatened not only to Germanise Austrian Italy, but to spread itself right along the Adriatic" (296) and offended by Italy's "moribund" Parliament (296), with its "'peace-at-any-price" posture (296), "non-existent" foreign policy (297), and "cap-in-hand attitude towards Germany and Austria" (297). To counter these developments, "The Young Nationalists, as they called themselves," set "to work to outline a definite, positive policy" (297). Tireless propagandizing increased their cause's popularity, until eventually, "[t]he more responsible people in the land began to sit up and take notice; and . . . a large number of prominent public men, while declining directly to associate themselves as Nationalists . . . openly endorsed the[ir] principles" (301–02). In contrast, McCullagh's Nationalists helped breed the jingoistic spirit responsible for the barbarous war for a desert that he protests:

> Almost unobserved, a new Chauvinist party has been growing up during the last few decades in Italy. The members of this party call themselves Nationalists . . . The[y] . . . are jingoists of an extreme and candid type. They believe in war for war's sake. They believe that the shedding of blood makes a nation virile, unifies it, intensifies the patriotism of its inhabitants. Their motto is: "If you feel decadent, go out and murder somebody." (3–4)

Moreover, both Lapworth and McCullagh, like Sickert writing at almost the same moment,[11] present Futurism as strongly patriotic and intimately involved with the Italian Nationalist movement. Calling Marinetti "one of the many minor poets who are now thumping the jingo drum," McCullagh explicitly equates the Nationalists' "extraordinary doctrine" of "war for war's sake" with the Futurist slogan, by mid-1912 already (in)famous in England: "'We wish to glorify war, – the only health-giver of the world'" (4 n.).[12] Lapworth in contrast approves the Futurists. But he too emphasizes their patriotism, praising them as "young ardent poets . . . men who turn towards life and movement, and whose distinguishing note is a buoyant hopefulness and confidence in their own and their country's future" (255). While Lapworth never explicitly equates the Futurists' celebration of war with the Young Nationalists', he suggests the connection. Explaining the Nationalist war policy, as propounded by Enrico Corradini, editor of the nationalist weekly *L'Idea Nazionale*, Lapworth's rhetoric becomes positively Marinettian:

> Corradini has . . . written a great deal on the need for a quickening in Italian life by the development of a real Nationalist spirit . . . [Italy] must develop a combative spirit; what she wants is a tonic, and a war would do her health good. (299–300)

Indeed, throughout Lapworth's account – published in March 1912, the same month the Futurist exhibition opened in London – he attributes to Italy and the Young Nationalists the very values and characteristics that English visitors to the Sackville Gallery were reading about as belonging to the Futurists. While Marinetti was promoting a new art movement, "the young, the strong, and the living *Futurists!*,"[13] Lapworth was promoting a "new nation" (13), "Young Italy," "glor[ying] in a new found strength" (32), animated by "a potent breath of new life" (254), "her face towards the future" (316). While Marinetti was insisting that the Futurists "would free [Italy] from the numberless museums which cover her with as many cemeteries,"[14] Lapworth was asserting that "Italy is no longer merely a museum of past glories, but a factor of great potentiality in continental development – a Power indeed to be reckoned with" (13–14). While Marinetti was "sing[ing] . . . of factories suspended from the clouds by their strings of smoke; . . . of adventurous liners scenting the horizon; of broad-chested locomotives prancing on the rails,"[15] Lapworth was praising Italy's "surprising" "industrial development" (233), its "lines of first-class passenger-boats" (236), its "kilometres of light steam railways and electric tramways" (235).

As Lapworth's readers learn that the voluble young Italian artists whose exhibition at the Sackville Gallery is causing such a stir are animated by the same "patriotic spirit" that inspired Italy's Tripoli campaign, McCullagh's learn that the leader of those artists is a fanatical supporter of Italy's War for a Desert. "If the reader wants to get a good idea of the monstrous length to which the cult of the cannon has been carried by Italian jingoes," he explains sarcastically, "I would advise him to read 'la Bataille de Tripoli,' by the 'poet' Marinetti" (397). McCullagh then quotes a passage from this short volume of war correspondence from the Libyan front, in which Marinetti brings Futurism's theatrical enthusiasm to the celebration of Italian military feats: in this narrative, the patriotic polemicist feverishly "'embrace[s] the ensanguined brow of this soldier who hugs in his arms his hot rifle, as a mother embraces a feverish child,'" wonders as an "'artilleryman . . . stammers painfully, with his torn jaws: "Eight! I have killed eight of them!"'" but shows his greatest excitement at "'the epic splendour of this sergeant who, his mouth closed by bloody gashes, lifts his two hands towards me each instant to indicate by his ten outspread digits that he has killed ten'" (quoted on 397).

Attempting to exploit any anti-Futurist sentiment the Sackville exhibit inspired, McCullagh attacks Marinetti's "wild paean" and Italy itself with the same rhetoric of ethical corruption disapproving English critics had used to assail the Futurists' artwork and action. As the critics were calling Futurism "degenerate," "a morbid form of destructive revolution,"[16] McCullagh was arguing that Marinetti's

> adoration of slaughter is almost as great a sign of degeneracy as the Futurist movement itself. Healthy nations take it for granted that their soldiers and their

sailors have ordinary male courage: it is only morbid and cowardly degenerates who go into paroxysms of excitement and sing wild paeans when they see an artillerist pointing a cannon at an enemy three miles off and unable to reply. (397)

McCullagh presents Futurism as yet another symptom of the national corruption that has gripped Italy, driving its government and people to wage a useless war with unparalleled "butchery." The wild paeans of one "jingo poet" have global repercussions, especially for those living in an aging empire itself perhaps degenerating. "When we realise that the men who write this sort of drivel are not only circulating without a keeper, but are dictating the policy of Italy," he warns, "we shall understand the danger to which Europe is exposed" (398).

To understand why McCullagh casts as so threatening the spirit animating a small group of Italian artists and the effort of Europe's "weakest Power" to conquer "an enormous waste of bare rock and sand," we need to understand the Young Nationalist doctrine of *Pan-Italianismo*. Pan-Italianism was an extension of the earlier nationalist doctrine of *Irredentismo*, first popularized during the years of Italian unification (1859–70). While Irredentists advocated Italy's incorporation of all foreign dominated territories populated by a majority of "ethnic" Italians, especially Austrian-controlled Trentino and Trieste, Pan-Italianists went further, advocating not only the "redemption" of Trentino and Trieste, but also a policy of general imperial expansion to make Italy another of Europe's "Great Powers."[17] To clarify such ambitions, Lapworth quotes a Young Nationalist "philosopher" who had argued that, " 'Italy must be Imperialist in order to prevent the closing up of all those openings whence the nation receives its oxygen' " (quoted on 303–04).[18]

The danger McCullagh warns against is a series of additional reckless and destabilizing imperialist wars under the banner of Pan-Italianism, which might precipitate the European conflict the English had been dreaming of and dreading for over a decade.[19] To underscore the threat, McCullagh tellingly quotes Marinetti's neglected political manifesto, "Italian Tripoli," first declaimed in the conflict's early days:

"The tiresome memory of Roman glory must at length be wiped out by an Italian grandeur a hundred times greater . . . We invite the Italian Government, now become Futurist, to increase all the national ambitions by despising the stupid accusations of piracy and proclaiming the birth of Panitalianism."[20] (quoted on 399)

The quotation confirms both that Marinetti himself publicly affiliated Futurism with the Young Nationalists' Pan-Italianist advocacy of war and imperial expansion and that evidence of the affiliation was available in England by mid-1912. This neglected association between the Futurists and the Nationalists suggests that Marinetti's advocacy of war as "the only hygiene of the world" expresses not only the general fascination among young Europeans with violence and irrationality,[21] but also a particular national political attitude determined by Italy's unique domestic and international situation.

Whether or not they approve Italy's military action, English analyses of the Turko-Italian War present the Futurists as active collaborators in Italian imperial policy. Such accounts contend that in Italy the nationalistic desire to transform a "young" nation into a "Great Power," a modern nation-state which could compete economically, imperially, and culturally with its European neighbors, animated new political groups like the Young Nationalists *and* new art groups like the Futurists. As the Italian government invaded North Africa to put Italy on the map imperially, in this view, the Futurists "invaded" Europe's capitals and art markets to put Italy on the map culturally. Both projects aimed to extend Italy's influence beyond its borders; the government's war would increase its imperial reach, Futurism's European tours would increase its cultural reach.

This image of the Futurists as imperialists casts interesting light on the founding of Vorticism in 1914 as an aggressively nationalistic art movement. Viewed with a consciousness of the expansionist military policies epitomized in the Turko-Italian war, the Futurists' theatrically aggressive appearance in London, only five months after the conflict began, might well have appeared the first move in a campaign to "colonize" England's art market.[22] That conquest would require not guns and lives, of course, but modern methods of propaganda, promotion, and performance. Understood in this way, the Futurists' three promotional tours in England – during spring 1912, fall 1913, and spring–summer 1914 – might well have seemed an application of Pan-Italianism to the realm of art – a strategy in effect of art imperialism.[23]

It was just such an understanding of Futurism at a time of perceived imperial decline and increasing international competition in England, we will see, that helped push the English Vorticists in the early summer of 1914 to reject Marinetti's effort to recruit them by mocking Futurism in their patriotic art quarterly, *BLAST*, as "AUTOMOBILISM,"[24] excoriating "Latins" generally as "the most romantic and sentimental 'moderns' to be found" and Italians in particular for "their Futuristic gush over machines" (41), and asserting defensively that modern art is "more the legitimate property of Englishmen than of any other people in Europe" (41) – a dubious claim at best since England could boast of no modern art movement as aggressively successful as Futurism. Animated by a sense of patriotic indignation at Futurist pretensions to being Europe's leading art movement, and mobilized by a sense of cultural defense, *BLAST* sought to overthrow Futurism, place its superior "native" movement at the forefront of modern European art, and thereby bolster Britain's (artistic) prestige.[25] The Vorticists ultimately based this nationalist program on the argument that Britain was by rights the world's "Greatest Power," a tactic that illuminates not only the hazy lines of complicity between avant-garde movements and European imperialism, but also the limits of that complicity.

VITALIZING BRITANNIA

It is now well-established that the Vorticist movement finally consolidated itself in response to Marinetti's public effort to identify the so-called English Rebel Artists as "Futurists" in his controversial "Vital English Art" manifesto of late May 1914 (co-authored by the Italian's only self-proclaimed English disciple, the painter Christopher Nevinson).[26] As has been noted frequently, the Rebels reacted angrily to this unexpected honor by composing a letter that denounced Marinetti and Futurism, sternly "dissociat[ing]" the Rebels from the Italian movement.[27] Less studied is Wyndham Lewis's jingoistic polemic, "Automobilism" (*New Weekly*, 20 June 1914), which continued the attack, confirming that a reading of the Futurists as art imperialists played a crucial part in Vorticism's formation.[28]

Lewis's neglected anti-Futurist screed shows that the Rebels understood Marinetti's attempt to co-opt them as an imperialistic act, and responded to that attempt publicly by embracing a nationalistic cultural policy. "Automobilism" assails Marinetti's celebration of "Motor-cars" and "Aeroplanes" (33) and "his contempt and abjurations" for the English as "absurd" (34). It dismisses Futurist claims of artistic advancement by describing Italy as a cultural backwater: "[w]hile Italy was still a Borgia-haunted swamp of intrigue, England was buckling on the brilliant and electric armour of the modern world" (33). And by excoriating "Latins" for the "extraordinary childishness" of their love for "mechanical inventions" (33), Lewis's article denigrates the Futurists as modernity's gushing children and positions the Rebels as its only true representatives: "For everything that is rubbishly puerile in the Latin temperament, machinery has come as an immense toy. They are in a perpetual state of vulgar and gesticulating '*émerveillement*'" (33). So when Lewis calls Marinetti and Nevinson's "Vital English Art" a "stupid polemic" and asserts that "it is time for definition" (34), he is calling on his comrades to counter Italian art imperialism by founding a nationalist art group. Seen in this light, the Rebels' decision sometime in June to change their movement's name to Vorticism and revise their soon-to-be-published periodical to reflect the anti-Futurist tenor of the moment,[29] confirms not only that the Rebels embraced Lewis's patriotic plan, but that his exploitation of national loyalty helped consolidate the movement.

To appreciate the significance of the promotion of this aggressively nationalistic cultural doctrine, it is helpful to recall that at the time Lewis's chauvinistic polemic appeared a consensus existed among a broad-range of English intellectuals – among others, Ford Madox Ford's circle of Edwardian literati, the contributors to Harold Monro's *Poetry and Drama*, Roger Fry's Omega Workshop aesthetes, the radical socialists at Alfred Orage's *New Age*, as well as the Rebel Artists – that England's art and letters were less "developed," less "modern" than those being created on the Continent.[30] Many agreed with Matthew Arnold that English culture was fundamentally provincial.[31] Some viewed their continental contemporaries as allies in a global effort to revolutionize "art" and "life" – to transform artistic practice and cultural institutions, on one hand, and social and political order, on the other. Most shared the opinion that English artists and writers needed to learn from their European contemporaries, so they advocated a policy of cultural internationalism as the proper way to "modernize" English art and literature. As chapters 1 and 2 argue, however, the underlying ambition of this internationalistic doctrine was the rather nationalistic one of using new art and literature to bolster Britain's flagging international status and relieve fears of national decline and foreign competition. This lurking nationalism paved the way for the radical doctrinal realignment which the Rebel Artists began initiating in response to mounting evidence of Futurist success.

Thus *BLAST: The Review of the Great English Vortex* (July 1914) is of historical significance not simply because it marks the apex of the avant-garde in prewar England or features works that anticipate later modernist aesthetics.[32] Equally important, the periodical confirms that

England's most militantly oppositional art movement also portrayed itself as an active though critical collaborator in Britain's "official nationalism," the contemporaneous effort on the part of the government to counter rising evidence of domestic "degeneration" and imperial decline by revitalizing English society and fortifying Britain's increasingly contested imperial, military, and economic power.[33]

Such an understanding clarifies *BLAST*'s opening polemics. These three manifestos – "Long Live the Vortex!," "Manifesto I," and "Manifesto II" – indicate that the Vorticists' periodical had three intertwined nationalist goals: to publicize their movement as England's – and possibly Europe's – premier art group; to revitalize a declining empire as a defense against foreign competition and encroachment – especially the Futurists' efforts to "occupy" the English art market; and to place England's art and literature on a level commensurate with its status as the world's "greatest" power (a level of prestige, according to Lewis, similar to that England enjoyed when Chaucer and Shakespeare wrote). As articulated in *BLAST*, these three goals would reinforce one another: promoting Vorticism would modernize England's art and letters, revitalize English society, and elevate British prestige.

Taken seriously, the Rebels' nationalistic commitment to displace Futurism with a native movement helps us recognize that *BLAST*'s opening manifestos articulate a rough and somewhat elusive theory of English art and a program of national reform.[34] "Long Live the Vortex!" lays the groundwork for the theory and the program: it defines the Vorticists' philosophical, aesthetic, and ethical preferences. "Manifesto I" practices the theory and further develops the program: it "blasts" the characteristics, people, and institutions that the Vorticists oppose, "blesses" those they support, and thereby projects a renewed Vorticist nation. "Manifesto II" further articulates the theory and explains the program: it elucidates the previous manifestos, identifies the "most fundamentally English" "qualities and characteristics," and uses those "diagnostics" of the English "race" (35) to describe "the specific nature of the art destined to grow up in this country" (36), England's "necessary native art" (37).

BLAST's opening manifesto, "Long Live the Vortex!" (7–8), introduces the patriotic Vorticists as anti-Futurist defenders of the present. After celebrating the "great art vortex sprung up in the centre of this town" (7), it distinguishes the Vorticists from their contemptible Italian counterparts, whose excessive adoration of the future is deemed inappropriate for an art group native to modern England: "We stand for the

Reality of the Present – not for the sentimental future, or the sacripant Past" (7). Continuing the attack, it scorns the Futurists' frantic celebration of motorcars, "AUTOMOBILISM (Marinetteism) bores us. We don't want to go about making a hullo=bullo about motor cars, anymore than about knives and forks, elephants or gas=pipes" (8). While Lewis's *New Weekly* polemic had used chauvinistic anger to attack Futurism, *BLAST* uses patriotic humor. "Long Live the Vortex" ridicules the Futurists' "hullo=bullo about motor cars" by mimicking Marinetti's polemical enthusiasm even while emphasizing the familiarity – for the English – of everything Italians find so amazingly new. "Elephants are VERY BIG," it jokes deflatingly, "Motor cars go quickly" (8). This first manifesto evokes pro-English and anti-Futurist sentiment by suggesting that nothing about modern life, be it exotic animals or automobiles, can surprise the inhabitants of a nation so industrially developed, so imperially dominant.

"Long Live the Vortex," positions Vorticism not only as a presentist and anti-Futurist art movement, but also an "Individualist" one. When the polemic takes a swipe at the Fabian Socialists' patronizing obsession with the poor, it explicitly aligns Vorticism with the English Individualist movement, led by the former suffragette and anarcho-libertarian theorist, Dora Marsden. "Blast . . . will not appeal to any particular class," it explains, "but to the fundamental and popular instincts in every class and description of people, TO THE INDIVIDUAL" (7). This reference, and later assertions that the periodical aims "to make individuals" and present "an art of Individuals" (8) confirm the Vorticists' embrace of social and political ideals shared by the young intellectuals around Marsden's "Individualist Review," *The Egoist*, a group which included Lewis's fellow Vorticists Ezra Pound and Henri Gaudier-Brzeska, and their Imagist ally, Richard Aldington.[35] Marsden's journal propounded the anarcho-libertarian doctrine of the German nominalist Max Stirner, as articulated in his 1844 work *Das Einzige und Sein Eigentum* (translated as *The Ego and his Own* in 1907), and became a leading organ for radical politics and advanced art. Not only did it articulate a system of "individualist" political beliefs shared by many of England's leading young artists and writers, but also promoted the Imagist and Vorticist movements, publishing works by Aldington, Gaudier-Brzeska, Lewis, Pound, and others. As Marsden embraced these artistic rebels, they embraced her politics, especially her opposition to socialism, liberalism, and state institutions as repressive constraints on the unique and vital individual.[36] Following Marsden, the Vorticists' periodical assails a host of established ideals and institutions that obstruct individual vitality and creativity. "Long Live the Vortex," declares the Vorticists' "task" to be the effort "[t]o make the rich of the community shed their education skin, to destroy politeness, standardization and academic, that is civilized, vision" (7).

Subscribing to the Individualist movement's vitalist anti-statism, the Vorticists sought to maintain their avant-garde opposition to the established, institutionalized organs of the state and all those persons and parties responsible, in their view, for maintaining England's decrepit, academic, and sentimental culture. When "Manifesto II" (30–43) claims that the Vorticists intend to "Stir up Civil War among peaceful apes" (31), it announces a grand struggle over the fate of England between two alliances of opposed forces. On the side of reaction and decline are arrayed the "established powers" – Fabian socialists, Royal Academicians, Bloomsburyites and all others who defend the calcified state or promote *passéism* and sentimentality in art and life. On the side of reform and revolution fight a coalition of radical forces, like-minded "individuals" from all walks of life who embody the "fundamentally English" characteristics, and politics, of vitality, presentism, rebelliousness, and opposition to established art and political institutions.[37]

Identifying England's reactionary forces, the closing page of "Manifesto I" blasts over fifty persons and institutions that the Vorticists combat. It names Fabians and socialists for their paternalistic politics and sentimental obsession with the poor: Reverend Bernard Vaughan, a mission worker in the London slums (he termed the controversial Strand statues by the Vorticists' ally, Jacob Epstein "indecent and inartistic");[38] the "Socialist Countess" of Warwick (she promulgated socialism among the nobility); and Sidney Webb, the leader of the Fabian movement. Conservative writers and artists, who defend academicism and *passéist* art and literature, are also condemned: Cambridge lecturer and poet, A. C. Benson; popular Royal Academy painter, Frank Brangwyn; National Portrait Gallery director and editor of the academic *Burlington Magazine*, Lionel Cust; and Tory editor of the *Spectator*, John St. Loe Strachey. Finally, "Manifesto I" blasts a series of religious leaders and occultists Lewis and his cohorts deem sentimentalists: Abdul Bahai, the founder of the universalist Bahai faith; the socialist mystic, Annie Besant (lecturing at the Queen's Hall during May and June); popular Nonconformist minister, R. J. Campbell; author of religious romance novels, Marie Corelli; and the Indian Nobel laureate, Rhabindranath Tagore.

Against these sentimental reactionaries, *BLAST* conjures an alliance of vital revolutionaries, including not only political agitators like the Suffragettes, Ulster Protestants, and unionized workers, but also radical cultural groups like the Egoists, Imagists, and literary Impressionists, even prize-fighters, who express rebelliousness through acts of physical violence, and the aviators piloting England's conquest of the skies. "Manifesto I" blesses heroic Suffragettes: Lady Aberconway (she presided over a March Suffragist meeting); Freida Graham (recently sentenced to six months in prison for damaging pictures at the National Gallery); and the imprisoned Lillie Lenton (she repeatedly committed arson and had undertaken a hunger strike in May). It venerates the leaders of the Ulster unionist movement, Sir Edward Carson and Captain James Craig (they were fomenting armed rebellion in Northern Ireland to deter passage of the Liberals' Home Rule bill), as well as the *éminence gris* of the trade union movement, Robert Applegarth (he had celebrated his eightieth birthday in January). The prizefighters Collin Bell, Dick Burge, Petty Officer Curran, and Bandsman Rice are blessed as well, along with aviators Claude Grahame-White, England's most renowned flyer, and the missing Swedish expatriate Gustav Hamel, who had performed aerial stunts for the king in February but had disappeared during a channel flight in May. The manifesto also celebrates advanced cultural figures like James Joyce (whose *Portrait of the Artist* had been appearing in *The Egoist* since February), and *New Weekly* art critic Frank Rutter (as curator of the Leeds Art Club, he had sponsored the Rebel Artists' exhibition in May).[39] In addition to blessing its cultural allies, *BLAST* features works by a number of non-Vorticist authors and artists deemed to be fighting for the cause of national revival: Ford Madox Ford, the literary Impressionist; dissident feminist writer, Rebecca West; English Post-Impressionist painter, Spencer Gore; and the controversial sculptor, Jacob Epstein.

Though the Vorticists positioned their anarchistic art movement as part of an imagined coalition of oppositional groups all working for the common goal of national revitalization, utopianism and political naivety led them to ignore the vast differences among these radical movements' respective agendas and their practical incompatibility with Vorticism's conjunction of anti-statist politics and elitist aesthetics.[40] While Emmeline Pankhurst's militant Women's Social and Political Union committed numerous acts of violence against institutions of state-power (tactics far more radical in practice than any rhetorical or pictorial "anarchism" in Vorticist art and polemics), their political goal was by no means anarchist; they sought not the abolition of the English state like the Egoists, but the vote for bourgeois women.[41] Carson's Ulster Protestants advocated armed resistance to the Liberal government's efforts to establish Irish Home Rule, and even began running guns to Northern Ireland in the early summer of 1914, but their politics ultimately weren't anti-statist either; they sought to derail the Liberal government's Home Rule policy and restore Tory control. While some sectors of the trade union movement were anarcho-syndicalist, practicing forms of violent mass action, their political goals were comparatively modest: to secure fair labor laws and expand workers' rights. This coalition of contentious reformist groups exists only in *BLAST*'s pages: notwithstanding their different locations across the political spectrum, the Suffragettes, Ulstermen, and unionized workers were pragmatic gradualist political movements with little use for a utopian art movement like Vorticism.

Despite *BLAST*'s radical (if naive) political ambitions and its explicit alliance with Marsden's anti-statist movement, its polemics patriotically defend certain statist modes of British prestige, namely the navy, industry, and empire.[42] Given the historical commonplace that avant-garde movements are by definition opposed to established institutions, this effort to maintain oppositional politics while embracing a nationalistic artistic agenda seems contradictory. Avant-gardism's intellectual elitism, antagonism to established institutions, and artistic experimentalism clashes with official nationalism's populist ambitions and state control of national prestige. In England this tension was heightened by the intellectual heritage of anti-provincialism and the anarchist politics of those segments of the intelligentsia from which Lewis, Pound, and other Vorticists came.

To resolve these contradictions, *BLAST* practices a long-standing technique of nationalist polemic: it recasts the modes of state power it praises as national characteristics. Naval power, technological accomplishment, and imperial predominance become, in this view, expressions of national genius, "fundamentally English" traits. "Manifesto I" exemplifies the ways *BLAST* utilizes such tactics to win support for the movement: it recalls the doctrine of British naval supremacy to incite readers' national pride in Vorticism, justifying that supremacy on the grounds that the English are a race of "SEAFARERS" (22). Because, as Benedict Anderson puts it, the "British empire . . . was a grab-bag of primarily tropical possessions scattered over every continent,"[43] the government depended especially on naval power to protect its interests. During the nineteenth century, politicians and historians had made this military fact into a central tenet of British nationalism. "Britannia rules the waves" became a hallmark not only of imperial policy but also of the government campaign to win support for naval buildup to counter foreign competition (especially from Germany). Pursuing a similar strategy, *BLAST* drums up support for Vorticism with a pattern-poem that celebrates English ships:

> **BLESS ENGLAND!**
> **BLESS ENGLAND**
> **FOR ITS SHIPS**
> **which switchback on Blue, Green and**
> **Red SEAS all around the PINK**
> **EARTH-BALL,**
>
> **BIG BETS ON EACH.** (22)

As the government had promoted empire, *BLAST* provokes patriotism to promote Vorticism.

The Vorticist aesthetic of pictorial abstraction is likewise justified when *BLAST* naturalizes the technique as essentially English. "Manifesto I" associates England and the English with the "abstract" ocean and blesses "ALL SEAFARERS" because "THEY exchange not one LAND for another, but one element for ANOTHER. The MORE against the LESS ABSTRACT" (22). "Manifesto II" pursues the argument, asserting that the "English Character is based on the Sea . . . The particular qualities and characteristics that the sea always engenders in men are those that are, among the many diagnostics of our race, the most fundamentally English" (35). By associating abstraction with the sea and the sea with English character – a connection buttressed by the doctrine of British naval supremacy – the Vorticists annex abstraction as property exclusively English.

The end of "Manifesto II" most extravagantly manipulates nationalist doctrine to present Vorticism as England's "necessary native art." To prove England the only nation truly "fit" to lead the world's artistic revolution, it cites British imperial and industrial supremacy:

> 1 The Modern World is due almost entirely to Anglo-Saxon genius, – its appearance and its spirit.
> 2 Machinery, trains, steam-ships, all that distinguishes externally our time, came far more from here than anywhere else. (39)

The claim that "Anglo-Saxon genius" created modernity recalls the earlier nationalist tradition of Anglo-Saxonism, which nineteenth-century statesman, historians, and men-of-letters had used to justify enlarging the empire on the grounds of "racial" superiority. Because their forefathers had been courageous, freedom-loving, and nomadic Teutons, the argument ran, the modern English are the world's most individualistic, energetic, and freedom-loving people, racially destined to control its most powerful navy and largest, most "civilized" empire.[44] *BLAST* uses similar tactics to make supporting Vorticism a matter of "racial" pride and to predict England's inevitable conquest of international advanced art. "Manifesto II" closes by asserting imperialistically that the "consciousness towards the new possibilities of expression in present life" should "be more the legitimate property of Englishmen than of any other people in Europe" because "Englishmen have spread themselves all over the Earth," bringing "all the hemispheres about them in their original island" (39–40).

Not surprisingly, *BLAST*'s polemics expose tensions generated by this attempt to promote radical forms of art and life using official nationalist tactics. To make clear Vorticism's fundamental difference from the conservative state, "Manifesto II" sometimes works defensively to distinguish its revolutionary nationalism from statist nationalism. When the polemic insists "that there is nothing Chauvinistic or picturesquely patriotic about our contentions" (34), it opposes Vorticism to what Tom Nairn calls "romantic nationalism," epitomized by the archaic pastoral poetry of A. E. Housman and the Georgian poets and the historical painting of Academy artists like Frank Brangwyn.[45] So "Manifesto I" blasts Brangwyn (21) and criticizes England's poet laureate, Robert Bridges (12), who often wrote in the "picturesquely patriotic" fashion the Vorticists scorn. In "Dunstone Hill," for example, Bridges had nostalgically contrasted England's idyllic rural past to its lurid industrial present:

> Far down across the valley deep
> The town is hid in smoky sleep,
> At moonless nightfall wakening slow
> Upon the dark with lurid glow:
>
> Beyond, afar the widening view
> Merges into the soften'd blue,
> Cornfield and forest, hill and stream,
> Fair England in her pastoral dream.[46]

"Long Live the Vortex" counters by insisting that the Vorticists "want to make in England not a popular art, not a revival of lost folk art, or a romantic fostering of such unactual conditions, but to make individuals"

(8), while "Manifesto I" blesses modern England as an "industrial island machine" (23). By assailing the pastoral strain of nationalist doctrine while celebrating the more "modern" tenet of industrial supremacy, *BLAST* works to reconcile its competing ambitions to mythologize England's past and to celebrate modernity and initiate the future.

Despite this use of official nationalist tactics to inspire artists and the art public to embrace Vorticism, the Vorticists' aesthetic experimentalism limited significantly the movement's popularity, and therefore its ability to realize its program of revitalizing English culture and thereby elevating British prestige. Even associates and partisans like Ford and Aldington had difficulty dealing with Vorticist visual art and categorizing the movement's literary showpiece, Lewis's Vorticist "play" *Enemy of the Stars.* In a contemporary review of the piece, Ford explained that "I don't just figure out what it means, but I get from it ferociously odd sensations."[47] In his review for *The Egoist,* Aldington called *Enemy of the Stars,* "the most portentous, the surprising piece of work in the whole volume . . . It stirs one up like a red-hot poker. Of course, I don't 'understand' it, in the sense that I cannot tell you exactly what the characters looked like, what they dressed in, or quite what they did."[48]

For the Vorticists' coterie such antagonistic qualities were evidence of their art's value, compatible with a sense of nationalistic pride in the movement and support for its project of cultural revitalization. Aldington confirmed that, despite his intellectual resistance to chauvinism, he viewed *BLAST* as a major *national* achievement that inspired strong patriotic feelings:

> It seems incredible but there must be in all of us something of what is known as national sentiment. We are the children of our soil and climate, and however much we may detest them, however much we may feel that we really belong to other latitudes, something in this island – its soil and climate, as I say – still compels us to prefer those who are like us to any other people . . . I am extremely glad to welcome the appearance of "Blast" – a periodical which is designed to be the organ for new, vigorous art in England . . . [T]he paper is an effort to look at art from an Anglo-Saxon point of view instead of from a borrowed foreign standpoint.[49]

Responding initially with competing feelings of loyalty to England's tradition of cultural internationalism and the Vorticists' nationalistic call, Aldington is ultimately convinced by the periodical's "Anglo-Saxon point of view" and "vigorous" new art to exchange internationalism for nationalism. *BLAST*'s willful compounding of nationalistic rhetoric and experimentalist art provoked national pride in at least one of the Vorticists' allies.

For the most part, however, *BLAST*'s "necessary native art" did not succeed in winning partisans, inspiring patriotic loyalty, or elevating national prestige. Because the Great War displaced nearly all other concerns within two months of *BLAST*'s publication, it is difficult to evaluate the reception of the periodical and Vorticism. But initial responses indicate that for the few who commented on the journal at all, the paradoxical compounding of nationalist rhetoric and elitist art failed to inspire any sense of patriotic pride in this new English art. Commentators in the popular press most often reprimanded *BLAST* for being "Futurist," harsh criticism for a movement founded as a militantly English alternative to the Italian movement.[50] The periodical's contents were described as "irrepressible imbecility which is not easily distinguishable from the words and works of Marinetti's disciples," its contributors cast as "desperate iconoclasts infected by Milan."[51] And while *BLAST* did generate some support among segments of the art public usually drawn to the current *cause célèbre*, such support probably had less to do with a view of the Vorticists as innovators or patriots than with a view of them as fashionable and amusing oddities.[52]

While *BLAST*'s failure to generate much intellectual support or national loyalty confirms the practical incompatibility of Vorticism's competing aims, it also indicates an unwillingness to compromise avant-gardist aesthetic ideals even at the expense of nationalist politics. David Graver has anatomized *Enemy of the Stars'* "aesthetic turbulence," charting Lewis's yoking in the play of competing "aesthetic fields and clashing forms" to create a spinning literary Vortex that "does not converge."[53] Graver notes that in *Enemy of the Stars*, Lewis "is not so much defending an aesthetic position as playing with the idea of aesthetic positioning."[54] Similarly, *BLAST* aggravates the contradictions between Vorticism's agenda of social transformation and cultural elitism and its effort to win support for national consolidation, in part to play with the idea of positioning an avant-garde movement as an instrument of nationalist politics. While Marinetti tried to resolve those contradictions by creating a populist avant-garde movement, which used advertising and promotional techniques to win a mass audience,[55] Lewis and his comrades responded to the challenge by refusing to resolve them: they placed the competing claims of avant-gardism and nationalism at the core of Vorticist theory and practice, making *BLAST* an arena for their contention.

BLAST thereby articulated the structural contradictions of a nationalist avant-garde, positioning Vorticism as at once England's most insistently nationalistic and avant-gardist art group, but in so doing, also drastically foreclosed the possibility that Vorticism would ever achieve its political aims. In the end, *BLAST* did little if anything to elevate Britain's international prestige, failing even to put English art and artists at the forefront of modern European culture. But its promotion of a nationalistic doctrine of modern art did help legitimate patriotism among a group of artists and writers who had long championed cultural internationalism. When war exploded across Europe a few weeks after *BLAST*'s publication, some of those same young men rushed to their nation's call "as swimmers into cleanness leaping"[56]; the cultural competition which spawned Vorticism and helped legitimate cultural nationalism also prepared them to take that leap.

More importantly, the Vorticists shared with the British government a cynical sense that nationalism had strategic value as a tool to manipulate public opinion. Anderson argues that the governments under Victoria and Edward used state-controlled educational institutions and the technologies of print capitalism to stretch "the short, tight skin of the nation over the gigantic body of the empire," as a means of assuring increasingly rebellious colonial publics, especially in Ireland, Scotland, and India, that they were "'British," despite the fact that they could never enjoy the rights and privileges reserved for the empire's "native" rulers.[57] While related, the Vorticists' ambitions were neither as cynical nor grandiose. They used advertising and propaganda techniques to promote nationalism as a means of persuading England's art public to support their movement, and to that extent, were complicit with government strategies of nationalist manipulation. But the Vorticists' spontaneous patriotic reaction to Futurist encroachment suggests that their consciousness of nationalism's tactical value was limited by their genuine loyalty to Englishness and empire.

In general terms, then, this chapter has attempted to extend the point Renato Poggioli first made over thirty years ago, that European avant-garde art movements of the early-twentieth century were all to some extent parasitic on the liberal capitalist regimes in which they arose.[58] But by emphasizing in particular the engagement and complicity of these two radical art movements with the imperial politics of their respective nations, I have not been attempting to accuse them of hypocrisy or bad faith. Rather, I have been trying to point out, as the Futurists and Vorticists so often did, that their movements embraced nationalism and avant-gardism as a matter of policy, casting modern art as an instrument of imperial politics.

Realizing such a doctrine was not the same as formulating it, however. The Futurists' comparative success in promoting their movement internationally – in only three years most European capitals had held Futurist exhibitions and performances and developed their own "native" Futurist groups – throws into relief not only the Vorticists' comparative failure to popularize their movement and thereby elevate British (artistic) prestige, but the comparative failure of the Futurists' fatherland to transform itself into a great power by projecting either armed or artistic forces abroad. And that fact, in turn, throws into relief the all-too-concrete limits of avant-gardist art generally – with its aggressive commitment to experiment and individuality – to advance imperial power.

So even while stressing the neglected significance of early modernist commitments to official nationalism and complicity with European imperial politics, I have been trying to articulate the limits of that significance. It is in part because the outcome of the Great War so highlighted those limits, I suspect, that writers and artists like Marinetti, Lewis, and Pound, who during the *avant guerre* had been drawn to radical left-wing or anti-statist politics like syndicalism and anarchism,[59] became increasingly enamored by the charismatic leaders of Europe's emerging right-wing authoritarian parties. Perhaps men like Mussolini and Hitler would be better able to appreciate the value of modern art and the wisdom of modernists; perhaps their regimes would be better equipped to translate modernist political ambitions into reality. Unfortunately for these writers and artists, Europe's fascist and national socialist regimes in the end only reconfirmed their political marginality. No amount of artistic vision, political will, or polemical heat, it seems, could overcome the limitations of modernist art and writing to serve the goals of modern authoritarian politics.[60] As the following chapter shows, however, the startling explosion of the Great War did create – for a time – cultural and political circumstances in England that confirmed the Vorticists' doctrine of anarcho-imperialism in art and life more powerfully than at any time before the conflict; the reasons for and implications of that confluence of circumstance and doctrine, we will see, call on us to reassess certain aspects of the most familiar stories told about the politics of modernism.

CHAPTER 4

"Surrounded by a multitude of other Blasts": Vorticism and the Great War

> [T]here is certainly a new type of energy arrayed against them [the Germans] which they, with their eyes fixed on the past, had not suspected the growth of.
>
> Wyndham Lewis, "A Later Arm than Barbarity" (September 1914), 299

> [T]hat the Vorticist movement should have survived a year such as that we have just passed through argues a grimness and tenacity of purpose such as must needs reflect itself in the works of these contributors.
>
> Ford Madox Ford, "On a Notice of 'BLAST' " (July 1915), 144

A story is often told about the First World War and the politics of Anglo-American modernism. Following the lead of writers like Wyndham Lewis and Ezra Pound, it figures the war's impact on the Vorticist movement, which Lewis and Pound led, as a (if not the) critical factor in shaping the modernists' post-war politics. The war's senseless destruction, it explains, intensified the Vorticists' critique of Britain's liberal, parliamentary government, which they held responsible for all that waste, encouraging them to support the radical right-wing parties that arose across Europe between the wars. Given the ubiquity of the tale, one expects to find numerous studies of *BLAST* II: *War Number*, the second issue of the Vorticist periodical, published almost a year into the conflict (July 1915). Even a cursory reading reveals the journal's active and complex engagement with the war and home-front life, especially politics and popular culture: it provides a wealth of valuable evidence of the war's influence on the Vorticist movement, evidence that illuminates the trajectory of modernist art and politics. So it comes as something of a surprise that we find comparatively little critical interest in *BLAST* II, particularly in its political art and polemics.[1]

The scant discussion *BLAST* II has provoked sketches another, related story about Vorticism and the Great War. In this narrative, the *War Number* is a rather tragic document of artistic (and political) concession in the face of war; its less radical, less innovative artworks and polemics demonstrate not just a decline from *BLAST* I's more genuinely oppositional and progressive standards, or even the lamentable death of Vorticism (or the avant-garde), but perhaps, and most disturbingly, a tendency to anticipate modernism's later retrograde politics. At best, the *War Number* is a casualty of war, at worst, an ur-text of fascist modernism.[2]

There is truth in both of these accounts. Still, I concur with Samuel Hynes that *BLAST* II is more productively examined in light of British public discourse and popular culture during the first year of the Great War.[3] When read in this way, the document tells a different story about the transformations of modernist art and politics during the conflict, a story that raises its own interesting questions about the other two, more common tales. Insisting on the importance of its wartime context, the *War Number*'s opening editorial describes a magazine and a movement "surrounded by a multitude of other Blasts."[4] This chapter recovers a number of those other "Blasts" and articulates some of their consequences for our understanding of Vorticism and the development of modernist politics. Reading *BLAST* II as a failure – of aesthetic will or progressive politics – is to misunderstand its proclaimed doctrine, artistic practice, and the ways they dovetailed with the realities of British life during the war's first year. Because the Vorticists had from the start placed at the center of their doctrine the allegedly incompatible aims of avant-garde critique and nationalist politics, *BLAST* II turns out to have been well suited to the circumstances of the early war: the conflict created a cultural and political environment that validated more powerfully than at any time before the war the Vorticists' program of dissenting patriotism in art and politics.

The Vorticists responded to a wartime context in which the British government was expanding control of public discourse, clamping down on dissent, and promoting an anti-modernist cultural policy, by reorienting the principal foreign target of their opposition from Italian Futurism to German (or Prussian) imperialism. The accusations of *passéism*, sentimentality, and effeminacy that the Vorticists had aimed at the Futurists in *BLAST* I are now turned on Germany, which becomes in *BLAST* II the international locus of the cult of the past and romance, an account used to buttress the new argument that Vorticism is allied with Britain against Germany. This opportunistic assertion of alliance affirms that modern English art and artists are participating in life for the highest stakes – the Vorticists, *BLAST* II repeatedly implies, are willing to fight for modernism *to the death.* And at the same time, the realities of wartime life validate the Vorticists' aims in a new and more potent way. The government-sponsored war against modernism gives them a clear and implacable home-front enemy, ensuring that their art will never become too-fashionable (as, in their eyes, Futurism had), and thereby demonstrating more clearly than ever before the integrity of their opposition. The war against Germany, now cast as the principal foreign enemy of the only true modernist empire, gives the Vorticists a new means of affirming their patriotism: in their willingness to die for the nation's cause – also the cause of modernism – they can prove, beyond doubt, the integrity of their support for empire. And when the movement's resident sculptor, the Frenchman (hence British ally) Henri Gaudier-Brzeska, is killed in action, the Vorticists' paradoxical program receives its ultimate confirmation: the death of the modern soldier-artist in the two-front war against Germany and *passéism.*

THE HOME-FRONT WARS AND THE AUTHORIZATION OF VORTICIST DOCTRINE

Like most intellectuals who remain in England during the war's first year, the Vorticists participate actively in the period's public controversies. The configuration of their participation articulates the confluence of Vorticist doctrine and home-front life. This company of rebellious artists and writers take up arms in three competing polemical "wars" raging on the home front: the government-sponsored propaganda war against Germany and German *Kultur* directed by the Edwardian literary establishment, in which the Vorticists endeavor to stand alongside their elders as spokesmen for their generation in the battle against Germany; the avant-gardist war against established social, political, and artistic institutions, in which they try to maintain the prewar effort to revolutionize English "art" and "life"; and, lastly, the polemical war against modernism, also led by older artists and writers, in which *BLAST*'s contributors strive to defend modern art and literature against accusations of irrelevance, decadence, even "Junkerism." To affirm their dissenting patriotism while defending modernism, the Vorticists argue in *BLAST* II that their war against artistic and political *passéism* is an extension of the war against Germany. They fight against the German forces of reaction for the future of modern Britain and modern art.

The Department of Information's propaganda war against Germany and *Kultur* was directed by the well-known writer and Liberal MP, Charles Masterman.[5] Within a month of the declaration of hostilities, he held a meeting of "well-known men of letters" for the "organisation of public statements of the strength of the British case and principles in the war."[6] Two weeks later, the *Times* published a "Declaration by Authors" on "Britain's Destiny and Duty" in which fifty-two leading writers publicly proclaim their support for "the cause of the Allies . . . with a full conviction of its righteousness," declaring Germany an outlaw nation driven to aggression by the "iron military bureaucracy of Prussia."[7] Among the worthies whose names conclude the Declaration are H. Granville Barker, J. M. Barrie, Arnold Bennett, Robert Bridges, G. K. Chesterton, Arthur Conan Doyle, John Galsworthy, Thomas Hardy, Rudyard Kipling, Arthur Pinero, May Sinclair, and H. G. Wells, a veritable Who's Who of Edwardian culture.

True to their word, these patriotic literati take up their pens in support of the cause. In a letter to the *Times* (2 September 1914), Poet Laureate Robert Bridges defines the moral stakes of the conflict, pronouncing it "a holy war . . . between Christ and the Devil." The Laureate leaves little doubt as to the proper response: "The infernal machine which has been scientifically preparing for the last 25 years is now on its wild career like one of Mr. Wells's inventions, and wherever it goes it will leave desolation behind it and put all material progress back for at least half a century. There was never anything in the world worthier of extermination, and it is the plain duty of all civilized nations to unite to drive it back into its home and exterminate it there."[8] Bridges's comparison between Germany's war machine and "Mr. Wells's inventions," would not offend the author of *The War of the Worlds*. From the declaration of war, Wells too had adopted the persona of patriotic journalist, churning out in less than a month eleven propaganda pieces, one of which sums up the official case against "Prussian Imperialism":

> Ever since the crushing of the French in 1871 the evil thing has grown and cast its spreading shadow over Europe. Germany has preached a propaganda of ruthless force and political materialism to the whole uneasy world. "Blood and iron," she boasted, was the cement of her unity, and almost as openly the little, mean, aggressive statesmen and professors who have guided her destinies to this present conflict have professed cynicism and an utter disregard of any ends but nationally selfish ends, as though it were religion.[9]

Figure 1 Wyndham Lewis, *Before Antwerp, BLAST* II (July 1915), cover.

This diagnosis of German "evil" – a policy of imperialism, ruthless force, and materialism orchestrated by a Prussian elite of little, mean, aggressive statesman and professors – is reiterated, in one form or another, in nearly every patriotic article, poem, and poster produced during the first year of war.

Not surprisingly, the Vorticists join the fight, claiming that their avant-gardist war against *passéist* art and life is not only compatible with the war against Germany, but also an extension of it. The *War Number*'s cover articulates the argument visually with a Vorticist vision of the Allied defense by Lewis, its title, *Before Antwerp*, identifying the modernist soldiers as defenders of the Belgian city against German assault (fig. 1).[10] *Before Antwerp* is Lewis's pictorial rejoinder to a celebrated war painting by one of the nation's best-known painters, Walter Sickert, entitled *Soldiers of King Albert the Ready* (fig. 2).[11] Sickert's impressionistic tableau of Belgians poised for battle against German invaders appeared in a December 1914 exhibition at the New English Art Club, winning praise as a major work of war art.[12] Lewis's visual counterattack expresses commitment to the war against Germany and the war for modernism: his angular military men appear at once Allied soldiers braced against German assault and artistic soldiers braced against established art, especially the impressionistic realism that dominated prewar art, and lingered in works like Sickert's *Soldiers*. Little wonder Lewis's soldiers are placed to oppose Sickert's.

The *War Number*'s opening Editorial continues the strategy, going so far as to suggest that because "Romance" inspired Germany's aggression, *BLAST*, with its long-standing antagonism to all things romantic, is an essential weapon in the conflict: "Germany has stood for the old Poetry, for Romance, more steadfastly and profoundly than any other people in Europe . . . This paper wishes to stand rigidly opposed, from start to finish, to every form that the Poetry of a former condition of life, no longer existing, has foisted upon us" (5). Lewis had first begun developing this argument in a neglected polemic entitled "A Later Arm than Barbarity," published in *The Outlook* of September 1914. "Germany is sleep-walking in a bombastic dream of another time," he argues there, "German romance . . . is the goddess whose deity is just now at stake." Pursuing this logic, he reasons that the "nations allied against Germany are in reality opposing the interference of the past,"[13] but stops short of following the analysis to its implied conclusion, never explicitly identifying the avant-garde as one of the "later arms" arrayed against German "barbarity." What Lewis only implies in September of 1914, *BLAST* declares in July 1915: Germans fight for the past; the Allies and the forces of advanced art fight for the future.

The argument failed to convince most British journalists and intellectuals. Older writers generally attacked modernism, casting it a decadent distraction from the pressing realities of war, a symptom of the national

Figure 2 Walter Richard Sickert, *Soldiers of King Albert the Ready* (1914), oil on canvas.

malaise that contributed to Britain's international decline and Germany's attendant rise, or a product of the same alien *Kultur* menacing Europe.[14] Predictably, England's popular humor magazine, *Punch*, takes up arms in this war. An October 1914 issue, for example, includes an anti-modernist cartoon, entitled "How the Cubist, By A Mere Alteration of Titles, Achieved a Ready Sale of Unmarketable Pictures" (fig. 3).[15] It portrays a near-sighted, scrawny, slope-shouldered "Cubist," who succeeds in selling his abstract paintings (which in fact look more Futurist than Cubist) to an overweight, hook-nosed, richly dressed – that is stereotypically Jewish – art collector by retitling them, "Ruin of Window of Rheims Cathedral," "Louvain 1914," and "In the Wake of the Huns." The cartoon ridicules modernism, charging modern artists with taking advantage of the war to advance their careers, and exploits visual stereotypes to accuse them of degeneracy and their patrons of stupidity and Semitic origin. The "Cubist's" poor physique, weak chin, and receding forehead were conventional indicators in prewar poster art of the dissipated lunatic, while the collector's big nose, bald head, and facial hair were markers of the Jew.[16] This use of anti-Semitism to assail modernism shows that the modernists had no monopoly on this prejudice.

Anti-modernists fired polemical salvoes at the Vorticists in particular in a *Times*' review of a March 1915 art exhibition in which Lewis and his comrades Henri Gaudier-Brzeska, William Roberts, and Edward Wadsworth had shown works. Under the telling title, "Junkerism in Art," the anonymous reviewer pronounces the wartime case against the Vorticists, terming their "rigid" pictures "Prussian in . . . spirit": "These painters seem to execute a kind of goose-step . . . [I]f the Junkers could be induced to take to art, instead of disturbing the peace of Europe, they would paint so and enjoy it."[17] Lewis responds directly to this attack in *BLAST* II: "if [the Junker] . . . painted, [he] would do florid and disreputable canvasses of nymphs and dryads, or very sentimental 'portraits of the Junker's mother' . . . As to goose-steps . . . as an antidote to the slop of Cambridge Post Aestheticism . . . or the Gypsy Botticellis of Mill Street, may not such 'rigidity' be welcomed?" (78–79). Lewis repudiates accusations of Junkerism by reiterating the Vorticist line: the movement's sternly anti-sentimental pictures oppose the spirit animating both *passéist* art and the German war effort.

That *BLAST* II opportunistically casts Germany as a prisoner of the past helps clarify the lines of alliance that did exist between Vorticism and state policy. Historians like Modris Eksteins and Eric Hobsbawm have argued that understanding British responses to perceived German aggression during the period requires recognizing that by 1914 a consensus existed throughout Europe that, as Eksteins puts it, "in economic and military terms Germany constituted the most powerful country in

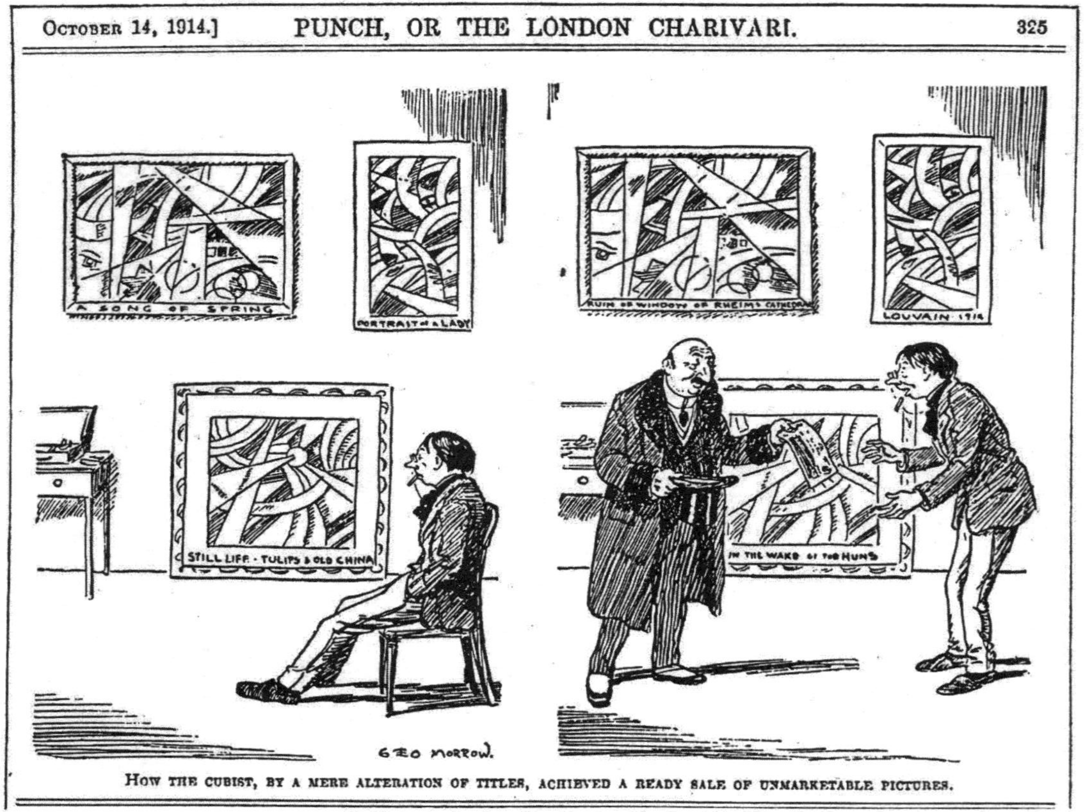

Figure 3 George Morrow, "How the Cubist . . . ," *Punch* 147 (14 October 1914): 325.

the world."[18] These perceptions led Germans to resent Britain in particular as the "archconservative power, intent on maintaining the status quo" against the "progressive, liberating force" that Germany represented.[19] In contrast, most Englishwomen and men, equating the rise of German power with the decline of British, resented Germany as an upstart nation, overly militaristic, materialist, and expansionistic. By associating Junkerism with *passéism* in *BLAST* II, the Vorticists work to affirm their avant-garde credentials while denying Germany's formidable, and for the British, ominous military and industrial achievements. This argument does not exactly replicate the government account of Germany as the world's evil aggressor, but it aims at the same goal: the containment of Britain's most threatening competitor.

The Vorticists' involvement with such official aims leads them at times to deploy the government's arsenal of propaganda tactics to defend modernism and assert their alliance with the national cause. In another *BLAST* polemic, Lewis attempts to channel popular repulsion at alleged German "atrocities" into support for modernism. Early in the war, examples of a potent new genre of propaganda began appearing, which lent the authority of fact to the popular picture of Germans as brutal barbarians – the Kaiser's Huns.[20] These works purport to supply documentary evidence of crimes the German army committed against innocent civilians and cultural treasures. By adducing additional "facts" of German barbarism, Lewis adapts the tactic to justify support for modern art:

> A fact not generally known in England, is that the Kaiser, long before he entered into the war with Great Britain, had declared merciless war on Cubism and Expressionism . . . I expect among his orders to his troops is one to "spare no Cubist prisoners, wounded or otherwise." – I am not implying that this should be a bond of sympathy between the British Nation and Cubists or Vorticists. I only mention it as an interesting fact. (9)

Yet as we will see, the war against modernism propels the Vorticists elsewhere in *BLAST* to protest the very strategy pursued here.

Because *BLAST* II insists that the Vorticists fight with the nation against Germany, its polemics assail in particular those attacks on modernism that exploit anti-German feeling. One of Lewis's "War Notes" aggressively opposes the tactic, which he deems the "Exploitation of Blood": "[t]here is a sort of blackguard that this time has produced – as an earthquake produces looters – who uses the blood of the Soldier for his own everyday domestic uses . . . [C]ritics . . . on the side of lucrative and established forms of art . . . who take this opportunity . . . to attack the [modern] movement in Painting . . . are an exact parallel to the Burglar in the earthquake" (24). By protesting such opportunism, Lewis slams both "patriotic" antagonists of new art, and intellectuals who sacrifice creative independence at the government's behest. But as we have seen, he too "exploits blood," using evidence of German atrocities to promote modernism. That such contradictory negotiations recur repeatedly in *BLAST* II demonstrates not just opportunism or hypocrisy, however, but also design: they map the dynamics of Vorticism's two-front war against Germany and *passéism*.

Accordingly, the *War Number* features polemics that deploy propaganda tactics alongside others animated by dissent. We can assess that dissension through *BLAST*'s responses to two questions especially pressing for British intellectuals priding themselves on their political commitment and cultural scope: how to justify war against Germany, and how to evaluate German culture in light of war. The answers *BLAST* provides show that the Vorticists believed it possible to support the national cause while resisting the official explanation. In their view, indeed, this paradoxical strategy is the necessary means to realize their politico-artistic project.

Despite its popularity, the British government's Manichean account of the conflict was disputed by a small number of dissenting writers of varying political persuasions. The most controversial such polemic of the early war is Bernard Shaw's "Common Sense about the War," a supplement to the *New Statesman* of 14 November 1914. In keeping with his reputation as socialist gadfly, Shaw rejects the official line that a Good England is morally obligated to defeat an Evil Germany, arguing that both nations are ruled by Junkers and Militarists bent on exploiting the poor. Still Shaw defends the socialist cause in terms as ethically polar as those of the war propagandists: "[w]ill you now at last believe, O stupid British, German, and French patriots, what the Socialists have been telling you for so many years: that your Union Jacks and tricolors and Imperial Eagles . . . are only toys to keep you amused, and that there are only two real flags in the world henceforth: the red flag of Democratic Socialism and the black flag of Capitalism, the flag of God and the flag of Mammon?"[21] Recognizing, nonetheless, that war against Germany had effectively suspended the war for socialism, Shaw concludes that the former conflict will have to be resolved before the latter can be resumed: his rejection of the government's justification as "hypocrisy and cant and humbug" has as its goal not the defeat of the international cartel of capitalist Junkers and Militarists as we might expect, but the efficient destruction of German power: "we in England are fighting to shew the Prussians that they shall not trample on us nor on our neighbors if we can help it, and that if they are fools enough to make fighting efficiency the test for civilization, we can play that game as destructively as they. That is simple, and the truth, and by far the jolliest and most inspiring ground to recruit on."[22] Not all dissident intellectuals of the early-war share Shaw's skeptical militarism, however. Members of the Cambridge and Bloomsbury circles embrace militant pacifism.[23] Among Bloomsbury pacifists, Clive Bell, for example, publishes the pamphlet, *Peace at Once*, which argues that no recourse to international law or power politics can justify the conflict: "War is mere destruction and butchery, a certain means to endless ill but never a means to more than a little adventitious good. Everyone suffers; . . . Everybody loses; sorrow, suffering, and death are the only winners. War is just a state of active and organised evil."[24] Bell turns against the government its tale of Holy War. In his account, peace becomes the necessary weapon to defeat the real evil menacing Europe; not Germany: war itself. In his editorials throughout *BLAST* II, Lewis too presents himself as a dissident, but one unique among leading dissenters. He concurs with his radical counterparts in certain respects. Like Shaw, he argues that German defeat is a military necessity; like Bell, he contends that war can not be justified on moral grounds.

What distinguishes Lewis's analysis, however, is its antagonism to conventional morality. For him, the conflict's devastation proves not the senselessness or immorality of war as such, but the human race's "fundamental" urge to murder and destroy. Considering Wells's oft-debated suggestion that the Great War will "end war," Lewis asserts:

> I feel that War won't go. It will be the large communities that make war so unmanageable, unreal and unsatisfactory, that will go . . . Everything will be arranged for the best convenience of War. Murder and destruction is man's fundamental occupation. (16)

When Lewis adopts the voice of the dissident in *BLAST* II, he does so not to evaluate the war's moral status but to acknowledge its existential reality. He finds in it dark and exhilarating truths about human aggression that confirm the Vorticists' prewar celebration of vitalizing violence, discrediting the categories of morality on which most arguments about the war, both for and against, depend.[25]

BLAST also departs from the official line on German culture. Whereas support for the war led many to totalizing dismissals of *Kultur*, the *War Number* defends Germany's artistic achievements even as those expressing similar views grow silent over time. The war posed a problem for cosmopolitan commentators, who before the declaration of hostilities had defended German art and literature, pitting their former devotion to cultural internationalism against a new-found patriotism. To reconcile these competing loyalties, such writers often bifurcate German history, distinguishing an older, better type of "German culture" from a more recent, more dangerous "Prussian *Kultur*." Ford Madox Ford, one of the Vorticists' closest allies in the Edwardian intelligentsia, employs the tactic in his anti-German polemic, *When Blood is Their Argument* (March 1915), praising "the old-fashioned German virtues of sentimentality, idealism, and romanticism," while excoriating the Prussian State for spreading "a religion of materialism and of egotism."[26] Written at Masterman's request, Ford's tract is a rejoinder to Shaw's "Common Sense" pamphlet. Predictably, Masterman viewed Shaw's polemic the way it came to be pictured popularly, as an unpatriotic, even treasonous document. He asked the Anglo-German Ford (then Hueffer) to respond to Shaw because of the former's intimate knowledge of Germany. No doubt Ford's background put him under particular pressure to verify his patriotism by obliging Masterman. At a time of increasing public suspicion of "alien enemies" – German spies in England – he could demonstrate his national loyalty by answering the government's call to action. But that decision would require maligning the nation of his father's birth, a nation he had defended until the eve of war.[27] In the end, Ford would choose England over Germany: his particular contribution to the propaganda war is a detailed assault on German culture, especially those "little, mean, aggressive . . . professors" officially deemed the architects of German aggression.[28]

Showing loyalty to Ford and the national cause, the *War Number* praises *When Blood is Their Argument* as a "Blast" against Germany (7). Yet while *BLAST* II implies support for Ford's negative reckoning of *Kultur*, it does not exactly reiterate the official denunciation. To be sure, it criticizes Germany, even divides German cultural history. But *BLAST* II splits Germany along somewhat unconventional lines, insisting that the official account unjustly ignores Germany's significant contributions to modern art and literature. The opening Editorial differentiates between "Official Germany [which] stands for . . . Traditional Poetry and the Romantic Spirit" and "unofficial Germany" (5). Though the populace of this "unofficial" nation is never clearly identified, the Editorial maintains that it had "done more for the movement" *BLAST* was "founded to propagate, and for all branches of contemporary activity in Science and Art, than any other country" (5). While the Vorticists are not unique in offering such a positive assessment of German culture, the timing of their argument makes it more provocative than similar claims made earlier. This kind of defense was originally formulated by a few dissident intellectuals in the war's opening months,[29] but by the time *BLAST* II appeared in mid-1915, with battle bogging down and the government clamping down on dissent, such praise for German culture ran more strongly against English opinion than had earlier defenses.

That a journal so devoted to defending modernism against allegations of cultural treason would begin with a polemic that invites just those indictments confirms both the Vorticists' commitment to political and artistic independence and their conviction that such dissent is compatible with the war against Germany. And as I hope to show, they were more correct in that contention than has been previously acknowledged. Because the government enlisted the aid of the intelligentsia in promoting its account of the conflict, it helped create a cultural environment that in forbidding political and artistic dissent authorized expressions of opposition. So by using their talents to resist Britain's official anti-modernist wartime culture, even as they supported the Allied cause, the Vorticists and their allies managed to produce a body of literary and artistic works that were at once propagandistic and experimental, imperialistic and avant-garde, Georgian and modernist. These works are further evidence of Vorticism's wartime fulfillment.

THE ARTS OF WAR

Lewis's principal literary contribution to *BLAST* II is the ambitious but incomplete war fiction, "The Crowd Master," an experimental-realist hybrid that modernistically portrays British mobilization on the homefront. Like much of the art and literature featured in the *War Number*, "The Crowd Master" engages wartime life, supports the war cause, but dissents in its literary and political approach.[30] Previous accounts tend to simplify and totalize this ambivalent, discontinuous, and incomplete text, treating it as univocally elitist in order to support a reading of the fragment as proto-reactionary.[31] It is better understood as a work that elucidates the conflicted responses of Lewis and his comrades to the huge crowds that rallied to support the British cause in late July and early August 1914, and the attendant claims of wartime patriotism.

Fictionalizing Vorticism's initial response to the stirrings of war, the story stages stylistic and thematic competition between mass patriotism and avant-garde critique, corporate action and intellectual elitism, conformity to state narratives and formal experiment. "The Crowd Master" deploys experimental literary techniques to affirm and interrogate the competing aims of Vorticist doctrine in war time.

Unlike press treatments of the British war crowds, which sought rhetorically to stir up patriotism and rally public support, Lewis's rendering in "The Crowd Master" works to analyze mass patriotism. Echoing period works of social psychology by English writers like Martin Conway, William McDougall, Wilfred Trotter, and Graham Wallas,[32] Lewis's text examines the role of mass behavior in the rush of popular support that attended war's approach. As historians like Eksteins and Hobsbawm have shown, the tumultuous days of late July, 1914, with their flurry of ultimatums and mobilization orders, provoked massive public demonstrations across Europe. These spontaneous displays surprised many European governments, which had expected greater popular resistance, and thus played a crucial role in encouraging the declarations of war that soon followed.[33] Anxieties about such resistance were especially pronounced in England due to an all-volunteer military policy, an over-dependence on foreign imports, and a prewar public mood of unprecedented dissent and agitation. Because politicians and members of the press were worried about public support, even when confronted with overwhelming evidence of it, they persisted in efforts to rally patriotism. Thus the *Times*' description of the London crowds that gathered in anticipation of war on 5 August, 1914, emphasizes above all the need for national unity:

> Towards midnight Trafalgar square, Whitehall, Parliament street, and Parliament square were filled with a solid mass of people. The cheering and singing which had marked the earlier hours of the evening died away as the hour approached at which the British demand must be answered by Germany. A profound silence fell upon the crowd just before midnight. Then as the first strokes rang out from the Clock Tower, a vast cheer burst out and echoed and re-echoed for nearly 20 minutes. The National Anthem was then sung with an emotion and solemnity which manifested the gravity and sense of responsibility with which the people regard the great issues before them.[34]

This report encourages the same patriotic "gravity and sense of responsibility" it describes. Recruitment propaganda disguised as objective reportage, the piece summons readers to join the mobilized crowd.

In comparison, Lewis's treatment of these public demonstrations is stylistically experimental and analytically penetrating. Translating the image of the mobilized crowd into a mode closer to the clipped declarative style of *BLAST* 1's manifestos, Lewis's text moves beyond encouraging national unity to explaining the patriotic willingness to die for one's country:

> THE CROWD
>
> THE CROWD Is the first mobilisation of a country.
>
> THE CROWD now is formed in London. It is established with all its vague profound organs au grand complet.
>
> It serpentines every night, in thick well-nourished coils, all over town, in tropic degustation of news and "stimmung."
>
> THE INDIVIDUAL and THE CROWD: PEACE and WAR
>
> Man's solitude and Peace; Man's Community and Row . . .
>
> We all shed our small skin periodically or are apt to sometime, and are purged in big being: an empty throb. (94)

As Paul Edwards notes, this mini-manifesto on crowd psychology conforms to period analyses.[35] Resembling theories like those of Conway, McDougall, Trotter, and Wallas that focused on the centrality of "impulse" or "instinct" in human social behavior, Lewis's text defines participation in a crowd as a state in which more primitive instincts subdue the promptings of reason. Wallas's groundbreaking work of political psychology, *Human Nature in Politics* (1908), for example, explains that "[i]n the case of human beings . . . the simpler impulses – especially those of fear and anger – when they are consciously shared by many physically associated individuals, may become enormously exalted, and may give rise to violent nervous disturbances."[36] Echoing especially Trotter's work on the role of the "herd instinct" in human social behavior, "The Crowd Master" attends in particular to the role of crowd psychology in mass patriotism. Trotter contends that in social animals, the "impulse to be in and always to remain with the herd will have the strongest instinctive weight,"[37] overwhelming even the "primitive instincts" of nutrition, sex, and self-preservation (47–48); Lewis argues similarly in "The Crowd Master" that the surrender of individuality entailed by participation in a crowd is an "anesthetizing" of self that can inspire persons willingly to die for country:

> [T]he Crowd in Life spells death . . . very often. The Crowd is an immense anaesthetic towards death. Duty flings the selfish will into this relaxed vortex . . . Wars begin with this huge indefinite Interment in the cities. (94)

These words can be read as exposing an elitist disdain for the unconscious feminized masses that manifests the besieged masculinism of the Edwardian establishment and anticipates what recent theorists have deemed the fascist unconscious.[38] But they can also be understood to initiate a rather prophetic analysis of the war's causes. Viewed in light of the government's rapid conquest of the public sphere during the war's opening months, and the attendant spread of propaganda and suppression of dissent, Lewis's effort to analyze rather than exploit crowd psychology seems an expression less of sexist psychosis or retrograde politics than of legitimate suspicion at expanding government control. It is perhaps not so surprising, then, that the key finding of Lewis's analysis – that "Wars begin" with the gathering of crowds – anticipates the account of mass patriotism's role in precipitating the Great War provided by today's historians.[39]

"The Crowd Master" is noteworthy not just because it analyzes rather than exploits mass patriotism. Through its rendering of Blenner, the soldier-turned-bohemian-egoist, it also portrays the effects of such patriotism on an oppositional Englishman like Lewis, divided between loyalty to nation and the individual ego. This "retired 1st Lieutenant" who now "writes a little, abusively as regards the army" learns of war (95), like his creator, while vacationing in northern Britain.[40] But upon reading the *Daily Mail* headline that "GERMANY DECLARES WAR ON RUSSIA," the skeptical Blenner cannot avoid feelings of dread and excitement:

> With the words came a dark rush of hot humanity in his mind. An immense human gesture swept its shadow across him like a smoky cloud. "Germany Declares War on Russia," seemed a roar of guns. He saw active Mephistophelian specks in Chancelleries. He saw a rush of papers, a frowning race. "'Ça y est," thought Blenner, with innate military exultation. The ground seemed swaying a little. He limped away from the paper-shop, gulping this big morsel down with delighted stony dignity. (95)

As Blenner assimilates the earth-shaking information with the reserve of a military professional, he feels exultation and delight at the prospect of national mobilization. Lewis's fragment responds similarly: fascinated by the swirl of patriotic activity of Britons being mobilized, it strives to maintain a critical distance.[41]

"The Crowd Master" shows this analytical fascination in its treatment of the type of the dutiful, good-humored, self-effacing British soldier portrayed in popular war literature. While the "Tommy Atkins" figure was originally idealized by Kipling and others before the century's turn, younger combatant writers like Herman Cyril McNeile and

Ian Hay Beith venerated the type in their efforts to portray the facts of the Great War realistically. These works render naturalistically war's trenches, mud, bullets, death, and the young men who confront them.[42] But Lewis's approach to the "Tommy Atkins" figure thematizes the complications of his paradoxical position as a civilian who had not yet joined the fighting troops and an avant-gardist trying to maintain commitment to artistic and political independence in the face of mass-patriotism and the pressure for national unity. Blenner's responses to the mobilized Scottish coal miners he encounters on the train to London epitomize the competition the text enacts between patriotic engagement and avant-garde critique. On one hand, Lewis's protagonist views the "pitmen" as embodying Britain's best qualities: "[h]ere were fellows to whom he could point to back up his chauvinistic enthusiasm for the country, and not doubt their shining and showing handsomely beside any men alive" (97). On the other, Blenner admires the pitmen because they remain individuals despite the patriotic crowds around them: "These Crowd-proof sailors were the first break in the continuity of the Crowd-spirit that Blenner had met since war began blowing up seriously" (97).

Confronted with the tumultuous realities of war's opening, Lewis was pulled, like his ambivalent protagonist, by the competing claims of self and nation, dissent and patriotism, nonconformity and collectivism. "The Crowd Master" is an illuminating document of the early war and the emergence of modernist politics because it does not resolve that competition in an unambiguous embrace of the elite ego. The contention between these claims, thrown into particular relief by mobilization, fascinates Lewis; he uses "The Crowd Master" to portray and probe it. The fragment is titled "The Crowd Master" less to celebrate such a person than to prompt readers to respond to the text as Blenner does to the identically named avant-garde manifesto by his egotistical friend Brown Bryan Multum, the "American poet" and provocateur:

> THE CROWD MASTER. What might that mean? . . . An opposition of and welding of the two heaviest words that stand for the multitudes on the one hand, the Ego on the other.
> That should be something!
> Did it really mean Master of the Crowd in the sense of a possessive domination by an individual? It meant something else, it seemed evident. (99–100)[43]

Taken as a whole, "The Crowd Master" neither celebrates a Crowd

Master nor masters the crowd. Like Blenner encountering the "opposition . . . and welding of" the two antithetical terms, it interrogates the dichotomy of individual and collective. By doing so Lewis's fragment expresses his vision of Vorticist doctrine in literary form: "The Crowd Master" works formally and thematically to show that avant-garde critique is compatible with patriotic collaboration. By embracing that ideal as an editorial policy, we will see, Lewis also managed to assemble a series of patriotic pictorial and literary works that, while by no means great, did depart aesthetically and politically from the pictures and poems sanctioned by the government, and to that extent validated (to the Vorticists at least) *BLAST*'s doctrine of patriotic dissent in art and politics.

The majority of visual works featured in *BLAST* II are formally comparable to those in *BLAST* I – dense angular fields of form, combining modes of abstraction and representation. Most do not engage the war (many were completed before it began): of the seventeen attributed illustrations, only five refer to the war at all, while just three portray war subjects. This imbalance demonstrates in part Lewis's claim that war poses no threat to modernism's prewar innovations: modern art "will be exactly the same after the War as before it," since "[a]ll art that matters is already so far ahead that it is beyond the sphere of these disturbances" (13). Yet the inclusion of war art in *BLAST* 2 also manifests the Vorticists' wartime conviction that art can and should engage the conflict using modernist visual techniques.

To appreciate *BLAST* II's war art as its contributors would have us, we need first to recover the popular war art the Vorticists oppose, the "weak and sentimentalized reactive" works the *War Number*'s commentaries assail (24). Generally speaking, four types of war art were produced during the conflict's first year: (1) commemorative history paintings of traditional military subjects – battles, on land and sea, often drawn from past wars England had won; (2) allegorical representations of combatant nations or the ideals at stake; (3) comic caricatures of unsavory German types; and (4) posters of heroic Allied soldiers and innocent victims of German aggression.[44] The first exhibition of war art, "Some Modern War Pictures" (New English Art Club, October 1914), featured grandiose renderings of great British military actions by the well-known history painters, A. Chevallier Tayler and R. Caton-Woodville. These paintings would, it was hoped, stir up patriotism and help recruit volunteers (Britain's military depended on volunteers until full conscription was mandated in May 1916).[45] More common and influential were the allegorical cartoons featured in popular magazines and newspapers like *Punch*. These typically portray Germany as the diabolical Kaiser being brutal and Britain as either the chubby and defiant John Bull or the British Soldier displaying loyalty and pluck (figs. 4 and 5). Some allegorical illustrations discourage class difference and encourage working-class volunteers by depicting conversations between the Soldier and the Worker in which the former appeals to the latter's sense of national duty (fig. 6). The best-known producer of allegorical cartoons was Bernard Partridge, who won immense notoriety during the war for illustrations in *Punch*.[46] Popular journals like *Punch* also featured the third category of war art: comic cartoons that caricature the enemy as a race of rigid militarists, filled with hate and adorned with various accoutrements of stereotypical Germanness – dachshunds, spiked helmets, beer steins, sausages (fig. 7). Making up the final category are war posters that work to recruit volunteers and solicit material support for the British military and for Belgian and French refugees. Typically, these portray gallant Allied soldiers resisting German aggression or innocent women and children displaced by it (fig. 8). The most renowned producer of this type of war art was the Academy painter Frank Brangwyn, who created scores of propaganda posters,[47] including one of the first, *Britain's Call To Arms*, which renders a soldier standing beside Belgian refugees pointing dramatically toward ruins from which, amidst the innocent dead, war victims flee.[48]

In his commentaries on art in the *War Number*, Lewis assails all these modes of war art, calling posters and popular art too representational (47) and modern caricature too literary and naturalistic (79). He blasts art that is "the ornament and current commentary of every day life," suggesting that "politically souled" artists who create naturalistic propaganda pictures at the government's behest reduce art's function to reflecting the status quo (72). Arguing against such a diminution, Lewis calls for an "abstract and universal" art (72) that refuses "plastic compromise" (70). Accordingly, *BLAST* II criticizes especially strongly three leading war artists: Caton-Woodville, whose historical paintings are deemed inane and formulaic (24); Partridge, whose *Punch* illustrations are assailed for their "endless tiresomeness and art school neutrality" (79); and Brangwyn, who is singled out above all English artists for assault – his is the first name on the list of those blasted (92).

But *BLAST* II doesn't just attack popular war art. It also features artworks that pursue the two front war against Germany and *passéism* by using techniques of pictorial modernism to render soldiers in scenes of

Figure 4 Bernard Partridge, "The Triumph of 'Culture,'" *Punch* 147 (23 August 1914): 185.

Figure 5 F. H. Townsend, "The Incorrigibles," *Punch* 147 (7 October 1914): 291.

Figure 6 Bernard Partridge, "A Glorious Example," *Punch* 147 (11 November 1914): 399.

STUDY OF A PRUSSIAN HOUSEHOLD HAVING ITS MORNING HATE.

Figure 7 Frank Reynolds, "Study of a Prussian Household Having its Morning Hate," *Punch* 148 (24 February 1915): 150.

Figure 8 John Hassall, *Belgian Canal Boat Fund* (poster).

war: Lewis's *Before Antwerp* (fig. 1), Christopher Nevinson's *On the Way to the Trenches* (fig. 9), and Jacob Kramer's *Types of the Russian Army* (fig. 10). Though formally inconsistent, these works share the common goal of presenting a modernist war art; Nevinson's *Trenches*, like Lewis's *Antwerp*, is a modern war poster, while Kramer's *Types* is a modern war caricature.

Kramer's cartoon can serve to clarify both the Vorticist view of it as an example of modern war art and the achievement of *BLAST* II's war art generally. *Types of the Russian Army* conforms well to Lewis's description, in "Modern Caricature and Impressionism" (79), of how modern war caricatures should look. The essay begins by criticizing English caricature art for relying too heavily on the techniques of Impressionism and naturalism, and goes on to argue, echoing Vorticism's prewar polemics, that the "naturalistic method, with its atmospheric slop and verisimilitude, makes a drab academic study of the best notion" (79). The piece deems *Punch*, England's major venue for war cartoons, a "national disgrace, from the point of view of drawing" and praises the late-nineteenth-century caricatures of Aubrey Beardsley – the only "important figure" England has "produced in the matter of imaginative drawing in the last generation" – for avoiding naturalism: "Beardsley's several versions of John Bull would be a good model to set against the endless tiresomeness and art school neutrality of some Albion or Lord Kitchener by Bernard Partridge" (79). In this light, Kramer's *Types* appears a modern caricature that avoids naturalist failings. It too rejects "the method employed by the degenerate Punch cartoonist" of finding a model, dressing-up and posing him, and "carefully cop[ying] . . . the required attitude" (79), portraying instead three Russian soldiers as freakish, unnatural grotesques: in the foreground, a large-headed, pigeon-toed midget; in the midground, a square-headed, hairy-faced cavalry man atop a tiny-legged horse; in the background, a rail-thin giant wearing a sword. Unlike most war art, Kramer's caricature is not an image to inspire faith in Britain's Russian allies or a willingness to die for the fatherland. In this it shares the Vorticist resistance to turning art into government propaganda.

Yet at the same time, Kramer's cartoon departs in particular ways from Vorticist visual practice and from certain political views announced in the *War Number*. Though the caricature inhabits a pictorial landscape occupied almost exclusively by abstractionist works, it is, as others have noted, neither particularly abstract nor Vorticist in pictorial technique.[49] And the disjunctiveness of Kramer's image does not end

Figure 9 Christopher Nevinson, *On the Way to the Trenches, BLAST* II (July 1915): 89.

with its visual style. Its apparently anti-Russian politics too are inconsistent with Lewis's proclaimed support for Russia. Endorsing Anglo-Russian alliance in one of his "War Notes," Lewis predicts hopefully that the "Slavic" empire will "get Constantinople," a principal aim of the Russian Government. The European incorporation of the artistically rich capital of the old Byzantine empire will, he explains, benefit "every good artist in Europe" (11). Kramer's rendering of Russian soldiers as distorted primitives is more consistent with the position of England's anti-Russian writers. For socialist intellectuals in particular, who had long-opposed the Tsar's regime as anti-democratic, aided the exiled Russian aristocrat-anarchist, Prince Kropotkin, and supported the first revolution of 1905–06, alliance with the Tsar's government seemed a serious mistake.[50] Bernard Shaw had made that case in the "Common Sense" pamphlet by excoriating the Tsar's autocratic government in terms as intense as those he used to condemn capitalism: "I . . . hate the infamous tyranny of which he is the figurehead as I hate the devil."[51] By rendering Russians freakishly, Kramer questions the government line aesthetically and politically, departing from the naturalistic conventions of popular war pictures as well as the pro-Russian policy

Figure 10 Jacob Kramer, *Types of the Russian Army, BLAST* II (July 1915): 31.

of the government and established press. The presence of Kramer's work in *BLAST* II also demonstrates Lewis's editorial willingness to feature dissident works even if they depart from the Vorticists' announced political views and aesthetic practice.

By including Kramer's *Types of the Russian Army*, Nevinson's *On the Way to the Trenches*, and his own *Before Antwerp*, Lewis placed engaged and fairly representational pictures into a body of artworks primarily abstract and aestheticist, non-Vorticist works into the propaganda organ of Vorticism, and artworks that voice contrasting political views at a time when only one political narrative, the government's account of the war, dominated public discourse. While these aesthetic and political inconsistencies have been read as evidence of Vorticism's wartime decline, Lewis and his cohorts would have taken them as indicators of aesthetic and political integrity: for them, such diversity measures the intensity of their modernist resistance to conformity at a time of rigid (artistic) consensus.

Reading *BLAST* II's war poems in the context of popular war poetry suggests that the Vorticists understood them too as demonstrating the movement's twin aims of patriotic political participation and modernist aesthetic experiment. While a few of the *War Number*'s non-political poems have been studied and praised, its war poetry is generally downplayed or dismissed.[52] Admittedly, when compared to prewar Imagism and the poetic masterpieces of high modernism, these sometimes blunt and polemical poems seem less aesthetically innovative and historically significant. But when the war poems are compared to the occasional poetry produced during the conflict's first year, we can begin to understand them as the Vorticists would have: as poems engaged in the serious work of demonstrating poetically Vorticism's competing commitments to art and politics, collaboration and dissent, patriotism and innovation at a time of political and poetic conformity.

Among the most celebrated patriotic poems of the early war are the "War Sonnets" of Rupert Brooke, the promising young Georgian poet, whose death in April on a boat to Gallipoli nearly coincided with the poems' publication, enhancing immensely both Brooke's stature as English patriot and the Sonnets' stature as major war poetry. We will have reason to return to the interesting subject of Brooke's death and its implications for wartime patriotism and for subsequent readings of Vorticism. For now, the "War Sonnets" will serve to represent the best that popular English poetry had to offer in response to the start of war. Brooke's most famous poem, "The Soldier," for instance, so earnestly brings the idealizing tropes of prewar ruralism and (new) Englishness to the (government's) wartime agenda of justifying the conflict, encouraging (especially upper-class) volunteerism, and celebrating patriotic self-sacrifice that it largely avoids the artlessness of most propagandistic poetry of the period.[53] Here is a Georgian pastoral patriotism at its most expressive:

> If I should die, think only this of me:
>   That there's some corner of a foreign field
> That is forever England. There shall be
>   In that rich earth a richer dust concealed;
> A dust whom England bore, shaped, made aware,
>   Gave, once, her flowers to love, her ways to roam,
> A body of England's, breathing English air,
>   Washed by the rivers, blest by suns of home.

And think, this heart, all evil shed away,
  A pulse in the eternal mind, no less
    Gives somewhere back the thoughts by England given;
Her sights and sounds; dreams happy as her day;
  And laughter, learnt of friends; and gentleness,
    In hearts at peace, under an English heaven.[54]

Brooke may not have signed Masterman's "Declaration of Authors," but the publication of the "Sonnets" confirms a comparable willingness to put his creative talents at the service of official propaganda.[55]

The majority of popular early war poetry lacks the aesthetic dimension that Brooke brings to defending the English cause: most is little more than government propaganda in rhyme that exhorts the public to join the fight at home or on the front lines by bluntly celebrating England and the Allied cause, or demonizing Germany, the Kaiser, and the conduct of the German troops.[56] Typical is humorist Barry Pain's "The Kaiser and God," which uses the Kaiser's public assertion that "God supported" the German army as an occasion to catalogue, in strutting tetrameter couplets, Germany's diabolical crimes:

Broken pledges, treaties torn,
Your first page of war adorn;
We on fouler things must look
Who read further in that book,
Where you did in time of war
All that you in peace forswore,
Where you, barbarously wise,
Bade your soldiers terrorize,
Where you made – the deed was fine –
Women screen your firing line,
Villages burned down to dust,
Torture, murder, bestial lust, . . .
Strange the offerings that you press
On the God of Righteousness![57]

In the context of poems like this, the war poetry of *BLAST* II is distinguished aesthetically and politically. Ford's *BLAST* II poem, "The Old Houses of Flanders" (37), for instance, would have been read by the Vorticists and their allies as an articulate and moving elegy on war's loss. Ford responded to the conflict using the modernist techniques of free verse and literary "Impressionism." He had recently described Impressionism in print as "a frank expression of personality,"[58] in which the "Impressionist gives you his own views, expecting you to draw deductions, since presumably you know the sort of chap he is" (168). If successful, the Impressionist would transmit "the sort of odd vibration that scenes in real life really have . . . giv[ing the] reader the impression that he was witnessing something real" (175). "The Old Houses of Flanders" strives to fulfill the Impressionist credo by personifying the destruction of the old Belgian houses. It thus renders war's destruction if not more "real," at least more affecting, than any list of atrocities in tetrameter:

The old houses of Flanders,
They watch by the high cathedrals;
They have eyes, mournful, tolerant and sardonic, for the ways of men,
In the high, white, tiled gables.
The rain and the night have settled down on Flanders;
It is all wetness and darkness; you can see nothing.
Then those old eyes, mournful, tolerant and sardonic,
Look at great, sudden, red lights,
Look upon the shades of the cathedral
And the golden rods of the illuminated rain,
For a second . . . .
And those old eyes,
Very old eyes that have watched the ways of men for generations,
Close for ever.
The high white shoulders of the gables
Slouch together for a consultation,
Slant drunkenly over in the lea of the flaming cathedrals.
They are no more, the old houses of Flanders. (37)

Because it portrays the speaker's feelings of personal regret rather than caricatures of German soldiers, descriptions of war crimes, or accusations of war guilt, Ford's elegy for Belgian culture distinguishes itself from much British war poetry in form and content. And when read in light of his own damning analysis of German culture in *When Blood is Their Argument*, the poem suggests that *BLAST* provided its contributors, more than many other journalistic venues, with a forum to express heterodox responses to the war.

It is not so surprising, then, that the *War Number* features one of the most unsettled and unsettling dissident poems of the early war: Helen Saunders's "A Vision of Mud" (73–74), a discordant, hallucinatory meditation on mud and poetry in wartime.[59] Saunders's particular poetic contribution is a restless reverie on the urge to bridge the chasm between home and the front in verse, and the ultimate impossibility of doing so. Consistent with *BLAST*'s attack on the sentimental realist techniques of war propaganda, Saunders's poem uses tropes of poetic naturalism to incite and then deny the empathy that propaganda art and poetry is supposed to provide.

"A Vision of Mud" proffers a disorienting series of images evoking facts of war: recruiting bands, beating drums, struggle, sickness, mud, bodies, blood, death. It opens, somewhat as the conflict did, on a note of exhilaration. Mud is presented as a medium of "mighty life": "There is mud all round / This is favourable to the eclosion of mighty life: thank God for small mercies!" (73). But the mud turns dangerous, overwhelming, as aggressors try to drown the speaker:

> I lie quite still: hands are spreading mud everywhere: they plaster it on what should be a body.
> They fill my mouth with it. I am sick. They shovel it all back again.
> My eyes are full of it; nose and ears, too. (73)

The poem presses us to read its images as representations of front life: here, a soldier suffocated in trench-mud by the enemy. The gambit recurs throughout the poem's first half. A whirl of images invites but never declares war; one moment a soldier seems to struggle in mud, the next, we hear sounds of mobilization: "It seems to be a recruiting band, / The drums thud and the fifes pipe on tip-toe" (73). For the poem's original audience, it would have been difficult not to read such lines as referring to the war. And as a "giant cloud like a black bladder with holes in it hovers overhead," pouring mud with "a little red" onto the narrator (73), remaining doubts about the poem's representational and rhetorical aims would disappear. Months after the war began, the German government launched a series of zeppelin attacks on Britain. April and May of 1915 witnessed eight air-raids; bombs rained down on Tyneside, East Anglia, Southend, Leigh, Westcliff, Ramsgate, and London.[60] These terrifying raids captured English imaginations. Few Britons could read Saunders's lines without recalling the deadly airships.

Yet as the narrator contemplates this rising "black mud" of war, the poem unexpectedly swerves:

> This mud has curious properties.
> It makes you dream. It is like poisoned arrows.
> (Such mud, naturally, is medicinal: that is why they have set up this vulgar "Hydro" here.
> It is a health-resort.) (73)

By matter-of-factly identifying the poem's mud as that of the "health-resort," Saunders startles her readers, rebuking those who would interpret her verse as providing access to the trenches, calling into question the basic assumptions of such an understanding: that reading about mud is in any way like being in it, that a mention of mud during wartime refers to the mud of the battlefield, that reading poetry is a political act, a form of participation in a distant and incomprehensible conflict. As most English poetry works insistently to support or render the conflict, "A Vision of Mud" questions the possibility of that project in a journal aimed to demonstrate it not only possible, but for modern writers and artists especially, necessary. The presence of Saunders's poem in *BLAST* II like that of Kramer's caricature of Russian soldiers, shows an editorial willingness to feature dissident artworks that deviate from the Vorticist line.

As Ford uses verse to lament war's cultural cost, as Saunders makes it question the project of writing war poetry, Ezra Pound turns it to protesting the war against modernism. "Et Faim Sallir Le Loup Des Boys" (22), presents poetry as a tool for rebutting period attacks like those of Alfred Orage, the dissident socialist writer and editor of *The New Age*. Before the war, as chapter 2 points out, Orage's *New Age* had been a leading organ for the promotion and analysis of modernism, publishing and praising works by numerous radical writers and artists, including Pound and Lewis. Yet Orage's wartime attacks on Imagism and Vorticism confirm that the conflict led him to take up arms against modernism. Like many of his contemporaries, Orage came to feel that the war made the modernists' grandiose claims for art seem at best overblown, at worst politically irresponsible. He begins the assault in early September of 1914, affirming that "Vorticism is dead": "It was, at best, only a big name for a little thing, that in the simmering of the prewar period suddenly became a bubble, and is now burst." Orage then applies to *BLAST* I the standard anti-modernist line of irrelevance: "[c]ompared with the war, it is incomparably feeble."[61] The polemic reaches its greatest intensity in an October assault on Imagism, however, where Orage further articulates his vision of modernism's extinction, going so far as to voice the "hope" that the Imagists might "all perish in the war,"[62] a wish more theatrically extreme than most found in the period's numerous anti-modernist polemics.

"Et Faim Sallir Le Loup Des Boys" responds by refusing poetically to abandon the modernist cause as the Vorticists defined it. Assailing in particular anti-modernist editors, Pound's narrator defends his closest allies by name, scorning dreams of dead Imagists:

> Cowardly editors threaten: "If I dare"
> Say this or that, or speak my open mind,

Say that I hate my hates,
  Say that I love my friends,
Say I believe in Lewis, spit out the later Rodin,
Say that Epstein can carve in stone,
That Brzeska can use the chisel,
Or Wadsworth paint;
                    Then they will have my guts;
They will cut down my wage, force me to sing their cant,
Uphold the press, and be before all a model of literary decorum.
                                        Merde! (22)

This defense resembles popular war poems in its use of poetry as a medium for polemic and anti-modernist polemic in its tendency to demonize antagonists. But the poem also distinguishes itself from the generalizations of both genres by asserting its emergence from a nexus of personal relationships.

In its closing tercet, as the narrator faces war's costs with defiance, "Et Faim Sallir Le Loup Des Boys" turns the besieged (but noncombatant) modern poet into modernist war hero:

Cowardly editors threaten,
Friends fall off at the pinch, the loveliest die.
That is the path of life, this is my forest. (22)

Acknowledging such costs is not the same as arresting them, however. Despite the speaker's determined embrace of artistic exile as the title's starving wolf in the woods, this poetic defense finally serves to emphasize the dynamic it seeks to resist: by admitting death into the poem, Pound articulates more powerfully than most anti-modernist polemics the limits of modern poetry in the face of war. Nonetheless, because Ford, Saunders, and Pound respond to the call to creative arms by resisting the conventions of popular war poetry, exploring instead their personal reactions to war's tumult, they uphold in poetry a modernist commitment to dissenting aesthetics at a time of militant political and aesthetic consensus. They manage thereby to produce distinguished war verse that expresses poetically the Vorticists' ideal of engaged dissent.

The broad dynamic this chapter has been tracing, in which Vorticist doctrine dovetails with wartime circumstances in such a manner as to authorize newly that doctrine, achieves its most intense and revealing expression in "Vortex Gaudier-Brzeska: (Written from the Trenches)" (33–34), the central polemical contribution of the talented young French sculptor whose death at the front in June 1915 casts a chastening pall over *BLAST* II. Rather than disputing the scholarly consensus that Gaudier's death, announced at the end of the polemic, anticipates and even symbolizes Vorticism's decline or demise during the Great War, I want to point out that his death was not understood by the Vorticists as merely a confirmation of one or another kind of failure or loss. On the contrary, "Vortex Gaudier-Brzeska" is the *War Number*'s culminating document: it extends Vorticism's program to its theoretical telos, recording and enacting the glorification of Gaudier in death, who by sacrificing his life in the Vorticists' two-front war against Germany and *passéism*, provides the ultimate authorization of Vorticist collaboration in the national cause and resistance to old-fashioned art.

"Vortex Gaudier-Brzeska" recreates in Vorticism's paradoxical image what George Mosse terms the "Myth of the War Experience"; it appropriates the myth's cult of the fallen young soldier whose death authorizes the national cause,[63] but makes its heroic soldier a modern artist. Robert Wohl has traced the development of the Myth in Britain through the case of Brooke, who made the perfect war hero, despite the fact that the cause of Brooke's death was less than heroic (blood poisoning attending the clap).[64] For as the First Lord of the Admiralty, Winston Churchill, explained in his eulogy, Brooke, "the poet-soldier," embodied all the best English qualities required for victory: "[j]oyous, fearless, versatile, deeply instructed, with classic symmetry of mind and body, he was all that one would wish England's noblest sons to be in days when no sacrifice but the most precious is acceptable, and the most precious is that which is most freely proffered."[65] In death, Brooke became a symbol for the generation of young Britons that he himself had praised for jumping into battle "as swimmers into cleanness leaping."[66] Wohl shows how Brooke's death validated the national cause, transforming him into "a patriotic monument of marble," "an icon in which an entire class could recognize itself and by means of which it could justify the sacrifice of its sons."[67] Similarly, by celebrating destruction even while insisting on his – and by extension Vorticism's – invincibility, Gaudier's "Vortex from the Trenches" lays the groundwork for the myth his death would fulfill: "WITH ALL THE DESTRUCTION that works around us NOTHING IS CHANGED, EVEN SUPERFICIALLY. LIFE IS THE SAME STRENGTH, the moving agent that permits the small individual to assert himself" (33). The demise of this defiant soldier-artist recuperates Vorticism's contradictory doctrine: his destruction is the final validation of his cause, transforming him into one of the heroic and monumental soldier-artists celebrated on the *War*

Number's cover, who dies in the fight for modern art and life against Germany and *passéism*.

In our context then, the Vortex's celebration of annihilation as the fullest proof of manly life does not serve to anticipate fascist modernism or uncover the masculinist psychosis of the fascist unconscious.[68] Instead, it bolsters the argument that during the early months of the Great War, England's leading modernist art movement positioned itself as an eager but critical collaborator with the British government. The crucial difference in their respective doctrines, as we have seen, is the role assigned to modern art and letters in the war for a British future. For the government, modernism plays a minor role, useful only insofar as its denigration validates official art and the official attack on Germany. For the Vorticists in contrast, it plays an essential role; they fight for a future in which Britannia rules not only waves, markets, and industry, but culture as well. As the *War Number* repeatedly insists, only the Vorticists, with their recognition that modernity requires a culture as advanced as it is patriotic, can lead the world's greatest empire against the forces of reaction to achieve that goal.

Such policy differences notwithstanding, however, the war exposes a deeper affinity. Gaudier's sacrificial death, like those of Brooke and other fallen soldiers across Europe, instantiates the paradoxical terminus of the prewar cult of masculine vitality that undergirds both Vorticism's project of avant-garde imperialism and the ideological edifice of the prewar nation-state system: the ultimate destruction of vitality as its ultimate affirmation.[69] This neglected affiliation calls into further question the still influential account of the avant-garde as a progressive – though only somewhat successful – antagonist of the nineteenth-century international system of bourgeois capitalism.[70] Not only does it extend the point Renato Poggioli first made over thirty years ago, that the avant-garde was always also a parasitic collaborator with that regime,[71] but suggests as well that the avant-gardists' neglected investments in the imperial politics and nationalistic psychology of the period played a role in facilitating their post-war political gyrations, at least as important as the opticalist aesthetics, (latent) anti-Semitism, or intellectual elitism usually cited.

The past four chapters have traced the complex articulation of an anarcho-imperialist politics among avant-garde artists and writers in England up and into the Great War as a means of opening some new avenues for understanding their post-war political interests. The following chapter moves closer still to the question of modernist theories of culture, power, and identity after the war by studying a fully-fledged modernist novel completed during the conflict which deals extensively with and further complicates period discourses of nationality, individuality, and sexuality. Chapter 5 clarifies avant-garde race thinking during the Great War as a means of enriching discussions of the ex-Vorticists' post-war involvements with radical forms of rac(ial)ism, racial intolerance, and race paranoia.

CHAPTER 5

Anti-Individualism and fictions of national character in Lewis's Tarr

The causes at the root of Tarr's present thrusting of himself upon Kreisler were the same as his later visits at the Lipmann's. A sort of bath of Germans was his prescription for himself, a voluptuous immersion. To heighten the effect, he was being German himself: being Bertha as well.

But he was more German than the Germans. Many aspects of his conduct were so un-German that Kreisler did not recognize the portrait or hail him as a fellow.

Wyndham Lewis, *Tarr*, 221

Such was Kreisler, but he was *himself* very cynically. He had explained this to Volker after the following manner: "I am a hundred different things; I am as many people as the different types of people I have lived amongst."

Lewis, *Tarr*, 256

No reader of *Tarr,* Wyndham Lewis's first-published, most-studied, and arguably best novel, can ignore the central role nationality plays. As its international characters interact chaotically on the streets and in the cafés of prewar Paris, they spend endless time contemplating their national characteristics and justifying their actions in terms of national character. They make so much of these topics that ever since *Tarr*'s first publication critics have periodically taken them as pivotal to the novel's meaning. Most such readings focus on the psychological drama of the novel's two German characters: Bertha Lunken, the over-sentimental lover of the English painter Frederick Tarr, and Otto Kreisler, the failed artist and financial parasite, whose obsession with the unattainable Russian-German beauty Anastasya Vasek drives him to rape Bertha, to kill accidentally Soltyk (the Russian-Pole he means to kill on purpose), and finally to hang himself. Critics analyzing the novel during times of anti-German sentiment in England and America – after the First and

Second World Wars – interpret *Tarr* as an anti-German tract, reading Lewis's overly-romantic and brutal Germans as literary instruments in a "racial critique," allegorical representations of their destructive fatherland. Rebecca West, in one of the earliest and most frequently cited commentaries on *Tarr*, deems it "a work of art of power and distinction" and Kreisler a "figure of vast moral significance."[1] Nonetheless, she reads the actions of Lewis's German characters as manifestations of national "ugliness":

> In watching Bertha Lunken, the acquiescent sentimentalist, and Kreisler, the murderous clown, whom she evokes by her spurious passions and inspires by her inertia to his most violent atrocity, we have the same baffled feeling with which Europe has watched Germany for the last four years: here are people the whole of whose beings are oriented towards ugliness.[2]

Writing after the Second World War, Geoffrey Wagner echoes West:

> Bertha and Kreisler . . . personify together the German romantic nihilism that is the racial criticism of the work . . . [T]hey are tellingly brought together in a brutal erotic clash, symbolic of the social rape Lewis thinks the Germans would like to effect in the society of nations.[3]

But by attributing a fixed repertoire of "German" traits to Bertha and Kreisler, West and Wagner simplify Lewis's bizarre characters and *Tarr*'s rather thick analysis of nationality and character, reducing thereby the novel's peculiar complexity, its interpretive challenge.

Wary of such limitations, Fredric Jameson, in his provocative 1979 study *Fables of Aggression*, offers a challenging new approach to *Tarr*'s treatment of nationality.[4] Like West and Wagner, Jameson interprets *Tarr* as a "national allegory" in which "the individual characters figure . . . more abstract national characteristics which are read as their inner essence." But he criticizes partisan interpretations like West's and Wagner's that focus on "a single foreign national essence alone" because such readings use "allegory . . . as the instrument of cultural critique." Lewis's treatment of national allegory is, he contends, more complicated: "a more complex network of interrelations and collisions emerges . . . [N]arrative meaning becomes relational, as momentary alliances develop and disintegrate."[5] Jameson introduces this complex conception of allegory to support his argument that *Tarr* enacts a transition from "national allegory to libidinal apparatus," an argument finally intended, he explains, to advance his larger project of studying the "political unconscious."[6] So while Jameson's is the most sophisticated and interesting analysis of nationality in *Tarr*, it is keyed more to his own preoccupations than to the novel's project.

In contrast, this chapter historicizes *Tarr* more finely, working to recover its critical aims and situate its treatment of nationality within the intellectual debates and literary practices of Lewis's closest contemporaries during the opening months of the second year of the Great War, when he was completing the novel. My reading draws on and is meant to complement Michael Levenson's, which begins the project of historicizing *Tarr* by analyzing it in the context of other modernist novels.[7] Levenson persuasively describes Lewis's fictional attack on nineteenth-century notions of personal identity. He locates Lewis with other practitioners of the modern British novel – James, Forster, Lawrence, Woolf – whose works "engage in self-conscious assault on a notion of character persistently associated with the nineteenth century."[8] Nevertheless Levenson differentiates Lewis's novel from those of his contemporaries because they still "sustain nostalgic longing for a whole self," while *Tarr* refuses such nostalgia. *Tarr* attacks the nineteenth-century ideal of "the autonomous ego, free and integral," Levenson maintains, as relentlessly as Lewis and his contemporaries attacked nineteenth-century conventions of narrative form.[9] *Tarr*'s rendering of personal identity and social interaction certainly assails nineteenth-century novelistic orthodoxies but Lewis aimed its fictional assault, we will see, more precisely than Levenson acknowledges.

Previous accounts of *Tarr* neglect the significance of its original appearance in Dora Marsden and Harriet Shaw Weaver's "Individualist Review," *The Egoist.* Though it has often been noted that the novel first appeared in serial form in *The Egoist,* very little effort has been made to relate its formal strategies and thematic concerns to the works appearing there. When *Tarr* is viewed in its original context, a number of the qualities that often trouble critics and readers (its two heroes, double plot, seemingly anti-German politics) become comprehensible – somewhat surprisingly – as strategies in a literary critique of the "Individualist" aesthetic, philosophical, and political positions articulated in *The Egoist* by some of Lewis's closest allies and contemporaries, including Marsden, Pound, and Joyce.

In *The Egoist, Tarr* acts as a harsh satire of a contemporary novel sub-genre that would later be canonized as one of that generation's central contributions to modern British letters, a sub-genre that articulates and idealizes the Individualist world-view. Not surprisingly, the best and most celebrated example of that genre, which can be considered an Individualist *Bildungsroman,* first appeared in *The Egoist.* Joyce's *A Portrait of the Artist as a Young Man* was serialized in the "Individualist Review" between February 1914 and September 1915. While Joyce's novel questions a number of the movement's tenets,[10] in the pages of *The Egoist, Portrait of the Artist* appears almost a translation of Individualist ideals into modern novel form: a *Bildungsroman* that portrays Stephen Dedalus's maturation into a deeply creative and fiercely independent artist – an ideal Individualist hero.[11] About six months after Joyce's novel began to appear in *The Egoist,* Lewis returned to an unfinished novel begun seven years earlier. He completed *Tarr* in November 1915; it appeared serially in *The Egoist* between April 1916 and November 1917.[12] In this context, *Tarr* works as a literary corrosive to the Individualist ideals *Portrait* seems to have embodied,[13] refuting the Egoists' representation of persons as self-defining beings capable of personal liberation, their narrative of such persons transcending the constricting forces of personal history to achieve independence, and their model of the novel as a *Bildungsroman* narrating the progressive education of a single subjectivity.[14]

Once the specificity of this novelistic assault on English Individualism is recovered, it becomes clear that *Tarr*'s rendering of nationality's relations to personal identity does not serve the reductive and partisan goals of racial critique. Lewis's novel deploys, scrutinizes, and disputes the two competing conceptions of national character being defended in intellectual and popular debates at the start of the war, both of which Lewis had himself previously (and sometimes simultaneously) embraced: on one hand, the racialist view of nationality as an internal and essential category, the result of an "heredity" that fundamentally defines the character of individuals of a particular "race" or nation; on the other, the Individualist view of nationality as an external, non-essential category, the result of a restrictive regime of cultural training that persons of sufficient energy, insight, and will can and should overcome.[15] *Tarr* portrays both of these accounts as reductive, simplifying, and inadequate to explain the disorderly facts of human identity and activity. The familiar critical picture of Lewis as essentially a racial essentialist, on which even Jameson's useful and complicating analysis relies, does not comport with the rendering of nationality in Lewis's first-published novel. If *Tarr* reiterates English stereotypes of Germans as members of a particularly brutal, aggressive "race," it also aggressively undermines the radically deterministic account of nationality reconquering popular and intellectual discourse throughout wartime Europe.

EGOISM AND THE INDIVIDUALIST NOVEL

According to the essays of its editor Dora Marsden, *The Egoist* was a libertarian and anti-socialist journal promoting the radical individualist philosophy of the German nominalist Max Stirner (1806–56). Stirnerian individualism had been popular with Anglo-American libertarians and anarchists since Stirner's anti-liberal tract, *Der Einzige und sein Eigentum* (1844), was first translated into English as *The Ego and his Own* in 1907.[16] The polemic assails "fixed ideas" like "God, immortality, freedom, humanity etc . . . drilled into us from childhood,"[17] as alien constraints on individual freedom: "a 'fixed idea' [is] . . . [a]n idea that has subjected . . . man to itself" (55). Stirner's egoist exposes all such false and restricting ideals by "putting to th[em] . . . the searching knife of criticism" (56); his ultimate aim is to release the individual ego from social and conceptual shackles: "[when] I no longer serve any idea, any 'higher essence,' then it is clear of itself that I no longer serve any man either, but – under all circumstances – *myself*" (482; original italics). Stirner's emancipated ego thus becomes the sole locus of value in the modern world: "I am *owner* of my might, and I am so when I know myself as *unique*" (490; original italics).[18] Inspired by Stirner, Marsden deployed similarly iconoclastic analytical methods to expose false ideas, escape repressive institutions, and empower the unique, decidedly manly, individual:

> The irony of "standing for" a thing lies in the fact that the first return the thing stood for makes is to bring its advocates kneeling before it. A man will lie down prone before the thing he "stands for" and serve it, and the one assertion of egoism is . . . that a man shall make it his concern with things to force them to minister to him. Standing for anything whatsoever means setting that thing on a pedestal, demanding that all around it shall pay it tribute . . . The egoist stands for nothing: his affair is to see to it that he shall not be compelled to kneel.[19]

The Egoists' idealization of the (manly) individual and attendant distrust of external constraints leads them to advocate a radical form of "Anarchistic" politics that opposes all conventionalizing collectives – especially the liberal state and its various institutions – in favor of a utopian social organization based on the independent coexistence of strong individuals.[20] Marsden's editorials relentlessly criticize the British state for inhibiting individuality. The Egoists, she affirms, "strive after the abolition of 'The State' . . . [and] the subtler and far more perniciously repressive agency of Conscience with its windy words and ideals."[21] Huntly Carter, a regular contributor on art and literature, uses

Stirner's language of self-possession in describing the goal of Egoist politics: "If human beings are to move significantly in any direction they must not be tied up in inseparable bundles, called groups, guilds, and communities. Each must belong wholly to himself or herself. Each must be free to feel, act and choose a path of his or her own."[22]

This distrust of the state and faith in the individual encourages the Egoists to read nationality as another of the repressive and conventionalizing external forces that strong persons can and should overcome in the struggle for egoistic liberation. Their view opposes the determinist conception of nationality prevalent in the late-nineteenth century and given "scientific" sanction by "eugenicists" and "anthropo-sociologists":[23] an hereditary category that essentially defines the character of individuals of a particular nation or "race." Sir Francis Galton, father of English eugenics, had encapsulated this radical hereditarian account in a founding document of eugenic theory, his 1865 "Hereditary Talent and Character." "The Hindu, the Arab, the Mongol, the Teuton, and very many more," Galton explains, "have each of them their peculiar characters . . . [which] are transmitted, generation after generation, as truly as their physical forms."[24] In contrast, the Egoists interpret nationality as a cultural construct, the result of the institutional training persons receive in particular national contexts. Such training is inherently anti-individual, in their view, because it aims to conventionalize persons, to replace unique characteristics with "national" traits validated by the state. As Stirner had rejected obedience to "the fatherland" (37) on the grounds that it was yet another "'fixed idea' . . . that has subjected . . . man to itself," Marsden, in an editorial at the start of the war, attacks the "State's men" for exploiting patriotism in order to defend the "status quo" and discourage individuality:

> [A] steady pressure . . . latterly has been put upon the young (the old matter less) to substitute without questioning *l'esprit de corps* for the egoistic spirit . . . Th[e] constructive sense which the cult of *esprit de corps* utilises with such widespreading effects . . . provides the underlying design of "Order," of which laws, regulations, the entire maintenance of the status quo, are but the subsequent steps taken to keep such orders permanent.[25]

According to *The Egoist*, artists are especially inclined toward individualism and resistant to restrictions on creativity and action. Leigh Henry, the journal's music critic, describes artistic creation as an essentially individualistic process: "The works of a creative artist are necessarily the statement of his personal desires and the record of his personal experience and achievement, and their value is proportionate to the development of his individuality." Since creativity is "proportionate" to individuality, "it is absurd to attempt to limit creative activity by existing standards, as such limitation can result only in an inadequate mode of expression."[26] The task of the modern artist must be to realize the ideal of personal liberation in art, to resist and overcome any and all external and conventionalizing influences. Occasional contributor and Imagist poet John Cournos, in an article celebrating the recently deceased Gaudier-Brzeska, casts the late sculptor's life as such a struggle for creative independence against external constraints: "Gaudier-Brzeska's career . . . illustrates the difficulties which beset the path of the modern artist, groping to extricate his personality from the existing confusion of influences and movements."[27] Reflecting this vision, *The Egoist* promotes artistic and literary movements similarly committed to creative independence and resistance to established aesthetic conventions and cultural institutions, especially Imagism and Vorticism.[28]

Given *The Egoist*'s agenda, it is little wonder that Marsden and Weaver agreed to serialize *A Portrait of the Artist as a Young Man.*[29] They easily could read *Portrait* as a translation of the movement's ideals into the form of a modern novel, the Individualist education story of Joyce's young provincial protagonist, Stephen Dedalus. In Joyce's *Bildungsroman*, the Egoists could find a formal correlate to their narrative of the autonomous, individuating ego: *Portrait* follows Stephen from his childhood to young adulthood, tracing his development from the son of a conventional middle-class, Irish Catholic family into a creative, unique, and fiercely independent young artist. In his search for a "mode of life or of art whereby [his] spirit could express itself in unfettered freedom,"[30] Stephen follows Satan's (Stirnerian) motto, "*non serviam: I will not serve*" (117). He successively "frees" himself from the constraining "nets" of family and religion. And as Stephen prepares to begin a last liberating flight from the constraints of fatherland, he explains his distrust of the Irish nationalist cause to his patriotic friend, Davin, in terms consistent with an Egoist critique of national training: "[w]hen the soul of a man is born in this country there are nets flung at it to hold it back from flight . . . nationality, language, religion. I shall try to fly by those nets" (203).[31] Stephen believes exile will fulfill his personal and artistic destiny. Reflecting its protagonist's optimistic spirit, *Portrait* concludes with an ending that is a beginning; time opens outward onto a vital future, full of hope and the promise of individual, creative potential:

26 *April:* Mother is putting my new secondhand clothes in order. She prays now, she says, that I may learn in my own life and away from home and friends what the heart is and what it feels. Amen. So be it. Welcome, O life! I go to encounter for the millionth time the reality of experience and to forge in the smithy of my soul the uncreated conscience of my race.

27 *April*: Old father, old artificer, stand me now and ever in good stead. (252–53)[32]

Of course, *Portrait* prompts a skeptical reading of these words and of Stephen's ability to realize his ideals.[33] But because it first appeared in *The Egoist,* Stephen's dream of artistic liberation and the novel that portrays his personal journey were given the Individualist movement's sanction and publicly affiliated with their doctrine. By undermining the tenets of Individualist *Bildungsroman* as demonstrated in *Portrait, Tarr* could thus strike at the heart of Egoist theory.

THE ANTI-INDIVIDUALIST NOVEL

As chapter 3's discussion of *BLAST's* first issue confirms, Lewis had associated himself publicly with the ideals of his Individualist compatriots at least since the Summer of 1914. *BLAST's* opening manifesto insists that the journal will appeal "TO THE INDIVIDUAL" and will "make individuals" by presenting "an art of individuals."[34] The periodical proceeds, in a fashion more dramatic but no less iconoclastic than Marsden's, to "BLAST" a slew of hallowed English ideals and institutions that allegedly obstruct individual vitality and creativity, patriotically exhorting readers to overthrow England's conventionalizing class system, educational establishment, and provincial cultural heritage in order to revitalize English art and society, and create a nation of hard-boiled and independent individuals.[35] And while chapter 4's account of Vorticism during the opening year of the Great War shows that wartime circumstances dovetailed with Vorticist doctrine in ways that newly authorized it, this chapter's reading of *Tarr* in *The Egoist* context indicates that the facts of wartime life also provoked Lewis to question Individualist theories of character, society, and politics. We know that as early as 1907, he had begun writing a self-consciously "European" novel, with a Goethian German hero and a Dostoyevskian sense of life's absurdity.[36] The following account suggests strongly that part of what drew Lewis back to the unfinished novel, aside from a desire to leave some major literary work behind him in the event of death at the front, was a (new-found?) desire to refute the Individualist ideals he periodically affirmed in *BLAST* 1. While revising the novel for publication in the autumn of 1915, Lewis seems to have expanded it to reflect that desire. Because the Egoists had sanctioned the genre of the novel as an appropriate literary form to articulate and celebrate their ideals,[37] it would serve well as an instrument with which to attack Individualism. And since the form had traditionally been used to render the lives of characters inhabiting dense social environments, it could be used to assail at once Individualist approaches to psychology, social interaction, politics, and aesthetics.

By the time Lewis completed *Tarr* in November 1915, it had become (in part) a rigorous fictional critique of the Individualist world-view, a satire of the Individualist *Bildungsroman* as epitomized in *The Egoist* by Joyce's *Portrait of the Artist.* To the Individualist view of persons as autonomous beings capable of independent action and personal liberation, *Tarr* opposes a picture of persons as overdetermined beings incapable of controlling the maelstrom of competing forces that constitute human identity. To the Individualist narrative of persons transcending the restrictions of personal history and national training to become creative and independent individuals, it opposes a narrative of persons struggling vainly to stabilize their disorderly lives in an equally chaotic social world. To the Individualist vision of the modern novel as an optimistic *Bildungsroman* that represents the continuously developing subjectivity of a single protagonist, it opposes a disjunctive formal hybrid which yokes together two contrary novel sub-genres – the education story of psychological development and the *Sturm und Drang* novel of psychological disintegration – assailing the formal conventions of narrative and psychological continuity that had dominated the genre since the early-eighteenth century.[38]

Tarr's fictive assault begins by extending the Individualist *Bildungsroman* beyond its open-ended conclusion to show the protagonist failing to fulfill the Egoists' ideal of personal and artistic liberation, and thereby challenging the autonomous ego at the heart of Individualism. *Tarr* begins where *Portrait of the Artist* ends; its "Overture" is, in effect, an epilogue to the Individualist novel. *Portrait* concludes with Stephen Dedalus poised to begin a new life on the Continent as an autonomous artist; *Tarr* takes up the story of its intellectually precocious young artist-protagonist, Frederick Tarr, after he has been living on the Continent for some time. Tarr finds himself in an exemplary Individualist predicament: embroiled in a stifling romantic relationship with an overly dependent young German woman, the "bourgeois-bohemian" art student Bertha Lunken. According to Individualist doctrine, artists achieve personal and artistic freedom by eliminating all restrictive attachments. Yet despite Tarr's rhetoric of artistic independence and antagonism to bourgeois conventions, he fails to fulfill the ideal: he is exposed as a deeply insecure and conflicted young man, unsure of his desires, attracted to the allure of bourgeois-bohemianism, incapable of separating himself from Bertha.

On a Paris street, Tarr unexpectedly encounters Alan Hobson, a Cambridge educated compatriot. During their antagonistic give-and-take, Tarr keeps positioning himself as an Individualist artist, immune to the appeals of conventional bourgeois life, and Hobson keeps assailing those claims, casting Tarr as a self-aggrandizing hypocrite. Tarr responds so angrily to Hobson's accusations and so many of his explanations sound defensive that by the end of the conversation he seems less a true Individualist than a person playing at Individualism. At first he assumes a posture of imperious superiority, blasting Hobson's bohemian accoutrements: shabby tweeds, German acquaintances, and long hair. "'[W]hy so much hair?'" Tarr prods. "'I don't wear my hair long. If you had as many reasons for wearing it long as I have, we'd see it flowing round your ankles!'"[39] To counter this pose of detached superiority, Hobson introduces incriminating evidence of Tarr's own bohemian entanglements:

> "Tut! Do you still see Fräulein Lunken – is it? – as much as ever?"
>
> "Oh, you know her? = Yes, I forgot that. = Yes, I still see her."
>
> "It seems to me you know more Germans than I do. = But *you're ashamed of it.* You do everything you can to hide it. Hence your attack on me a moment ago. = I met a Fräulein Brandenbourg the other day, a German, who claimed to know you. I am always meeting Germans who know you. She also referred to you as the 'official fiancé of Fräulein Lunken.' = Are you an 'official fiancé?' And if so, what is that, may I ask?"
>
> Tarr was taken aback, it was evident.
>
> Hobson laughed stridently. (24)

As Tarr scrambles to counter Hobson's palpable hit, the text flags his infantile defensiveness:

> "As you know," he soon replied, "'engagement' is an euphemism. And as a matter of fact my girl publicly announced the breaking off of our engagement yesterday."
>
> He looked a complete child, head thrown up as though proclaiming something he had reason to be particularly proud of. = Hobson laughed convulsively, cracking his yellow fingers. (24–25)

Hobson's exposure of the engagement provokes from Tarr a rapid-fire series of theories intended to explain his "association" with Bertha while reaffirming his status as independent artist. Despite these efforts, Tarr's defensive theorizing discloses a model of personal identity far more encumbered than the Individualists' autonomous ego. His first account echoes *The Egoist* line that artists are especially individualistic beings, more resistant to constraints than others. "'I am an artist,'" he proclaims, mouthing the conviction that persons define their own identities. Next he distinguishes artists as especially vital and self-creating beings, immune even to the physical claims of sexuality: "'With most people, not describable as artists, all the finer part of their vitality goes into sex . . . The artist is he in whom this emotionality normally absorbed by sex is so strong that it claims a newer and more exclusive field of deployment. = Its first creation is *the Artist* himself, a new sort of person; the creative man'" (29).[40] This account threatens Tarr's proclaimed identity as a "creative man," however, by contradicting the fact that he is "'associated sexually'" with Bertha (29). How can this sexually engaged young man be an artist, if artists' vitality expresses itself in art rather than sex? To resolve that problem, Tarr proposes a more complex theory of artists' sexuality that inversely correlates visual style with sexual behavior. Artists "'whose work is very sensuous or human,'" he explains, have a "'sex instinct'" that is "'more discriminating,'" while those whose work is "'ascetic rather than sensuous'" are less discriminating sexually. Under this account, Tarr cites the "'invariable severity'" of his painting to justify his "'coarse . . . foolish, slovenly taste . . . in women'" (30). This rationale evidently fails to alleviate his worries about artistic integrity, however. Within moments of proposing a theory to reinforce his status as "creative man," Tarr acknowledges the "secret" that his identity is in fact deeply conflicted:

"You have understood the nature of my secret? = Half of myself I have to hide. I am bitterly ashamed of a slovenly, common portion of my life that has been isolated and repudiated by the energies I am so proud of. 'I am *ashamed* of the number of Germans I know,' as you put it. = I have in that role to cower and slink away even from an old fruit-tin like you." (31)

Tarr's description of his identity as split, a divided entity in which one "portion" struggles to "hide," "isolate . . . and repudiate" another, overturns the Individualist picture of the autonomous ego as an integral and coherent entity that must resist not internal selves but external constraints.

In a subsequent discussion with his friend Butcher, Tarr embraces an exemplary Individualist strategy to reaffirm autonomy and salvage his battered persona as "creative man": he resolves to "*dis-engage*" himself from Bertha. But Butcher's cautionary response to the plan casts serious doubt on Tarr's ability to realize it. Butcher knows that the disorderly facts of human life tend to confound such stratagems:

> Butcher filled his pipe, then he began laughing. He laughed theatrically until Tarr stopped him.
>
> "What are you laughing at?" . . .
>
> "I was laughing at you. You repent of your thoughtlessness and all that. Your next step is to put it right. I was laughing at the way you go about it. You now proceed kindly but firmly to break off your engagement and discard the girl. That is very neat."
>
> "Do you think so? Well, perhaps it is a trifle overtidy." (43)

The specter of complexity Butcher raises begins haunting Tarr as soon as he attempts to execute the "overtidy" scheme. His tumultuous meeting with Bertha defers all disengagement plans, plunging him into a chaos of human intimacy.

Positioned as the climactic scene of the "Overture," Tarr's encounter with Bertha undermines the Individualist ideal of self-liberation. Were *Tarr* an Individualist *Bildungsroman*, this scene between lovers would have come at or near the end of the story, climaxing with the protagonist's separation from the unwanted woman, a symbolic assumption of emotional, sexual, and artistic independence. Another celebrated *Bildungsroman* of the *avant guerre*, Lawrence's *Sons and Lovers* (1913), defines the pattern. In the final pages of Lawrence's novel, the artist-hero, Paul Morel, courageously terminates his dependent relationship with the intense, devoted Miriam despite her love for him and his lingering desires for her. Though Morel recognizes that by leaving Miriam, he is "defrauding her of life," he also knows that staying will "stifl[e] . . . the inner . . . man," even "deny . . . his own life." Refusing "to give life to her by denying his own," Morel separates from Miriam, thereby fulfilling the Individualist ideal of personal liberation.[41] Tarr fails miserably to follow Morel's example. He keeps trying to escape the stifling relationship with Bertha, but each effort is subverted by his own internal confusion and her perplexing responses. Lawrence's individualistic picture of a dependent young woman who obediently submits to the superior will of an independent young man is countered with a bleak emotional stalemate in which neither woman nor man can triumph over inter-dependency:

They progressed from stage to stage of this weary farce. Confusion increased. It resembled a combat between two wrestlers of mathematically equal strength. Neither could win. One or other of them was usually wallowing warily or lifelessly on his stomach, the other tugging at him or examining and prodding his carcase. (60)

Tarr's debate with Hobson assails the Individualist ego from within by exposing the self as a fractured entity; his exchange with Bertha attacks that ego from without by rendering human intimacy an infectious contagion that can penetrate and distort the self. After extensive wrangling – Tarr striving to evade his emotional attachment to Bertha; she striving to maintain relations despite his "callous" (73) efforts at separation – Tarr begins to acknowledge Lewis's frigid vision of intimacy. To account for his inability "to walk out of the door at once and never come back" (59), Tarr entertains one bleak and paranoiac interpretation of intimacy after another. First, love is a contagious mental disease, spreading obsession from lover to beloved:

What is *love?* he began reasoning. It is either *possession* or a possessive madness. In the case of men and women, it is the obsession of a personality. He had presumably been endowed with the power of awaking love in her. He had something to accuse himself of. He had been *afraid of giving up* or repudiating this particular madness. (72)

Under this account, Tarr cannot break off the relationship with Bertha because he is infected by her obsession, having in effect internalized her fear of separation. Recognizing that fear in himself, Tarr attempts to explain its sources. He moves from a conception of love as a communicable form of madness, to one of the lover as a thief of personality; from the figure of the lover as thief, he moves to that of the beloved as hostage:

His tenderness for Bertha was due to her having purloined some part of himself, and covered herself superficially with it as a shield. Her skin at least was Tarr. She had captured a bit of him, and held it as a hostage. (72)

This vision of the beloved as the lover's victim not only contradicts the Individualist picture of the active ego, free and independent, but casts a new and grisly light on love. The romantic notion of love as a union between two persons spawns a picture of separation as a form of mutilation:

People can wound by loving; the sympathy of this affection is interpenetrative. Love performs its natural miracle, and they become part of us; it is a dismemberment to cast them off. Our own blood flows after them when they go. (72)

And in a final morbid effort to explain his failure to act and exculpate himself for that failure, Tarr re-embraces a theory of love as communicable disease, but this time as a physical illness. Under this account, he can blame his inability to "walk out . . . the door . . . and never come back" on a diseased and contagious Bertha:

> Or love was a malady; it was dangerous to live with those consumed by it. He felt an uneasiness. Might not a wasting and restlessness ensue? It would not, if he caught it, be recognisable as love. Perhaps he had already got it slightly. That might account for his hanging about her. He evidently was suffering from something that came from Bertha. (72)

The spread of this contagion of intimacy is not limited to persons in love, however. As Tarr contemplates the disease, it contaminates *all* human contact: "Everybody . . . all personality, was catching. We are all sicknesses for each other. Such contact as he had with Bertha was particularly risky" (72).

Thwarted by uncooperative inner selves and contaminating others, the would-be Individualist never establishes independence. This conflicted, porous, and shifting subjectivity effectively forecloses Tarr's ability to take *any* definitive action. In *Tarr*, human subjectivity appears dynamic, as in *Portrait of the Artist* and *Sons and Lovers*, but its movement is always tortuous, futile: a vortex of conflicting forces that spins violently and gets nowhere, sweeping away the Individualists' advancing ego. The meeting between Bertha and Tarr can only conclude inconclusively. He leaves Bertha's flat without leaving her, still attracted to the bourgeois-bohemian conventions he reviles, hounded by doubts and recriminations, "[s]omething follow[ing] him like a restless dog" (74).

With the start of *Tarr*'s second section, "Doomed, Evidently – the Frac," the aesthetic form of the Individualist novel comes under attack. The model of the modern novel as a *Bildungsroman* recording the developing identity of a single hero is displaced as the narrative of a would-be Individualist is displaced by another, alien and antagonistic to the education story: a pessimistic German Romantic tale of *Sturm und Drang*. Once called a novel of *zerrissenheit*, or disintegration, this sub-genre typically records the trials of an oversensitive young artist, full of storm and stress, being slowly torn apart by the conflicting claims of the social world he inhabits and his tumultuous inner-life. His disintegration is provoked by an inability either to win the ideal woman who obsesses him, as in Goethe's *The Sorrows of Young Werther* (1774, final version 1787), or to reconcile a dream of creating transcendental art with the philistine realities of bourgeois life and taste, as in the works of E. T. A. Hoffmann, especially those concerning the eccentric musician-composer Johannes Kreisler – the "Kreisleriana" (1810–14) and *Murr* (1820–21).[42] Lewis's tale of *zerrissenheit* features a disintegrating German "artist" who shares the surname of Hoffmann's too-romantic composer and the suicidal fate of Goethe's too-romantic lover:[43] the expatriate Otto Kreisler, whose sick and unrequited obsession with Anastasya Vasek eventually drives him to take his own life. Hoffmann's influence pervades Lewis's narrative of disintegration; Otto's story shares with Johannes's a number of themes and formal strategies: mental life as chaos, human behavior mechanized by passion, and personal conflict as strange theater.[44]

In *The Egoist*'s pages, this yoking of antithetical narrative types into one conflicted whole not only refutes the agenda of the Individualist *Bildungsroman* formally, but questions more general conventions of narrative and psychological continuity that underlay the *Bildungsroman and* the tale of *zerrissenheit*. In *Tarr*'s shadow, both narratives appear unjustifiably to simplify and stabilize human identity and interaction. Though each represents the protagonist in an opposing trajectory of action – one's ego in ascent; the other's in decline – both assume an integral and dynamic self. *Tarr*'s fractured narrative pulls identity apart.

Otto Kreisler's sudden appearance intensifies *Tarr*'s critique of Individualism, as individual psycho(patho)logy contaminates social interaction. In the argument with Hobson, Tarr describes his identity as torn between two antagonistic selves, one artistic, the other sexual. During the struggle with Bertha, that identity is further split as intimacy with a lover subdivides the shattering ego between self-involvement and dependence on another. With the arrival of Kreisler, personal identity and social life sink into a maelstrom of transitory and disjunctive "selves" colliding within individual minds and upon the social stage of bourgeois-bohemian Paris.

"Doomed, Evidently – the Frac" plunges the reader into Kreisler's tumultuous life. The failed artist desperately wants to get his evening coat out of hock. He needs the "frac" to attend a dance where he hopes to encounter the mysterious woman he has recently met and become obsessed with, the Russian-German beauty Anastasya Vasek. Kreisler fantasizes himself and Anastasya as the principals in a tale of *zerrissenheit:* he the oversensitive artist overwhelmed by hopeless love; she the ideal and unattainable dream-woman. But his efforts to see Anastasya again and fulfill the fantasy are foiled by internal compulsions and unexpected external events. He has no money to recover the frac. Having abused the generosity of his rich (Jewish) friend Volker and hocked nearly all his possessions, Kreisler awaits a check from his father in Germany. This predicament fills him with rage.[45] He hates his father not just because of financial dependence, but also because his father has just married Kreisler's own former fiancée. Of course, the check fails to come in time, leading an increasingly incensed Otto to attempt ever more drastic means of acquiring funds. He tries to hock a suitcase, but cannot get enough for it. He runs into an English acquaintance and contemplates asking him for the cash. They converse, but Kreisler paranoiacly imagines his request rejected and drops the idea, filled with boundless anger for the oblivious Briton (112–15).

Just as the German reaches a state of raging distraction, overwhelmed by feelings of persecution and resentment, he runs into Anastasya. She is accompanied by the suave Russian-Polish art-dealer, Soltyk, who has superseded Kreisler as the honored recipient of Volker's money. This fact, for Otto, is a last straw. Having spoken with Anastasya very briefly only once before and knowing nothing about her relations with Soltyk, he jumps to the conclusion that she and the Russian-Pole are romantically involved, taking the encounter as ocular proof that she – a woman he barely knows – has betrayed *his* affections. Outraged and humiliated, Kreisler changes plans. He will still attend the dance, but now with the purpose of punishing Anastasya and Soltyk. The inability to get the frock out of hock now becomes a distinct advantage: his shoddy appearance will only intensify the "indignity" he intends for Anastasya and Soltyk (133). On his way to the dance, Kreisler gleefully rubs against a newly painted wall in hopes that the stain will enhance his planned "misconduct" (125).

The Bonnington Club dance is the textual event where *Tarr*'s critique of Individualism achieves its fullest and most comic articulation: the scene assails at once Individualist notions of identity, interaction, and politics. During the dance, Kreisler spreads disorder, venting his rage on nearly everyone at the dance. He abuses his dance partners: "Several young women . . . he lured to the conservatory. = They all came out with scarlet faces" (151). Twice he goes so far as to turn himself and his partner into a "disturbing meteor" (148), which he drives violently into groups of unsuspecting guests. He turns a well-planned social event, where multi-national bourgeois-bohemians are meant to interact in an orderly and respectful fashion according to codes of cosmopolitan etiquette, into a comic and turbulent chaos:

Their hostess also was dancing. Kreisler noted her with a wink of recognition. =

Dancing very slowly, almost mournfully, he and his partner bumped into her each time they passed. The widow felt the impact, but it was only at the third round that she perceived the method and intention inducing these bumps. She realised they were going to collide with the other lady. The collision could not be avoided. But she shrank away, made herself as small as possible, bumped gently and apologized over her shoulder, with a smile and screwing up of the eyes, full of meaning. = At the fourth turn of the room, however, Kreisler having increased her speed sensibly, she was on her guard, and in fact already suggesting that she should be taken back to her seat. He pretended to be giving their hostess a wide berth this time, but suddenly and gently swerved, and bore down upon her. The widow veered frantically, took a false step, tripped on her dress, tearing it, and fell to the ground. – They caused a circular undulating commotion throughout the neighbouring dancers, like a stone falling in a pond. (155–56)

Metaphorically, the "maelstrom" Kreisler is "producing and conducting" (154) collides with the Egoists' anarcho-libertarian politics. In *Tarr*, anarchy is not the utopian form of social order that maximizes individual liberty the Egoists imagine. It is the defining condition of human identity, a state of turbulent and destructive *dis*order. The psychological bedlam and social commotion of Lewis's humanity forecloses all possibility of realizing the anarchist dream of independent egoists inhabiting a stateless society.[46]

As the Individualists' ideal of political anarchism is displaced by this picture of psychological anarchism, their notion of the authentic self is displaced by that of the theatrical self. In Individualist narrative, the hero's ultimate task is to discover his true identity, to achieve authenticity. In *Tarr,* because identity is a transitory concatenation of contradictory desires and compulsions, the task of personality becomes a desperate but ultimately futile series of efforts to find such an authentic self. Unable to locate it within, characters keep trying-on social identities they wish were authentic in hopes that by performing such pseudo-selves they might somehow acquire real ones.[47] So Tarr, by no means an Individualist artist, keeps pretending to be one, and Kreisler, who is no Romantic hero, keeps trying to play that part.

These frantic but finally futile efforts to adopt an authentic identity turn social life itself into a theater of anarchy, a chaotic spectacle of missteps and misperformances. As *Tarr*'s characters frantically don roles they think appropriate to the social "scenes" they encounter, unexpected disturbances always render their roles obsolete. All performances flop. Sometimes a disturbance comes from outside a character: others, involved in their own private dramas, may subvert a performance. As Kreisler searches the dance-floor to punish the treacherous Soltyk,

he caught sight of Anastasya dancing with (he supposed) some Englishman.
He stopped, paralysed by her appearance. = This reality intercepted the course of his imaginary life (of which his pursuit of Soltyk was a portion). He stood like somebody surprised in a questionable act. (153)

Such disturbances also originate within: a character's determination to maintain a chosen role may be overwhelmed by the swarm of conflicting drives infesting identity. On discovering Anastasya in the arms of yet another man, Kreisler is overwhelmed by a fury so potent that it literally takes control of him:

He had not reckoned on being met by her before his present errand was finished. = The next moment he was furious at this interference; at her having the power to draw him up . . . Hell and Heavens! he was not going to stop there looking at her . . . He took her partner roughly by the arm, pushing him against her, hustling him, fixing him with his eye. He passed beyond them then, through the passage he had made. His blood was flooding him . . . *He was . . . as surprised at his action . . . as she was.* (153; emphasis added)

Since persons can control neither their raging desires nor the actions of others, social activity becomes as chaotic as Kreisler's fanatic dances. Every scene, every interpretation, every plan of action invariably goes horribly wrong.

Thus while Kreisler arrives at the dance intending to inflict "some indignity or other" on Anastasya and Soltyk, he fails miserably to do so. Despite all the abusive behavior, he punishes everyone *except* the pair he means to abuse. Soltyk pays no attention and Anastasya finds Kreisler's antics curious and finally laughable:

Anastasya freed herself at once from her partner, and pale and frowning . . . was looking after Kreisler curiously. She would have liked him to stop. He had done something strange and was as suddenly going away. That was unsatisfactory. = They looked at each other blankly. He showed no sign of stopping: she just stared. = Suddenly it was comic. She burst out laughing. (153)

An evening Kreisler planned would end in "a climax, of blows, words, definite things" (159), unravels instead in a typical Lewisian anti-climax, leaving him the primary victim of his own cruel shenanigans. Echoing Tarr's slinking departure from Bertha's flat in the "Overture," Kreisler beats a hasty retreat from the dance: "[t]he turmoil of the evening remained his, the solid part of it, unshared by anybody else . . . All he wanted now was to get away from the English Club as soon as possible" (159).

In *Tarr*'s anarchic medium the ideals of Individualism, though illusory, still exert immense appeal. Anastasya becomes the locus of desire for Kreisler and (later) Tarr because she shows the self-possession they lack. Yet her individualist appearance is misleading. Because *Tarr* exposes the autonomous and authentic ego as a hoax, self-realization in Lewis's text, if such a concept has meaning at all, can consist only in the consummate performance of pseudo-selves. During her first conversation with Tarr, Anastasya cockily describes her identity as a series of such performances: "'I don't like being anything out and out, life is so varied. I like wearing a dress with which I can enter into any milieu or circumstances. That is the only real self worth the name'" (133). Anastasya's casting of identity as a kind of costume which covers an absent self suggests the limits of her "individualism." She appears a self-realized individualist because she is the best performer in *Tarr*'s theater of personality, revealing little evidence of subjection to the chaos that mars other characters' role playing. She is the idol of Individualism that Kreisler and Tarr worship; her appearance of stability offers them the illusion of fixity in a world of flux. "[T]he maelstrom" that Kreisler "produc[es] and conduct[s]" at the Bonnington Club "require[s] her for its heart" (154); while for Tarr, she is "a touch-wood and harbour from his perplexed interior life" (314). Yet Anastasya is a consummate performer less because she has defined herself as such, more because she has been pushed into the role by the objectifying treatment of men: "[q]uite used to being looked at, she had become resigned to inability to avoid performing" (100). As the passivity of this language confirms, Anastasya's facility as a performer is the result of being made the subject and locus of male desire. Her final appearance on Lewis's stage only confirms her victimization.

The closing paragraphs bring *Tarr*'s corrosive project to its culmination in a vision of dehumanization and temporal compression that mocks the open-ended conclusion of the Individualist *Bildungsroman.* Stephen Dedalus emerges at the end of *Portrait of the Artist* believing himself a creative and independent individual on the threshold of a promising new life. Joyce's novel concludes with the story of its hero's future still to be told, narrative suspension enacting formally Stephen's hopes for the life to come. *Tarr* counters that open-ended finish with a pinched conclusion that squeezes years of Tarr's future into six terse sentences:

> Tarr and Anastasya did not marry. = They had no children.
> Tarr, however, had three children by a lady of the name of Rose Fawcett,

who consoled him eventually for the splendours of his "perfect woman." = But yet beyond the dim though solid figure of Rose Fawcett, another rises. This one represents the swing back of the pendulum once more to the swagger side. The cheerless and stodgy absurdity of Rose Fawcett required the painted, fine and inquiring face of Prism Dirkes. (320)

This contracted finale not only renders Tarr's future one of degradation and dependence, but contorts the novel's characters into anonymous and attenuated figures in a mechanical process of sexual and narrative repetition.[48] As would-be-Individualist becomes a mindless instrument of his own schizophrenic sexual desires, caught swinging between dehumanizing "relationships," Bertha and Anastasya are reduced to sex objects, no more than clever names in a bleak scheme of sexual reiteration, destined for replacement by an endlessly alternating series of bourgeois-bohemians like Rose Fawcett and swagger-sexes like Prism Dirkes (whose names themselves suggest endless replication).[49] *Tarr*'s characters end up grotesques trapped in a disjunctive and distorting narrative that scorns Individualism and its dreams of psychological, social, and aesthetic continuity and progress.

FICTIONS OF NATIONAL CHARACTER

Tarr treats literary form and conceptions of nationality similarly. As it conjoins two opposing models of the modern novel to challenge the assumptions underlying both, it brings together in a corrosive clash the opposing conceptions of national identity competing for authority at the start of the Great War. Discrediting Individualist *and* determinist views of nationality's influence in personal identity, *Tarr* portrays both as inadequate to explain the facts of human life. Tarr functions to undermine the Individualist view that self-realized persons can escape nationality, while Kreisler and Bertha together undermine the determinist view that persons are defined by nationality: Tarr fails to overcome "Englishness" as Kreisler and Bertha fail to conform to "Germanness." Each succumbs, in his or her own way, to Lewis's maelstrom of personal identity, that dynamic and distorting "condition" in which the vagaries of individual psychology, social intercourse, and national training converge, transforming persons into human grotesques.

During the debate with Hobson, Tarr plays the Individualist part by ridiculing the conventionality of English character. But his attack masks an envy for Hobson that springs from a fascination with the bourgeois-bohemian life he condemns. Animated in part by an Individualist contempt for what he calls the "'whole of English training'" (42), Tarr lambastes Hobson for submitting to England's standardizing systems of education and class in terms that strongly echo Marsden:

" – You have bought for eight hundred pounds at an aristocratic Educational establishment a complete mental outfit, a programme of manners. For four years you trained with other recruits. You are now a perfectly disciplined social unit, with a profound esprit de corps." (34)

Yet Tarr's personal history as a young man lacking Hobson's financial support and educational pedigree (he resembles the young Lewis in this), complicates his efforts to overcome the influence of English training. He has the ambivalences of the outsider. He resents Hobson's bourgeois accoutrements because he lacks them, enthralled by those institutionally inculcated national traits because he has not been fully trained as an "Englishman."

Tarr's relations with Bertha expose these ambivalences. Attempting to explain his involvement with her to Butcher, he articulates the dilemma. He is embroiled with the German bourgeoise, he tells his friend, because she displays at once the exoticism of a foreigner and the banality of the Englishwoman:

"That bourgeois, spoiled, ridiculous element was the trap. I was innocently depraved enough to find it irresistible. It had the charm of a vulgar wall paper, a gimcrack ornament. A cosy banality set in the midst of a rough life. Youthful exoticism has done it, the something different to oneself." (39)

For Stephen Dedalus defining personal liberation is a comparatively uncomplicated task; it consists in rejecting the oppressive sources of Irish training (family, religion, fatherland). For Tarr, whose national training is incomplete, the desire to "fly by those nets" is always tainted by attraction for them. His individualistic efforts at self-liberation, including the aim of transcending nationality, are always thwarted by a desire for the "cosy banality" of bourgeois life, epitomized for him above all by England and Englishness.

Disgusted by this continuing attraction for persons and things English and bourgeois, Tarr gravitates to the exotic Anastasya. She becomes the locus of his desire to escape Englishness because she seems so un-English. Her "racial" differences become for him a source of erotic attraction:

He felt immensely pleased with himself as he walked down the Boulevard Clichy with this perfect article rolling and sweeping beside him. No bourgeoise this time! = He could be proud of this anywhere! Absolute perfection! Highest quality obtainable. " – The face that launched a thousand ships." A thousand ships crowded in her gait. There was nothing high-falutin' about her, Burne-Jonesesque, Grail-lady or Irish-romantic. Perfect meat, perfect sense, accent of Minnesota, music of the Steppes! And all that was included under the one inadequate but pleasantly familiar heading, *German*. He became more and more impressed with what was *German* about her. (297)

The humor of this analysis derives from the disjunction between Tarr's increasing impression of Anastasya's "Germanness" and the fact, which he glimpses, that none of her enthralling characteristics appear even remotely to result from her birth in Berlin (213). By subsuming all that she represents for him – an alternative to the bloodless, pre-Raphaelite image of the ideal English woman – under the inadequate rubric "German," Tarr confirms that he desires Anastasya less because she is German, more because she is not English. He hopes that through intimacy with this cosmopolitan woman ("No bourgeoise this time!"), he will achieve finally the elusive goal of individual liberation.

Of course, Tarr never realizes the Individualist dream through intimacy with Anastasya. Their relationship does not facilitate his transcendence of emotional dependence, sexual obsession, or nationality; it culminates by exposing him as a mindless sexual mechanism, swinging schizophrenically between relationships with swagger sex and bourgeois-bohemian women. That Tarr's sexual life has this contradictory structure confirms his ultimate failure as an Individualist. The ambivalences exposed during the opening debate with Hobson define Tarr's sex life at the novel's conclusion. On one hand, he wants to become an independent artist and so despises everyone and everything English and bourgeois-bohemian; on the other, he is attracted compulsively to bourgeois-bohemia because he lacks the proper educational, class, and financial pedigree. Thus he alternatively desires women like Anastasya, who have nothing English or bourgeois about them, and women like Bertha, who display the "cheerless and stodgy absurdity" so common to his compatriots. It is no coincidence that Anastasya is succeeded in Tarr's personal history by Rose Fawcett, a bourgeoise with a very English-sounding name.[50]

If Tarr serves to discredit the Individualist account of nationality, Kreisler and Bertha function to attack the determinist view that nationality fundamentally defines identity. *Tarr* begins to erode that account by showing that conventional national stereotypes, which may seem especially desirable "roles" through which to constitute a stable identity, are often, like the humans who construct them, incoherent and unstable. Kreisler's efforts to fix his identity by playing the role of the ideal German fail in part because a single monolithic conception of German national character did not exist. Two contradictory models of Germanness had been competing in the English imagination for historical authority since the wars of unification: Germans as sensitive romantics; Germans as patriotic militants.[51] As we have seen, the first conception was older and based on the Romantic cultural tradition, in which writers like Hoffmann portrayed Germans as sentimental idealists, full of storm and stress, being slowly torn apart by the conflicts between their minds and environments. The authoritarian conception, on the other hand, was less literary or cultural in origin than ideological and institutional: it was based on Bismarck's code of "blood and iron" and the ideals of the educational establishment that Germany's Prussian rulers consolidated after unification. Under that account, Germans were a "race" of disciplined, obedient soldiers, committed to making Germany the world's greatest military and imperial power, and thereby securing for their fatherland, in Kaiser Wilhelm's famous words, "a place in the sun."[52]

Even *Tarr*'s readers have been tempted, we have seen, to stabilize Lewis's complex Germans by interpreting them as national stereotypes. But Kreisler and Bertha resist such efforts at containment: their traits and behaviors are reducible to neither the passive and self-destructive sentimentality of the Romantic model of German character, nor the aggressive militarism of the Prussian model. While Kreisler and Bertha repeatedly try to conform to these stereotypes, displaying certain conventional "national" characteristics, their lives are far less stable, far more complex than either stereotype permits.[53] They suffer their respective fates not because of nationality, as a reading of *Tarr* as an anti-German tract requires, but because they are individuals whose particular personal histories, psychological compulsions, and social experiences lead them to try to fix the chaotic flux of identity on the ground of national training, an effort that in Lewis's anarchical world is doomed to failure.

Kreisler has a psychological complexity that foils any account of him as simply an allegorical manifestation of either German romanticism or Prussian militarism. *Tarr* locates the origin of his brutality more in personal history than nationality. The troubled relationship with his father accounts not only for his acts of spiteful aggression but also for other traits that do not fit the stereotype: his peculiar obsession with money, his special antagonism toward Soltyk, his compulsive attraction for Anastasya. As Paul O'Keeffe has argued, Kreisler's behavior springs from the conflicted emotions he feels toward the father who has usurped his fiancée and withholds needed money and the former fiancée who has married his father. O'Keeffe explains that this "Oedipal nightmare" drives Kreisler to channel his compulsive feelings of hatred, envy, and desire toward surrogate fathers and surrogate fiancées. His emotions regarding his father are displaced onto his wealthy compatriot, Volker, for withholding money and onto Soltyk for usurping Anastasya, while those regarding his ex-fiancée are displaced onto Soltyk for usurping the role as recipient of Volker's money and onto Anastasya for "preferring" Soltyk.[54]

Kreisler is rendered compulsive and confused to show that while humans may attempt to fix the chaotic flux of identity by conforming to national stereotypes, they will always finally perplex and confound those conventionalizing forms. In the frantic struggle to secure identity, persons will try to surrender their agency to any role that promises a sense of substantiality. Though a dizzying array of candidate roles may present themselves, the stereotypes of nationality exert particular allure owing to their institutional construction, cultural authority, and popular appeal. But when Lewis's characters attempt to fit national stereotypes, they find themselves enmeshed in the process of deformation that *Tarr*'s conception of identity entails: all efforts to conform are thwarted by their particular psychological compulsions, transforming them into national caricatures, distortions of national types. Despite his best efforts to fulfill a monolithic national ideal, Lewis's unstable German appears by turns a militaristic Prussian officer devoted to a heartless honor cult, a hopeless Goethian suicide self-destructively obsessed with an unattainable woman, and a Freudian case study tormented by an Oedipal nightmare that leads him compulsively to envy and despise men, to worship and abuse women. Thus a character who strives mightily to embody Germanness, turns into the kind of wildly unstable psychological compulsive more familiar to English readers (especially via Dostoyevsky) as "Russian."[55]

Kreisler's efforts to stabilize himself upon the conventions of German nationality, whether the passive Romantic or the active Prussian model, are repeatedly thwarted by the action of his "very complicated, mysterious and turbulent existence" (251). During his frantic ratiocinations on the pending duel with Soltyk, he invokes his German training and pedigree, "arbitrarily reviv[ing] the title of Freiherr that, it was rumoured in his family, his ancestors had borne" (263), to justify his jealous and destructive rage against the Russian-Pole. But as "Freiherr" Kreisler plays the role of honorable Prussian nobleman, his compulsive hatred for Soltyk twists his desire to act with honor into a chaotic practice of senseless brutality. His pursuit of Soltyk climaxes not in the exemplary chivalric duel, with two men meeting at an appointed time, choosing their weapons, marching twenty paces in opposite directions, and firing. Instead, the "duel" degenerates into a farcical parody of its chivalric model, contorted by Kreisler's fickle mind. Once the German finds himself at the appointed time and place, facing his adversary, he loses interest: "'I am willing to forego the duel at once on one condition. If Herr Soltyk will give me a kiss, I will forego the duel!'" (272). This bizarre offer, which both insults Soltyk's "manhood" and exposes the conflicted nature of Kreisler's feelings for his opponent, provokes the Pole to fury. He lunges at Kreisler. They scuffle briefly, but are soon separated. Soltyk and his friends begin to withdraw. Kreisler, his mind changing again, stops them to resume the duel. He levels a gun at Soltyk, ordering him to take up a weapon. Soltyk's second, Saretsky, rejects the offer. As Kreisler bends to pick up a gun and give it to his opponent,

> Saretsky aimed a blow at his head. It caught him just in front of the ear, on the right cheek bone. He staggered sideways, tripped and fell. The moment he felt the blow he pulled the trigger of the Browning, which still pointed towards his principal adversary. Soltyk threw his arms up, Kreisler was struggling towards his feet. He fell face forwards on top of him. (275)

This "climax" would be wildly funny if it were not so grotesque: the "honorable" Prussian nobleman struggles in the dirt with the corpse of an innocent man he had steamrolled into a meaningless "duel" and shot by mistake.

This bleak dynamic, whereby circumstance, psychology, and national training converge, disfiguring personality and behavior, achieves its most disturbing manifestation in Kreisler's rape of Bertha. The rape marks the culmination of the trajectory begun on their walk to the Bonnington Club dance. During that fateful trip, Bertha, inspired by the atmosphere of the dark Parisian night, had embraced the role of a self-sacrificing romantic:

> For Bertha the darkened trees rustled with the delicious and tragic suggestions of the passing of time and lapse of life. The black unlighted windows of the tall houses, held within, for her, breathless and passionate forms, engulfed in intense eternities of darkness and whispers . . . Her strange companion's

dreamy roughness, this romantic enigma of the evening, suddenly captured her fancy . . . She took his hand. = Rapid, soft and humble she struck the deep German chord, vibrating rudimentarily in the midst of his cynicism.

"You are suffering! I know you are suffering. I wish I could do something for you. = Can not I?" (141)

The text identifies Bertha's embrace of sentimentality as a submission to national training by identifying her act with "the deep German chord." This sentimental young woman who aims to sacrifice herself in order to save her "suffering" companion does not end up the heroic martyr for love that the Romantic stereotype dictates, however. Even though she distrusts Kreisler, Bertha unwisely pursues the sacrificial role by agreeing to pose for him. In Kreisler's flat, the illusion is abruptly shattered: unprovoked, he assaults her. And by a similarly twisted logic, Kreisler is driven to rape Bertha, a woman he has no real feelings for, by a schizophrenic desire to love and destroy an entirely different woman. As Kreisler seizes her, Bertha glimpses the distorting dynamics of human agency in *Tarr:* "[h]er tardy words, furious struggling and all her contradictory emotions disappeared in the whirlpool towards which they had, with a strange deliberateness and yet aimlessness, been steering" (193–94).[56] Bertha and Kreisler are not stereotypical Germans. Caught between personal compulsions and national conventions, between Individualist activity and determinist passivity, they become human grotesques, farcical caricatures of the national types of the self-sacrificing romantic and the disciplined militarist. No "racial critique" of Germans then, *Tarr* renders its moment's accounts of nationality the comforting fictions of a race of beings too chaotic to realize their dreams of stability.

Ever since the appearance of Hugh Kenner's groundbreaking 1954 study of Lewis's works,[57] an increasing number of critics, including among others Jameson, Levenson, and Peter Bürger, have argued for the significance of *Tarr* and for Lewis's crucial role in the history of British modernism. Despite such efforts, the novel, though generally viewed as one of Lewis's best, has, as Bürger states, "still not been admitted to the canon of modernist literature by writers concerned with the subject."[58] Lewis's achievement in *Tarr* has been underestimated in part because critics have not historicized the work adequately, failing to acknowledge the novel's active engagement with specific debates among leaders of the English avant-garde concerning issues of personal identity, political action, literary aesthetics, and national character.

Retrieving *Tarr*'s assault on the English Individualist movement has allowed us to recognize Lewis as an antagonist within the Egoist circle, a kind of Kreisler figure disturbing their doctrinal consensus, willing to pursue his critical vision despite their contrary views. As Marsden and her comrades strove to preserve the prerogatives of the free and autonomous individual, to defend an anarcho-libertarian politics, and to articulate an Individualist aesthetics, Lewis offered in *Tarr* a pessimistic alternative to their vision, insisting on the chaos and complexity of personal identity, social life, and modern literature. Engaged in this fictive assault on Individualist doctrine, *Tarr* was a powerfully oppositional work, critical even of the views of Lewis's closest associates in the avant-garde. In this, our account revises the prevailing consensus that Lewis became the "enemy" of literary modernism only in the late-twenties.[59] As we've seen, he began disputing the opinions and literary practices of his artistic contemporaries before the end of the Great War, before the orthodoxies of modernism had solidified.

And by recovering in particular Lewis's literary attack on the Individualist *Bildungsroman*, as epitomized in *The Egoist* by Joyce's *A Portrait of the Artist as a Young Man*, we have been able to better assess *Tarr*'s formal achievement. This disjunctive, hybrid novel should be seen as an important modern text not only because it questions the conventions of narrative and psychological continuity that had prevailed in novels since the early-eighteenth century, but also because it was among the earliest Anglo-American literary works to apply to literature the formal techniques of fragmentation and assemblage that visual artists had been deploying for nearly a decade before the Great War. Years before Joyce, Eliot, and Pound wrote their major works, Lewis, by combining two different narrative forms in a single novel, had created a text characterized, as Bürger puts it, by "radical discontinuities" of the sort that would eventually distinguish the canonical works of literary modernism.[60]

Lewis's achievement in *Tarr* has also been misunderstood because analysts have not accompanied him to the conclusion of his critical journey. That failing has usually taken two forms. Most often, critics – including insightful readers like Jameson and Bürger – have taken the novel's English protagonist not as Lewis portrayed him, but as Tarr wants to be read, namely as a successful Individualist artist.[61] By exempting Tarr from Lewis's corrosive attack, such readers have been able to interpret the novel as a more straightforward and positive work than the text itself indicates. As we have seen, no character escapes the corrosive implications of *Tarr*'s anti-individualist vision.[62] Other analysts, like

West and Wagner, have restricted the scope of Lewis's critical assault to characters of only one nationality, interpreting the novel as a racial critique of Germans. These readings neglect the ways in which *Tarr's* German characters fail to conform to national stereotypes, ignore the novel's criticisms of its English characters, and thus, misconstrue Lewis's complex analysis of nationality's role in personal identity.

Readings of *Tarr* as a racial critique portray Lewis at best as a jingoistic advocate of anti-German stereotypes and at worst as an unreflective dupe of "racial" determinism. Our reading of the novel challenges both portraits: in context, Lewis's literary treatment of nationality is as striking as his attack on Individualism. *Tarr* refutes both the Individualist and determinist analyses that defined the range of orthodox views of nationality during the *avant guerre.* One might even argue that Lewis's literary investigation of national character anticipates much later "deconstructions" of the category of nationality and its reductive stereotypes by uncovering their implication in established regimes of power, by exposing their inadequacy to account for and determine human activity, and by explaining their persistent appeal. As we have seen, *Tarr* diagnoses the allure of national determinism *and* English Individualism. Persons embrace and attempt to conform to such simplifying accounts of human identity and activity, according to Lewis's novel, because they promise coherence and order. But since human life is irreducibly chaotic, implacably antagonistic to all such efforts of explanation and containment, those efforts are doomed to fail. That Lewis in *Tarr* resolutely disputed the nineteenth-century groundwork of Individualism, the emerging aesthetic and political consensus of British modernism, and the *avant guerre's* orthodox analyses of nationality, could be offered, it seems to me, as compelling evidence that *Tarr* deserves to be recognized as a major modern novel and Lewis as a major modern author.[63] But our reading of *Tarr* is finally motivated less by a desire to demonstrate the novel's literary value, despite its arguably brutal ideological content, than to provide a fuller and more finely grained explanation of the ways in which the novel responds to particular debates on literary form, identity, and nationality among Lewis's closest contemporaries. I want to conclude therefore by making a final point about the novel's treatment of period theories of race.

This chapter began with the claim that when properly contextualized *Tarr* calls into question the familiar picture of Lewis as essentially an essentialist. That claim now needs some clarification. Our account indicates that even as Lewis's novel disputes the theory that persons are essentially defined by nationality, it also confirms that Lewis was a kind of "racial" determinist, if by "race" we understand not the different and competing (sub)species nineteenth-century racialists believed inhabited the nationalized, Darwinian world, but rather the single human race. *Tarr* portrays human nature as a kind of racial virus, a force rendering the whole human species irredeemably chaotic, ugly, and absurd. The predominance of this more explicitly universalist brand racial determinism in Lewis's novel helps underscore two (neglected) points concerning early modernist theories of nationality more generally. First, there were at least three quite different (some might say incompatible) conceptions of human character that avant-garde writers and artists could (and did) subscribe to (sometimes simultaneously): identity as defined by blood heredity, identity as defined by individual will and cultural training, identity as defined by human nature. And thus second, if we want to provide convincing accounts of the evidence of radical racial determinism found in the writings of particular modernists after the Great War, we must first acknowledge the presence and analyze the consequences of this early-century ability to believe, at (nearly) the same time, that all human beings are essentially the same, that different groups of humans are essentially different (some superior to others), and that a few select individuals are essentially different from and superior to all other individuals and races.

Conclusion

The last chapter concluded with a fairly specific argument about the particularities of race thinking in Lewis's novel *Tarr*, an argument that is, I tried to demonstrate, more responsive to the text and its original (political) context than previous accounts; one that shows Lewis's views on nationality and race during the early war to be more nuanced and interesting than any construal of modernist race thinking as straightforwardly racist would allow. By taking into account such complexities in a particular writer's political ambitions and the ideological universe where they were originally articulated, moreover, this argument points to the need for continued reconfiguration of the discursive field around modernism, and in particular of the analytical categories through which modernist race thinking and politics are often discussed. I want to conclude by suggesting how the methodology and findings of this study contribute to such a reconfiguration, how they help yield new accounts of avant-garde politics, modernist notions of race and nationality, and modernism's post-war political complexities.

As we have seen, *Tarr* entertains, ridicules, and ultimately rejects period conceptions of national identity either as the permanent product of blood heredity or as a cultural construct susceptible to modification, even overcoming, by persons of sufficient character and determination. The basis for this double rejection is a theory of human racial character as essentially anarchical, antithetical to the stability necessary to sustain both a racialized national identity or a self-realized ego free of cultural accoutrements. That the novel carries out a fairly elaborate fictive critique of period conceptions of nationality but ends up embracing a vision of the human race as fundamentally ugly and anarchic, at once radically determined and radically unstable, suggests why accounts of modernist race thinking as simply essentializing and discriminatory can only fail to account for the early views of at least one of the most notorious "reactionary" modernists.

The implications of this finding for current discussions of modernism and modernist politics and theories of race seem to me fairly significant; it suggests that far from being either flat-footed essentialists or heroic self-liberators, these writers, during the early century at least, are better described as at once, or alternately, totalizers and atomizers, essentialists and constructionists, collaborators and resistants. This point gives some interesting perspective on the accusation of high-modernist racism: it prompts us less to ask whether a specific modernist was racist, more to consider the implications of evidence of modernist race thinking more conflicted, less coherent, more complicated than straightforward racial determinism and discrimination. Even if we entertain for a moment the view that Lewis and Pound eventually did become full-fledged racists, this evidence urges us to consider how their earlier, more mongrelized conceptions of nationality might have contributed to that later development. Alternately, one might respond to our argument about representations of national character in *Tarr* by asking whether the "reactionary" modernists' post-war views on nationality and race ever were any less complex and unstable than those we have discovered in Lewis's novel and the writings of other self-consciously avant-garde writers during the *avant guerre.* Perhaps the modernists' later, more notorious claims about race, and the hatreds that fuel them, depend in part upon an ability to hold antithetical visions of human identity simultaneously: to celebrate the strong individual (whether politician or artist), even while stereotyping Jews or blacks.

The point is not to deny the presence or downplay the significance of essentializing, deterministic, or discriminatory claims or attitudes about other races in the post-war writings of Lewis, Pound, or others, but to question whether an analysis of such claims as demonstrating racism is adequate. We may be too tempted to embrace condemnatory readings – of a particular author's poetry, fiction, or political theory or of modernism in *toto* – that attribute foundational significance to racism because they seem to offer the opportunity to demonstrate in a comparably foundational manner our own exemption from racism. I am wary of taking such a position because it encourages the belief, in my view a fiction, that by condemning modernism or racism we have in any sense escaped them; that we are therefore immune to errors of arrogance, confusion, and intolerance of the sort to which numerous modernist writers – and, not coincidentally, modern nations – succumbed. I am fascinated by the possibility that, for example, even when Pound was at his most offensive, raving incoherently about conspiracies of Jewish financiers contaminating economic health and freedom, he still displayed (political) commitments that in other contexts might seem enlightened, progressive, good: to improve the condition of workers; to devise new forms of government and economic organization that are just and efficient; to facilitate the careers of talented artists and writers and thereby enrich culture; to support the cause of one's (adopted) nation; to avoid the sort of senseless waste of life and youth perpetuated during the Great War. This more complex understanding is, I believe, more interesting and challenging than the rather uncomplicated, and comforting, charge of racism because it makes it more difficult to close the questions of modernist race thinking and modernist politics; more difficult to suppose that we are in any necessary sense immune to falling into comparable errors in judgment. This study's findings compel me, at least, because they discourage too complacent an approach to modernism's most perplexing problems.

The shifting and paradoxical political commitments we have recovered in avant-garde writings are, I would affirm, more interesting than those more commonly described in part because they complicate the problem of understanding how radical writers could come to admire the regimes of Hitler and Mussolini. What happens to the anarcho-libertarian distrust of the state, the Egoist idolatry of the creative individual as constitutionally antagonistic to all and any restrictions on creativity and action once we decide that these writers are fascist? What happens to the mongrel vision of (national) identity as construct and essence, which affirms the primacy of the individual as often as it reaffirms the primacy of heredity? Can we hope to comprehend "fascist modernism" without answering these questions?

Even as my findings irritate the challenges of coming to terms with modernist politics, I think they deepen and nuance understandings of those politics. The avant-gardists' early investments in empire and the cult of the nation certainly illuminate their later attractions to the militantly nationalist, aggressively imperializing regimes of Nazism and Fascism. Their prewar linking of radical (left-wing) political modes (anarchism, syndicalism) to the cause of nation and empire surely helps explain a post-war interest in political movements that couple, in particular ways, socialism and radical nationalism. Their prewar construal of identity as hybrid and unstable – which enabled the Vorticists to term themselves "Individuals" unfettered by nationality, even while proclaiming their creative works "fundamentally English" – doubtless sheds light on later attractions for right wing movements *not* of English or American origin – radical nationalist regimes in relation to which Anglo-American writers like Lewis, Pound, or Eliot, as non-natives, would always, in some crucial sense, be alien and alienated.

In early twentieth-century England, avant-garde writers and artists were obsessed, like the larger society in which they lived, by the topics of nation, empire, and nationality. Their boisterous polemics defined a radical artistic subculture in terms of these topics, conjuring eventually and paradoxically an anarchistic art movement avowedly imperialist in ambitions. This study has been motivated primarily to demonstrate how these young thinkers came to understand that paradoxical project as logical, necessary, and patriotic, how their political ambitions shaped avant-garde cultural doctrine from the death of Victoria through to the conclusion of European war nearly twenty dizzying years later. That task has been successful if our analysis has made more clear the lines of complicity and resistance between the historical avant-garde and early century imperialism and has clarified the ways in which period debates about nationality, group character, and individual identity shaped emerging modernist doctrine and practice in the years leading up and into the Great War.

By retrieving avant-garde views on nationality and radical culture, by reconstructing some more properly political aspects of English literary doctrine, by tracking the extent and limits of collaboration between the avant-garde and Britain's political establishment, between avant-garde polemics and popular discourse before and during the Great War, this study has also worked to complicate, at times contest, both heroizing accounts of the avant-garde as aesthetically and politically internationalistic, anti-establishment, and progressive, and more negative readings of it as at best a failure of radical will, at worst elitist, authoritarian, protofascist, and thereby to supplement familiar explanations of the ex-Vorticists' interest in rightwing, authoritarian politics. The works of the early century's self-styled cultural revolutionaries continuously and vigorously demand to be understood in relation to period political debates and discussions of nationality and empire. By reading their most political writings in that way, *Literature, Politics, and the English Avant-Garde* has attempted to supplement prevailing accounts of the phenomenon of the avant-garde, early modernist conceptions of group character, and their roles in the formulation of modernist politics and doctrine after the Great War. If the book also furthers reflection on the ways in which continuing investments in the debates, categories, and terminology of modernism condition the ways in which we discuss it, it will have exceeded my best expectations.

Notes

INTRODUCTION: NATIONS, EMPIRES, AND THE HISTORICAL AVANT-GARDE

1 The most influential articulation of this kind of account is Fredric Jameson, *Fables of Aggression: Wyndham Lewis, the Modernist as Fascist* (Berkeley: University of California Press, 1979).

2 Wyndham Lewis, *Hitler* (London: Chatto & Windus, 1931).

3 For a sense of the extent and duration of this debate, see the bibliography to Robert Casillo, *The Genealogy of Demons: Anti-Semitism, Fascism, and the Myths of Ezra Pound* (Evanston: Northwestern University Press, 1988). Not only is this bibliography the most complete on the subject, but Casillo's effort to demonstrate the centrality of Pound's anti-Semitism to his fascism and his poetics is also, to date, the most comprehensive (one might say obsessive) critical condemnation of modernist reaction.

4 Alan Munton, "'Imputing Noxiousness': Aggression and Mutilation in Recent Lewis Criticism," *Wyndham Lewis Annual 1997*, ed. Paul Edwards (Bath: Wyndham Lewis Society, 1997): 5–20, provides an intelligent analysis of such projection in recent criticism on Lewis; Munton writes that "Lewis is so widely reviled that almost any claim about him, or his work, can be made. That he, or his work, is violent, fascist, misogynist and pathologically insane has become, not the end-point of argument, but the point of departure . . . Lewis criticism, like no other in the study of modernism, is the arena in which critics have found that they can act out their desires. The nature of those desires is consistently antipathetic towards understanding, sympathy or tolerance" (5). David Peters Corbett, "Introduction: 'The Subject of Modern War,'" in *Wyndham Lewis and the Art of Modern War*, ed. Corbett (Cambridge University Press, 1998), proposes as a solution to such antipathetic readings a responsible historicism, explaining that "Lewis may have been concerned with violence and aggression as central themes and principles of his work, he may have had anti-Semitic views, but the only way of gaining an understanding of these things and judging them properly, is to see them historically" (5; see also 13). As this introduction indicates, I concur with Corbett's suggestions.

5 See, for example, Peter Bürger, *The Theory of the Avant-Garde*, trans. Michael Shaw (1974; Minneapolis: University of Minnesota Press, 1987), and Andreas Huyssen, *After the Great Divide: Modernism, Mass Culture, Postmodernism* (Bloomington: Indiana University Press, 1986).

6 See Miriam Hansen, "T. E. Hulme, Mercenary of Modernism, or, Fragments of Avantgarde Sensibility in Pre-World War I Britain," *ELH* 47 (1980): 355–85; Alan Robinson, *Symbol to Vortex: Poetry, Painting and Ideas, 1885–1914* (New York: St. Martins Press, 1985), esp. 90–118; Tim Redman, *Ezra Pound and Italian Fascism* (Cambridge University Press, 1991), esp. 17–50; Charles Ferrall, "*The New Age* and the Emergence of Reactionary Modernism Before the Great War," *Modern Fiction Studies* 38 (Autumn 1992): 653–67; Andrew Hewitt, *Fascist Modernism: Aesthetics, Politics, and the Avant-Garde* (Stanford University Press, 1993); Robert von Hallberg, "Libertarian Imagism," *Modernism/Modernity* 2 (April 1993): 63–79; David Kadlec, "Pound, *BLAST*, and Syndicalism," *ELH* 60 (Winter 1993): 1015–31; Michael Tratner, *Modernism and Mass Politics: Joyce, Woolf, Eliot, Yeats* (Stanford University Press, 1995); Cinzia Sartini Blum, *The Other Modernism: F. T. Marinetti's Futurist Fiction of Power* (Berkeley: University of California Press, 1996); Bruce Clark, *Dora Marsden and Early Modernism: Gender, Individualism, Science* (Ann Arbor: University of Michigan Press, 1996).

7 Giovanni Cianci, "A Man at War: Lewis's Vital Geometries," in *Volcanic Heaven: Essays on Wyndham Lewis's Painting and Writing*, ed. Paul Edwards (Santa Rosa: Black Sparrow, 1996), 11–24, wisely warns, "[w]e must guard against projecting back on to these euphoric years [before the First World War] what happened in the twenties and thirties. These were not yet the years of social and political organization, but the exuberant, heroic years of the avant-garde's utopian phase" (14). I am a bit less sanguine than Cianci, though, about the avant-garde's Utopian phase.

8 I concur with Josephine M. Guy, *The British Avant-Garde* (London: Harvester Wheatsheaf, 1991), that it is time "to view avant-garde politics in their cultural and historical specificity" and that "the achievements of radical and innovative artists and writers" are best "measured in terms of their *own* culture and not ours – in terms, that is, of the specific intellectual, political, or aesthetic orthodoxies to which those artists and writers were opposing themselves" (2).

9 Even recent revisionist studies on the politics of Anglo-American modernism, which usefully recover neglected sources for the postwar political commitments of writers like Lewis and Pound, still tend to underestimate the influence for English avant-garde politics and aesthetics of the most popular political concerns and obsessions of prewar Britain. Vincent Sherry, *Ezra Pound, Wyndham Lewis and Radical Modernism* (Oxford University Press, 1993) retrieves the important role played by continental (mostly French) theorists of aesthetic style and art's social functions – especially Benda, de Gourmont, le Bon, and Sorel – in the modernists' "new standard of visual immediacy in words," a standard which, Sherry contends, encour-

aged them "to esteem (what they saw as) a superior directness in the political cultures of Nazism and fascism" (7). But because Sherry's story aims (internationalistically) to establish the influence of a nineteenth-century continental intellectual tradition on English modernist politics, it overlooks the equally important influence of early twentieth-century British politics and political argument.

10 One can get a sense of the breadth of the avant-garde phenomenon by consulting the massive exhibition catalogue, *Futurism and Futurisms*, ed. Pontus Hulten, trans. various hands (New York: Abbeville, 1986).

11 Umberto Boccioni, Carlo D. Carrà, Luigi Russolo, Giacomo Balla, Gino Severini, "Futurist Painting: Technical Manifesto" (11 April 1910), *Exhibition of Works of the Italian Futurist Painters* (London: Sackville Gallery, 1912); rpt. in *Futurism*, ed. Joshua C. Taylor (New York: Museum of Modern Art, 1961), 126.

12 Blaise Cendrars, *Inédits secrets*, ed. Miriam Cendrars, vol. 16, *Oeuvres complètes*, 16 vols., ed. Raymond Dumay and Nino Frank (Paris: Le Club français du livre, 1968–71): 16: 360–61; quoted in Marjorie Perloff, *The Futurist Moment: Avant-Garde, Avant Guerre, and the Language of Rupture* (University of Chicago Press, 1986), 9–10.

13 Lewis, "A Man of the Week: Marinetti," *New Weekly* 1 (30 May 1914): 328–29; rpt. Lewis, *Creatures of Habit and Creatures of Change: Essays on Art, Literature and Society 1914–1956*, ed. Paul Edwards (Santa Rosa: Black Sparrow, 1989), 31.

14 The most influential articulation of this view is Bürger, *Theory of the Avant-Garde*. Other accounts that draw on Bürger include Perloff, *Futurist Moment*, Huyssen, *After the Great Divide*, Terry Eagleton, *The Ideology of the Aesthetic* (Oxford: Basil Blackwell, 1990), 366–417, esp. 370–72.

15 Perloff, "Violence and Precision: The Manifesto as Art Form," *Futurist Moment*, 80–115; compare Raymond Williams, *The Politics of Modernism: Against the New Conformists* (London: Verso, 1989), 33.

16 Bürger, *Theory of the Avant-Garde*, explains that "the attack of the historical avant-garde movements on art as an institution has failed, and art has not been integrated into the praxis of life" (57); Eagleton, *Ideology of the Aesthetic*, concurs with Bürger that the "revolutionary" avant-garde's "attempt to hook art up once again with social praxis" (370) ultimately "failed, rolled back by Stalinism and fascism" (372). Perloff, *Futurist Moment*, echoes Bürger's claim that "montage may be considered the fundamental principle of avant-gardiste art" (72), when she calls "collage and its cognates (montage, assemblage, construction)," perhaps "the central artistic invention of the *avant guerre*" (xviii).

17 Perloff, *Futurist Moment*, xviii.

18 Among scholars who emphasize that the avant-garde should be understood in the context of bourgeois capitalism and its institutions are Bürger, *Theory of the Avant-Garde*; Eagleton, *Ideology of the Aesthetic*; Ferrall, "'Melodramas of Modernity': The Interaction of Vorticism and Futurism before the Great

War," *University of Toronto Quarterly* 63 (Winter 1993/94): 347–68; Huyssen, *After the Great Divide*; Perloff, *Futurist Moment*; Renato Poggioli, *The Theory of the Avant-Garde*, trans. Gerald Fitzgerald (1962; Cambridge University Press, 1968); and Williams, *Politics of Modernism*; of these only Williams shows much appreciation of the significance of nation, nationality, and empire in the avant-garde phenomenon. In *Politics of Modernism*, 49–63, he acknowledges wisely that "[w]ithin the range of general possibilities [of political direction available to avant-gardists] it mattered greatly what was happening in the different countries in which the avant-garde movements were based, or in which they found refuge" (59), but does not carry out a case study of the avant-garde within a single national context, as I do here. Williams's emphasis on the national specificity of avant-garde movements is echoed by Guy, *British Avant-Garde*, 41, 43–44.

19 See Tom Nairn, *The Break-up of Britain* (London: Verso, 1977); Ernest Gellner, *Nations and Nationalism* (Ithaca: Cornell University Press, 1983); Benedict Anderson, *Imagined Communities: Reflections on the Origin and Spread of Nationalism* (London: Verso, 1983); E. J. Hobsbawm, *Nations and Nationalism Since 1780* (Cambridge University Press, 1990).

20 F. T. Marinetti, "Initial Manifesto of Futurism" (20 February 1909), *Exhibition of Works of the Italian Futurist Painters*, rpt. in Taylor (ed.) *Futurism*, 124.

21 Boccioni *et al.*, "Futurist Painting: Technical Manifesto," 125.

22 Lewis (ed.), *BLAST*, 22, 39, 41. Italian Futurists and English Vorticists were not alone in proclaiming their nationalistic aims; the Russian "Cubo-Futurists" were also aggressive patriots. Alexei [Aleksander] Kruchenykh, "New Ways of the Word (the Language of the Future, Death of Symbolism)" (1913), rpt. in *Russian Futurism through its Manifestos, 1912–1928*, ed. Anna Lawton, trans. Anna Lawton and Herbert Eagle (Ithaca: Cornell University Press, 1988), asserts: "[w]e hold a high opinion of our motherland! Do not give yourself to the imitation of things foreign. Do not use foreign words in your literary works, they are fitting only in one case: when you want to give them a pettily derogatory meaning" (76–77).

23 Edward W. Said, *Culture and Imperialism*, (New York: Knopf, 1994), xiv. Jameson, "Modernism and Imperialism," in Eagleton, Jameson, and Said, *Nationalism, Colonialism, and Literature* (Minneapolis: University of Minnesota Press, 1990), 43–66, contends that "the structure of imperialism also makes its mark on the inner forms and structures of that new mutation in literary and artistic language to which the term modernism is loosely applied" (44). My study supplements efforts by a number of scholars of British modernism to analyze the responses of modernist writers – especially, and for obvious reasons, Conrad, Forster, Joyce, Woolf, and Yeats – to nationalism and imperialism; it differs from most others in its exclusive focus on the early century avant-garde moment and its consideration of writers and artists who were less skeptical of British imperialism than Conrad, Forster, Joyce, or Woolf, and who, unlike Joyce and Yeats, theorized self-consciously *English* forms of nationalist art. See Patrick Brantlinger, "*Heart of Darkness*:

Anti-Imperialism, Racism or Impressionism?," *Criticism* 4 (Fall 1985): 363–85; Eagleton, Jameson, and Said, *Nationalism, Colonialism, and Literature*; Michael North, "W. B. Yeats: Cultural Nationalism," *The Political Aesthetic of Yeats, Eliot, and Pound* (Cambridge University Press, 1991), 21–73; Emer Nolan, *James Joyce and Nationalism* (New York: Routledge, 1994); Kathy Phillips, *Virginia Woolf against empire* (Knoxville: University of Tennessee Press, 1994); Said, *Culture and Imperialism*, 19–30 (on Conrad), 186–90 (on Modernism), 200–6 (on Forster), 220–38 (on Yeats); Stephen Regan, "W. B. Yeats and Irish cultural politics," in *Cultural Politics at the Fin de Siècle*, ed. Sally Ledger and Scott McCracken (Cambridge University Press, 1995), 66–84.

24 Nairn, *Break-up of Britain*, 341.

25 Nairn, *Ibid.*, 348.

26 Throughout this study, I use the term "imperialism" as it was most often used at the time; as Jameson, "Modernism and Imperialism," explains "during this period the word 'imperialism' designates, not the relationship of metropolis to colony [as it usually does in postcolonial discourse and theory], but rather the rivalry of the various imperial and metropolitan nation-states among themselves" (47).

27 Williams, *Politics of Modernism*, affirms that "the late nineteenth-century was the occasion for the greatest changes ever seen in the media of cultural production" and that "in response" to these changes "there arise . . . defensive cultural groupings, rapidly if partially becoming competitively self-promoting" (33); my study confirms that these "defensive" and "competitively self-promoting" cultural groupings also arose in response to perceived changes in the relative international prestige of the different nations from which they came.

28 Anderson, *Imagined Communities*, 41–9.

29 Anderson, *Ibid.*, 82.

30 Accounts that detail Futurism's complicity with Italian Imperialism include Walter Adamson, *Avant-Garde Florence: From Modernism to Fascism* (Cambridge: Harvard University Press, 1993); Hewitt, *Fascist Modernism*; George Mosse, "The Political Culture of Italian Futurism," *Confronting the Nation: Jewish and Western Nationalism* (Hanover and London: Brandeis University Press, 1993), 91–105; Emilio Gentile, "The Conquest of Modernity: From Modernist Nationalism to Fascism," trans. Lawrence Rainey, *Modernism/Modernity* 1 (September 1994): 55–87. I have found no comparable accounting of avant-garde imperialism in England.

31 Gellner, *Nations and Nationalism*, 48

32 Anderson, *Imagined Communities*, contends that the "idea of a sociological organism moving calendrically through homogeneous, empty time," upon which the "old-fashioned novel" depends, "is a precise analogue of the idea of the nation, which also is conceived as a solid community moving steadily down (or up) history" (31); Said's account in *Culture and Imperialism* argues that "cultural forms like the novel" were "immensely important in the

formation of imperial attitudes, references, and experiences" (xii).

33 Scholars of Italian Futurism like Adamson and Hewitt have led the trend, but some of the most influential accounts of the avant-garde downplay or ignore these aspects. Perloff, *Futurist Moment*, convincingly traces the cosmopolitan ambitions of the avant-gardists and the internationalistic nature of the avant-garde phenomenon, but underestimates the competing influence of nationalism. While Perloff acknowledges that the "hostile statements Lewis and Pound made about Marinetti and the Futurists" were marked by "the aggressive nationalism of the *avant guerre*" (171), her declared interest in the dynamics of international creative exchange encourages her to leave unexamined the ways in which nationalism cohabited with internationalism in the avant-garde and to describe the "stubborn nationalism" of the *avant guerre* as little more than the source of the "poignancy" in the poetry of the period (xix). And because Perloff's treatment of the British avant-garde aims to elaborate the links between Futurism and Vorticism (an internationalist argument I accept), she overlooks the importance of English nationalism and British imperialism for the development of Vorticism in particular and British modernism in general.

34 William C. Wees, *Vorticism and the English Avant-Garde* (University of Toronto Press, 1972), and Richard Cork, *Vorticism and Abstract Art in the First Machine Age*, 2 vols. (London: Gordon Fraser, 1976), were the first Anglo-American studies to recover the role of the Futurists' success in the formation of Vorticism, but neither is much interested in the nationalism of the Vorticists or Futurists. Compare Giovanni Cianci, "Futurism and the English Avant-Garde: The Early Pound Between Imagism and Vorticism," *Arbeiten aus Anglistik und Amerikanistik* 1 (1981): 17–27.

35 See Perloff, *Futurist Moment*, 162–93, and Reed Way Dasenbrock, *The Literary Vorticism of Ezra Pound and Wyndham Lewis* (Baltimore: Johns Hopkins University Press, 1985), 28–85. A more recent, explicitly political, reassessment of the relations between Vorticism and Futurism, like Ferrall's " 'Melodramas of Modernity,' " underestimates the importance of nationalism and imperialism to the avant-garde; while Ferrall concludes that "in the end, Futurism and Vorticism do not so much oppose the Capitalist societies of prewar Europe as exemplify their most militarist, nationalist, and misogynist tendencies" (364–65) – a view not entirely incompatible with the argument of chapter 3 below – his account, like his formulation here, grants priority to capitalism (Marxist style), and tends to treat militarism, nationalism, and misogyny as secondary symptoms of "modern industrial society" (364), a view which does not adequately acknowledge the priority the Futurists and Vorticists (like the societies from which they came) granted to nation, empire, and nationality.

36 See R. K. Webb, *Modern England From the 18th Century to the Present* (New York: Harper & Row, 1968); Richard Shannon, *The Crisis of Imperialism 1865–1915* (London: Paladin, 1974); Jonathan Rose, *The Edwardian Temperament, 1895–1919* (Athens: Ohio University Press, 1986).

37 On the European politics of the moment, see Eric Hobsbawm, *The Age of empire 1875–1914* (New York: Random House, 1987).

38 George Dangerfield, *The Strange Death of Liberal England* (1935; New York: G. P. Putnam, 1980).

39 Tratner, *Modernism and Mass Politics*, considers the role played by continental (mostly French) theorists of mass psychology and modern collectivism – especially le Bon and Sorel – in the development of postwar modernist writing of both the left (Joyce, Woolf) and right (Eliot, Yeats), and even discusses the anti-imperialism of Joyce and Woolf and the shifting nationalism of Yeats and Joyce. But Tratner's (conventional) decision to focus on Joyce, Woolf, Eliot, and Yeats – writers today canonized as comprising the great tradition of British (high) modernism – leads him to underestimate the significance of the important prewar manifestation of collectivism in art and politics, the "historical avant-garde" with its collectivist movements, magazines, and manifestos. My more tightly focused account of the English avant-garde and its leading figures – writers now viewed as minor modernists, like Huntly Carter, Ford Madox Ford, Dora Marsden, Alfred Orage, and Wyndham Lewis – shows that the collectivist experiments of the avant-garde in England, which certainly influenced the development of British modernist art and politics after the war, were inextricably involved with the anxious nationalism and defensive imperialism of Edwardian and Georgian Britain.

40 Studies that contribute, in one way or another, to this view, include David Ayers, *Wyndham Lewis and Western Man* (New York: St. Martins, 1992); Andrea Freud Loewenstein, "The Molten Column Within: Wyndham Lewis," in *Loathsome Jews and Engulfing Women: Metaphors of Projection in the Works of Wyndham Lewis, Charles Williams, and Graham Greene* (New York University Press, 1993), 119–87; Casillo, *Genealogy of Demons*; Anthony Julius, *T. S. Eliot, Anti-Semitism, and Literary Form* (Cambridge University Press, 1995). See Muton's "'Imputing Noxiousness,'" for a rejoinder to such criticism. Paul Edwards, "'The Strange Actor' and 'Semitic Discourse,'" in *Wyndham Lewis Annual 1997*, 32–38, grapples with Lewis's complex involvement with "Semitic Discourse" in "The Strange Actor" (an essay published in the *New Statesman* of 1924 and reprinted in Lewis, *Creatures of Habit and Creatures of Change*, 89–95), and comments smartly that "the idea of modernist writing expressing any 'essence' . . . seems false to the procedures and spirit of modernism, particularly as practised by Lewis; though being a 'modernist' doesn't mean that a writer cannot be the dupe of an idea" (33). For another helpful account of Lewis's entanglements with period anti-Semitism, see Geoff Gilbert, "Shellshock, Anti-Semitism, and the Agency of the Avant-Garde," in *Wyndham Lewis and the Art of Modern War*, 78–97.

41 George W. Stocking, Jr., "The Persistence of Polygenist Thought in Post-Darwinian Anthropology," in *Race, Culture, and Evolution: Essays in the History of Anthropology*, 2nd. edn. (1968; University of Chicago Press, 1982), 42–68; provides ample evidence that this conception was widespread among Vic-

torian anthropologists and argues that the notion was enabled by the resilience of older Lamarckian and polygenist notions into the age of Darwin; compare Stocking, "The Turn-of-the-Century Concept of Race," *Modernism/Modernity* 1 (January 1994): 4–16. For an invaluable collection of essays that explore constructions of Englishness during the period and the varied ideological work to which they were put, see Robert Colls and Philip Dodd (eds.), *Englishness: Politics and Culture 1880–1920* (London: Croom Helm, 1986).

42 For a sense of Edwardian anxieties about national decline and "degeneration," see Samuel Hynes, *The Edwardian Turn of Mind* (1968; London: Pimlico, 1991), 15–53; for a sense of Edwardian efforts to counter decline by vitalizing British life, see Rose, *Edwardian Temperament*, 74–116. On the tradition of intellectual collaboration with imperialism in Britain, see Nairn, *Break-up of Britain*, 38–44, and Said, *Culture and Imperialism.*

43 Ford Madox Ford, *Thus to Revisit* (1921; New York: Octagon, 1966), 59.

44 On the influence of Stirner's text on British modernism, see Michael Levenson, *A Genealogy of Modernism: A Study of English Literary Doctrine 1908–1922* (Cambridge University Press, 1984), 63–8; von Hallberg, "Libertarian Imagism"; and Clark, *Dora Marsden and Early Modernism.*

45 Lewis (ed.), *BLAST*, 7–8, 11–20.

46 Robert Crawford's account of "Modernism as Provincialism," in *Devolving English Literature* (Oxford University Press, 1992), 216–70, is scrupulously attentive to comparable paradoxes in the alleged "Englishness" of the "High Modernism" of Eliot, Lawrence, and Pound; I find Crawford's account of Eliot's "poetics of the *metoikos*" especially compelling (219–34).

47 While Ferrall, "*The New Age* and the Emergence of Reactionary Modernism Before the Great War," for example, notes the "contradictory combination of the traditional and radical" that "characterizes the culture of reactionary modernism," he reads it as a combination of "right-wing politics and experimental aesthetics" (665), neglecting that the politics themselves combined right- and left-wing elements. William Chase, *The Political Identities of Ezra Pound and T. S. Eliot* (Stanford University Press, 1973), is distinguished among "political" analyses of Anglo-American modernists (especially given its publication date) because it begins by "confront[ing]" not only the "well-known" fact that Pound and Eliot were "reactionaries" (xiii), but also the seemingly contradictory fact, "often not confronted," that Pound and Eliot were "also radicals" (xiii–xiv). More recently, Kadlec, "Pound, *BLAST*, and Syndicalism," has attended to the ideological complexity of Pound's aesthetic ambitions before the war, explaining that Pound's "technical efforts to restore ethical power to poetry, and his frustration with the marginal place of the arts in British society, were conceived not only along militant anarcho-syndicalist lines, but also in terms similar to those of reactionary political efforts to construct a more richly 'organic' society" (1024). For a summary of the ways in which the Italian Fascist state failed to fulfill the "authoritarian" statism epitomized by Hitler's National Socialist

state, see Paul Morrison, *The Poetics of Fascism: Ezra Pound, T. S. Eliot, Paul de Man* (Oxford University Press, 1996), 6.

48 Williams, *Politics of Modernism*, 62.

49 Compare Morrison, *Poetics of Fascism*, 4; among other analyses that argue against this view of left-wing politics as categorically different from and immune to the errors of right-wing authoritarianism are Marc Shell, *Children of the Earth: Literature, Politics, Nationhood* (Oxford University Press, 1993); Etienne Balibar and Immanuel Wallerstein, *Race, Nation, Class: Ambiguous Identities*, trans. Etienne Balibar, Chris Turner (1988; London: Verso, 1991).

50 On the Edwardian cult of vitality, see Rose, *Edwardian Temperament*, 74–116; on the ubiquity of a masculinist ideology in late-Victorian and Edwardian culture, see Philip Dodd, "Englishness and the National Culture," in *Englishness: Politics and Culture*, 5–7; Robert Colls, "Englishness and the Political Culture," in *Englishness: Politics and Culture*, 37–38; and Jane Mackay and Pat Thane, "The Englishwoman," in *Englishness: Politics and Culture*, 191–229.

51 Doubtless the most influential of such accounts is Sandra M. Gilbert and Susan Gubar, *No Man's Land: The Place of the Woman Writer in the Twentieth Century*, 3 vols. (New Haven: Yale University Press, 1988–1993). Huyssen, *After the Great Divide*, contends that such defensive masculinist dynamics characterize the responses of "high modernism" in general to mass culture (44–62). Lisa Tickner, "Men's Work? Masculinity and Modernism," *differences: A Journal of Feminist Cultural Studies* 4.3 (1992): 1–37, examines these dynamics in British modernist visual art before the Great War.

52 Poggioli, *Theory of the Avant-Garde*, 220–21.

53 Cianci, "A Man at War," explains that the avant-gardists "adopted a strategy of confrontation, and were quite relentless and uncompromising in their agitation. Where they met resistance, they made an open declaration of war, albeit only a metaphorical war, without bloodshed. They waged it through an art politics whose militaristic connotations were already implicit in the term 'avant-garde'" (13).

54 Bürger, *Theory of the Avant-Garde*, 91–92.

55 Rupert Brooke, "Peace," in *The Collected Poems of Rupert Brooke: With a Memoir* (London: Sidgwick & Jackson, 1918), 5.

56 Hynes, *A War Imagined: The First World War and English Culture* (New York: Macmillan, 1990), 65–67.

57 Klaus Theweleit, *Male Fantasies*, vol. 2, *Male Bodies: Psychoanalyzing the White Terror*, trans. Erica Carter, Chris Turner, and Stephen Conway (Minneapolis: University of Minnesota Press, 1989); for a recent reading of Futurism in this mode see, Blum, *Other Modernism.*

58 For an exemplary articulation of this argument, often made by historians but only recently taken up by literary scholars, see Mosse, *Nationalism and Sexuality: Middle-Class Morality and Sexual Norms in Modern Europe* (Madison: University of Wisconsin Press, 1985); compare Mosse, *The Image of Man: The*

Creation of Modern Masculinity (Oxford University Press, 1996).

1 CONJURING NEW CHARACTER

1 The *Return to Yesterday* version is almost identical in detail (except for the comparison to Guy Fawkes) to the first version of the tale Ford published, "Mr. Wyndham Lewis and 'Blast,'" *Outlook* 34 (4 July 1914): 15–16. When Ford edited *The English Review*, he was still known as Hueffer; I follow current convention of using the surname Ford. Arthur Marwood was Ford's co-editor at the *Review*.

2 The best treatment of Ford's effort to embody through *The English Review* the (Arnoldian) ideal of "disinterestedness" is Mark Morrisson, "The Myth of the Whole: Ford's *English Review*, the *Mercure de France*, and Early British Modernism," *ELH* 63 (1996): 513–33.

3 Philip Dodd, "Englishness and the National Culture," in *Englishness: Politics and Culture 1880–1920*, ed. Robert Colls and Philip Dodd (London: Croom Helm, 1986), 1–28, provides an accounting of the preoccupation of "the institutions and practices of a cultural politics" in Englishness and the "English Spirit" between 1880–1920.

4 Michael Levenson, *A Genealogy of Modernism: A Study of English Literary Doctrine 1908–1922* (Cambridge University Press, 1984), 49.

5 Ford, *Thus to Revisit* (1921; New York: Octagon, 1966), 58, 60.

6 Ford, *Return to Yesterday*, 391.

7 Throughout this chapter, I use the capitalized form of Liberal to indicate the political party that came to power in the election of 1906 and the lowercase forms of liberal and liberalism to indicate the moderate left-wing political ideology that prevailed among English elites between 1906 and 1910.

8 F[ord], "The Critical Attitude: Blue Water and the Thin Red Line," *English Review* 2 (April 1909): 137.

9 Arnold, "The Function of Criticism at the Present Time," *Essays in Criticism, First Series*, ed. Sister Thomas Marion Hoctor (1875; University of Chicago Press, 1968), 15. See Dodd, "Englishness and the National Culture," 11–14, for an account of the ways Arnold used his "culturalist argument" to facilitate the "colonisation by the English of the Celts," the "bestowal of identity by the core on the periphery" (14).

10 [Ford], "The Functions of the Arts in the Republic. I. Literature," *English Review* 1 (December 1908): 159.

11 [Ford] E. R., "The Functions of the Arts in the Republic. IV. The Plastic Arts," *English Review* 1 (March 1909): 797.

12 Arnold, "The Literary Influence of Academies," *Essays in Criticism*, 35.

13 *Ibid.*, 35.

14 *Ibid.*, 36 and 37.

15 *Ibid.*, 39.

16 *Ibid.*, 36 and 37.

17 [Ford], "Functions of the Arts in the Republic. IV. The Plastic Arts," 797.
18 [Ford] E. R., "The Critical Attitude: On the Objection to the Critical Attitude," *English Review* 4 (February 1910): 531.
19 Arnold, "Function of Criticism," 29; italics original.
20 *Ibid.*, 25 and 21.
21 *Ibid.*, 19.
22 Arnold, "Literary Influence of Academies," 41.
23 *Ibid.*, 52.
24 Arnold, "Function of Criticism," 28.
25 F[ord], "Blue Water and the Thin Red Line," 135.
26 *Ibid.*, 139.
27 I agree in part with Morrisson, "The Myth of the Whole," that "Ford attempted to create a discursive space in *The English Review* that would embody his conception of disinterestedness," a conception "predicated upon Ford's vision of French letters as an expression of the Enlightenment, and . . . ultimately in the service of . . . the desire for a social and cultural cohesion based neither on middle-class philistinism nor on mass-market taste" (514). But, as will become clear, I think Morrisson reads Ford's "disinterestedness" as more disinterested than certain *Review* editorials indicate.
28 R. K. Webb, *Modern England From the Eighteenth Century to the Present* (New York: Harper & Row, 1968), 456–7; Webb describes this "record of Liberal accomplishment" as "remarkable" (456); compare Dennis Smith, "Englishness and the Liberal Inheritance After 1886," in *Englishness: Politics and Culture*, 258–64, esp. 261; and Colls, "Englishness and the Political Culture," *Englishness: Politics and Culture*, 5–54.
29 Webb, *Modern England*, 458–61.
30 *Ibid.*, 455.
31 *Ibid.*, 400; Webb points out, however, that despite the fact that "[i]n 1911 . . . the Liberals destroyed the veto by which the House of Lords could wreck their legislation, and passed the most sweeping welfare measure yet imaginable," the period 1911–14 was "as good as barren of progressive legislation." Webb accounts for this paradox in part as the result of "a strange political apathy which came over the country . . . born, in some at least, of well-being, in others, of exhaustion"; in part as the result the "great complexity" of passing Irish Home Rule and Welsh Disestablishment legislation; and in part because of "alarming international tension building up" and a series of "violent, irrational, dangerous and incomprehensible revolts" at home against "what had seemed the most solidly planted parliamentary democracy in the world" (460–61).
32 Nairn, *Break-up of Britain*, 29.
33 *Ibid.*, 30–33.
34 *Ibid.*, 31.
35 *Ibid.*, 32.
36 [Ford], "Political and Diplomatic: The Unemployed," *English Review* 1

(December 1908): 163, 161; the book Ford recommends by Stephen Reynolds is *A Poor Man's House* (1908; London: John Cape, 1928).

37 [Ford], "The Unemployed," 161–2.

38 Colls, "Englishness and the Political Culture," explains that the "English State took the same view of revolution as the Roman Church took of miracles. It believed in them – indeed it was founded on one albeit one of a different order – but it did not welcome them, and was in no hurry to acknowledge them" (34).

39 A[rthur] M[arwood], "British India," *English Review* 1 (February 1909): 569; further citations included in the text.

40 F[ord], "Blue Water and the Thin Red Line," 136.

41 *Ibid.*, 135–36.

42 On the Sheffield Outrages, see Webb, *Modern England*, 319–20; on the Hyde Park Riots, see Webb, *Modern England*, 324.

43 Nairn, *Break-up of Britain*, contends that "[u]nder British conditions the intellectuals were not radicalized: they moved more and more into that peculiar service of the old order . . . as an extensive, civil-based, autonomous corps of *chiens de garde*. Without the leadership of a militant radicalism, the masses were unable to break the system" (39).

44 For a related argument about how Ford, in *The Spirit of the People: an Analysis of the English Mind* (London: Alston Rivers, 1907), works to exsanguinate British imperial doctrine, making it more compatible with the prewar period's anxious liberalism, while preserving its principal tenet of Britain's "natural" supremacy, see my "Thinking Race in the *Avant Guerre*: Typological Negotiations in Ford and Stein," *Yale Journal of Criticism* 10.2 (1997): 376–81.

45 [Ford] E. R., "On the Objection to the Critical Attitude," 531.

46 See Ford, "On Impressionism," *Poetry and Drama* 2 (2 June 1914): 167–75, and "On Impressionism (Second Article)," *Poetry and Drama* 2 (December 1914): 323–34; for a fuller discussion of Fordian Impressionism, see Levenson, *Genealogy of Modernism*, 105–119. My understanding of Fordian realism has also benefited from comments in David M. Thompson, "Calling in the Realists: The Reputation and Revision of Lawrence's *Sons and Lovers*," *Novel* (Spring 1994): 246.

47 Ford, *The Critical Attitude* (London: Duckworth, 1911), 29. *The Critical Attitude* is a revised collection of Ford's editorials from *The English Review*.

48 [Ford] "Functions of the Arts in the Republic. 1. Literature," 160.

49 *Ibid.*, 159.

50 *Ibid.*, 160.

51 *Ibid.*, 160.

52 Colls, "Englishness and the Political Culture," esp. 49–54; Smith, "Englishness and the Liberal Inheritance After 1886," esp. 258–64.

53 Peter Brooker and Peter Widdowson, "A Literature for England," in *Englishness: Politics and Culture*, 116–63, provides an account of the ways in which a "sentimental love of the mother-country, particularly when traced

to recollections of youth and perceptions of rural England, proves central to expressions of Englishness in the literature of the period" (117).

54 J. W. Allen, "The Back of Beyond," *English Review* 1 (March 1909): 623.

55 A. M. Quinton, "Social Thought in Britain," in *The Twentieth Century Mind: History, Ideas, and Literature in Britain*, 3 vols., ed. C. B. Cox and A. E. Dyson (Oxford University Press, 1972), 1: 129.

56 As Marianna Torgovnick, *Gone Primitive: Savage Intellects, Modern Lives* (University of Chicago Press, 1990), explains "the needs of the present determine the value and nature of the primitive. The primitive does what we ask it to do. Voiceless, it lets us speak for it. It is our ventriloquist's dummy" (9).

57 [Ford] E. R., "The Work of W. H. Hudson," *English Review* 2 (April 1909): 157–64 (161).

58 Alun Howkins, "The Discovery of Rural England," in *Englishness: Politics and Culture*, 74.

59 W. H. Hudson, "Stonehenge," *English Review* 1 (December 1908): 62; further citations included in the text.

60 Howkins, "The Discovery of Rural England," 74.

61 Allen, "Back of Beyond," 618–24; further citations included in the text.

62 See Charles Booth, *Life and Labour of the People of London* (1880–1903; London: Macmillan, 1902–03); B. Seebohm Rowntree, *Poverty: A Study of Town Life* (1901; London: Macmillan, 1902); L. G. Chiozza Money, *Riches and Poverty* (1905; London: Methuen, 1906); Will Reason, *Poverty* (London: Headley Brothers, 1909). For further discussion of these texts, see Samuel Hynes, *Edwardian Turn of Mind* (1968; London: Pimlico, 1991), 54–57; Reba Soffer, "The Revolution in English Social Thought, 1880–1914," *American Historical Review* 75.7 (Dec. 1970): 1957–58; and Dodd, "Englishness and the National Culture," 7–11.

63 Dodd, "Englishness and the National Culture," 12.

64 The complicity I identify between Graham's "Andorra" and *The English Review*'s cosmopolitan imperialism is complicated by Graham's Scottish nationality and political history as socialist activist and Scottish Labour Party MP. Indeed, Chris GoGwilt, "Broadcasting News from Nowhere: R. B. Cunninghame Graham and the Geography of Politics in the 1890s," in *High and Low Moderns: Literature and Culture, 1889–1938*, ed. Maria DiBattista and Lucy McDiarmid (Oxford University Press, 1996), differentiates Graham's "nostalgic, utopian view of the South American pampa" from that of "his friend W. H. Hudson," because the former's persona and political ideals register "resistance to the global political realignments following the Spanish–American War – a resistance to a whole range of Anglo-Saxon imaginings, most notably Rudyard Kipling's address to Americans to 'take up the white man's burden'" (251). My account suggests, however, that despite Graham's personal history of such "resistance" to late nineteenth-century imperialism, his early-twentieth century travel writing in *The English Review* helped to support Ford's more "civilised" version of imperial privilege.

65 R. B. Cunninghame Graham, "Andorra," *English Review* 1 (January 1909): 205; further citations included in the text.

66 Norman Douglas, "The Island of Typhoëus," *English Review* 1 (February 1909): 414.

67 The best accounts of Lewis's early stories I have found are: Ian Duncan, "Towards a Modernist Poetic: Wyndham Lewis's Early Fiction," in *Wyndham Lewis: Letteratura/Pittura*, ed. Giovanni Cianci (Palermo, 1982), 67–85; and Walter Michel, " 'Inferior Religions,' the Wild Bod(ies), and the Early Stories," in *Wyndham Lewis Annual 1994* (Bath College of Higher Education): 15–23; see also, Paul Edwards, "Lewis's Myth of the Artist: from Bohemia to the Underground," in *Volcanic Heaven: Essays on Wyndham Lewis's Painting and Writing*, ed. Edwards (Santa Rosa: Black Sparrow, 1996), 27–30.

68 Compare Edwards, "Lewis's Myth of the Artist," 28.

69 Compare Giovanni Cianci, "A Man at War: Lewis's Vital Geometries," in *Volcanic Heaven*, 16.

70 Duncan, "Towards a Modernist Poetic," explains that "Lewis's Breton countryside in these early stories could not be further from a pre-industrial celtic pastoral; it is a clearly perceived post-industrial landscape, economically emarginated and stagnant, all sense of community as fragmented and dispossessed as in the metropolis" (77).

71 Wyndham Lewis, "The 'Pole,'" *English Review* 2 (May 1909): 255–65, rpt. Lewis, *The Complete Wild Body*, ed. Bernard Lafourcade (Santa Barbara: Black Sparrow, 1982), 209. Lafourcade's edition reprints all of the Lewis texts under consideration in this chapter: "The 'Pole,'" "Some Innkeepers and Bestre," *English Review* 2 (June 1909): 471–84; "Les Saltimbanques," *English Review* 3 (August 1909): 76–87; and "Our Wild Body," *New Age* 2 (5 May 1910): 8–10; further citations will be included in the text, page numbers will be from Lafourcade's edition.

72 Duncan, "Towards a Modernist Poetic," 79. Under Ford's editorship *The English Review* published two such translations: Leo Tolstoi, "The Raid (A Volunteer's Story. 1852)," trans. Constance Garnett, *English Review* 1 (December 1908; January 1909); Fyodor Dostoyevsky, "An Honest Thief," trans. Garnett, *English Review* 2 (May 1909) (the same issue in which Lewis's, "The 'Pole'" was published).

73 For a contemporary taxonomy of the constituent races of world nations, see Henry W. Nevinson, "Notes on the Balkans, with a Table," *English Review* 1 (December 1908): 187.

74 George W. Stocking, Jr., "The Persistence of Polygenist Thought in Post-Darwinian Anthropology," *Race, Culture, and Evolution: Essays in the History of Anthropology*, 2nd. edn. (1968; University of Chicago Press, 1982), 42–68.

75 Stocking, *Race, Culture, and Evolution*, 56–59.

76 Ford, "On Impressionism," 167–68.

77 Duncan, "Towards a Modernist Poetic," 78.

78 Hynes, *Edwardian Turn of Mind*, 15–53.

79 Duncan, "Towards a Modernist Poetic," thus speculates that "although

Lewis registered . . . alienation and antipathy as regards the contemporary post-industrial and technological culture, he is perhaps the first major English novelist to depart fundamentally from th[e] by now extreme and often vitiated romanticism" that "dominated English letters throughout the nineteenth and early twentieth centuries" (75–76).

80 Dennis Brown, *Intertextual Dynamics within the Literary Group – Joyce, Lewis, Pound, and Eliot: The Men of 1914* (London: Macmillan, 1990), explains that "[i]t is, in particular, Lewis's focus on masculinist assertion which makes his eccentrics somehow 'barometric' representatives of a powerful underlying aggression in society at large. In this world the sex-war is conducted almost entirely at the expense of women, whose most effective form of revenge on the tyrannical males is to cook badly. So although Lewis chooses the Breton countryside as setting, and eccentrics as characters, his tales resonate with the implications of contemporary European gendering" (32–33); I am less confident than Brown seems to be that Lewis's satirical anatomizing of "contemporary European gendering" overcomes his participation in and exaggerated replication of that gendering. See Dodd, "Englishness and the National Culture," 5–7, for a discussion of the ways in which the English public school system contributed to the period "identification of the English with the masculine" (5) and the "dominant English licensed to other groups and to other nationalities those 'female' qualities which it did not acknowledge itself to possess" (6). For a discussion of the ways in which Edwardian Liberalism gendered "Liberal freedom" masculine, see Colls, "Englishness and the Political Culture," 37.

81 James Clifford, *The Predicament of Culture: Twentieth-Century Ethnography, Literature, and Art* (Cambridge, Mass.: Harvard University Press, 1988), 92–113.

82 Compare Duncan, "Towards a Modernist Poetic," 74–75.

83 Accordingly, Ford, *Return to Yesterday*, continues the tale of Lewis's arrival by noting that "The 'Pole,'" "was about the indigent Slavs or make-believe Slavs who victimise willing boarding-house keepers in the French capital and Provinces. I became certain that Mr. D. Z. [as this version names Lewis] was himself a Pole" (390).

84 Edwards, "Lewis's Myth of the Artist," explains that "[w]hen it was no longer possible for artists to find examples of 'primitive' people uncontaminated by industrial and bourgeois values, they attempted to become such people themselves, managing to create in their own way of life a kind of urban version of the authentic, unscripted freedom they had looked for elsewhere. The decision that a way of life, particularly the way of life of artists, rather than works of art representing it, is to be the medium of creativity, is crucial to the history of the Avant-Garde" (30). For an account of the ways in which the aggression of Lewis's Bretons, especially Bestre, signifies a "revolt against rationality," see David A. Wragg, "Aggression, Aesthetics, Modernity: Wyndham Lewis and the Fate of Art," in *Wyndham Lewis and the Art of Modern War*, ed. David Peters Corbett (Cambridge University Press, 1998), 195–97.

85 Paul Edwards has suggested to me that Lewis may have been prompted to write "Our Wild Body" in response to F. T. Marinetti's April 1910 speech to the English (Marinetti, "Futurist Speech to the English: Given at the Lyceum Club of London," *Marinetti: Selected Writings*, ed. R. W. Flint, trans. Flint and Arthur A. Coppotelli [New York: Farrar, Straus and Giroux, 1972], 59–65); this possibility is intriguing in our context because it raises the possibility that Lewis's earliest efforts to fashion an English avant-garde were prompted by his Italian contemporary, and thus that the dynamics of national cultural competition which would drive Lewis and his closest allies to found the Vorticist movement in response to Marinetti's colonizing sallies into the English art world of 1912–14 (the topic of chapter 3 below) actually began as early as 1910.

86 See Cianci, "A Man at War," 17; Michel, "'Inferior Religions,'" 18; Vincent Sherry, "Anatomy of Folly: Wyndham Lewis, the Body Politic, and Comedy," *Modernism/Modernity* 4.2 (April 1997): 133; and Wragg, "Aggression, Aesthetics, Modernity," 193.

87 Lewis, "Our Wild Body," *New Age* 2 (5 May 1910): 8; rpt. Lewis, *Complete Wild Body*, 251; further references included in the text.

88 Sherry, "Anatomy of Folly," 133.

89 H. Stuart Hughes, *Consciousness and Society: The Reorientation of European Social Thought, 1890–1930*, 2nd. edn. (1961; New York: Vintage, 1977) and Carl Schorske, *Fin-de-Siècle Vienna* (New York: Alfred A. Knopf, 1980).

2 NARRATIVES OF AMBITION AND ANXIETY

1 Samuel Hynes, *A War Imagined: The First World War and English Culture* (New York: Macmillan, 1990), 4–5; the principal work on *The New Age* is Wallace Martin, The New Age *under Orage: Chapters in English Cultural History* (New York: Barnes & Noble, 1967).

2 Ezra Pound, "Affirmations II. Vorticism," *New Age* 16 (14 Jan. 1915), praises the journal for setting an example of editorial independence that "permits one to express beliefs which are in direct opposition to those held by the editing staff" (277).

3 This period view of the late-Victorian and Edwardian eras as a time of decline has been reiterated by later scholars like George Dangerfield, *The Strange Death of Liberal England* (1935; New York: G. P. Putnam, 1980), viii; and Hynes, *The Edwardian Turn of Mind* (1968; London: Pimlico, 1991), 9. Reba N. Soffer, "The Revolution in English Social Thought, 1880–1914," *American Historical Review* 75.7 (December 1970): 1938–64, counters such accounts by arguing that "from the 1880s until 1914 there was in England a genuine, vital revolution in the contents, methodology, and purposes of social thought" (1938). For our argument, however, whether or not the late-Victorian and Edwardian periods were actually times of decline is less important than the fact that most women and men in early century England worried that they were.

4 Huntly Carter, "The 'Blue Bird' and Bergson in Paris," *New Age* 9 (11 May 1911): 44.
5 Carter, "The Independants and the New Intuition in Paris," *New Age* 9 (25 May 1911): 82.
6 Carter, "Letters from Abroad: The Post-Expressionists," *New Age* 9 (26 October 1911): 617.
7 Carter, "The 'Blue Bird' and Bergson in Paris," 44.
8 T. E. Hulme, "Notes on Bergson 1," *New Age* 9 (19 October 1911): 587–88; rpt. *Further Speculations*, ed. Hynes (Minneapolis: University of Minnesota Press, 1955), 29–30. Hulme's enthusiasm for continental thought later led him to embrace the work of *L'Action française* writers Pierre Lasserre and Charles Maurras and of the German aesthetician Wilhelm Worringer. See Michael Levenson, *A Genealogy of Modernism: A Study of English Literary Doctrine 1908–1922* (Cambridge University Press, 1984), 39–47, 82–84, 98–101, and Alan Robinson, *Symbol to Vortex: Poetry, Painting, Ideas, 1885–1914* (New York: St. Martins, 1985), 63–80, 109–20, 124–32.
9 Holbein Bagman, "Englishmen and Aesthetic Sensibility," *New Age* 6 (18 November 1909): 59.
10 Carter, "Letters from Abroad: The New Idea of Dramatic Action. 1," *New Age* 9 (20 July 1911): 272.
11 John Middleton Murry, "Bergson in Paris" [letter], *New Age* 9 (1 June 1911): 116.
12 Jacob Tonson [Arnold Bennett], "Books and Persons," *New Age* 8 (8 December 1910): 135; quoted in Hynes, *Edwardian Turn of Mind*, 332.
13 Murry, "Bergson in Paris," 115.
14 E. Belfort Bax, "Bergson," *New Age* 9 (20 July 1911): 280; further citations included in the text.
15 Vincent O'Sullivan, "Paris as a Pleasure Resort," *New Age* 9 (15 June 1911): 161–62; further citations included in the text.
16 G. K. Chesterton in the *Daily News*, quoted in "Present Day Criticism," *New Age* 10 (14 December 1911): 158.
17 Suffragist polemics, for instance, cited French tolerance for prostitution as a contributing factor in the "epidemic" of venereal disease among European men (an accusation which would find evidence in the lives of a significant number of male modernists). The most controversial of these polemics was Christabel Pankurst's *The Great Scourge and How to End It* (1913), rpt. in *Suffrage and the Pankhursts*, ed. Jane Marcus (London: Routledge, 1987), 187–240, which used the claim that most men were infected with venereal disease to justify female celibacy; see Lisa Tickner, *The Spectacle of Women: Imagery of the Suffrage Campaign 1907–1914* (University of Chicago Press, 1988), 131–148; Janet Lyon, "Militant Discourse, Strange Bedfellows: Suffragettes and Vorticists before the War," *differences: A Journal of Feminist Cultural Studies* 4.2 (1992): 100–33.
18 Hynes, *Edwardian Turn of Mind*, 330–31.
19 E. Wake Cook [Letter], *New Age* 10 (30 November 1911): 119.

20 David Kadlec, "Pound, *BLAST*, and Syndicalism," *ELH* 60 (Winter 1993): 1015–31, cites articles in the London *Times* of 27 and 28 February, 1912, which warned of the British coal miner's "militant aggressive policy" and anarcho-syndicalist tactics (1015). On the influence of anarchism and syndicalism in England during the period, see Bob Holton, *British Syndicalism: 1900–1914* (London: Pluto Press, 1976); I owe Kadlec this reference. On the involvement of French Post-Impressionists with anarchism, see Joan Ungersma Halperin, *Félix Fénéon, Aesthete and Anarchist in Fin de Siècle Paris* (New Haven: Yale University Press, 1988) and Richard Sonn, *Anarchism and Cultural Politics in Fin de Siècle France* (Lincoln: University of Nebraska Press, 1989); on the involvement of the Cubists with anarchism, see Patricia Leighton, *Re-Ordering the Universe: Picasso and Anarchism, 1897–1914* (Princeton University Press, 1989). For further discussions of the intersections between Anarchism and Modernism, see the essays in the Anarchism issue of *Modernism/Modernity* 2.2 (April 1995) and David Weir, *Anarchy and Culture: The Aesthetic Politics of Modernism* (Amherst: University of Massachusetts Press, 1997).

21 W. B. Richmond, "Post-Impressionists" [letter], *Morning Post* (16 November 1910): 5; quoted in Hynes, *Edwardian Turn of Mind*, 330–31.

22 Robinson, *Symbol to Vortex*, discusses Kennedy in his (critical) analysis of the "New Classicism" which emerged at this time in the pages of *The New Age* and its significance for the modernists' turn toward classicist aesthetics (90–118).

23 For example, Hynes, *Edwardian Turn of Mind*, 15–53; my account of Edwardian anxieties of decline and the ways in which they were exploited by popular writers and politicians is informed by Hynes's.

24 Robert Baden-Powell, *Scouting for Boys* (London: Horace Cox, 1908), 208; further citations included in the text.

25 Hynes, *Edwardian Turn of Mind*, 27.

26 William Le Queux, *The Invasion of 1910* (London: Eveleigh Nash, 1906), 542.

27 M. D. Eder, "On German Spies," *New Age* 6 (20 January 1910): 271. A Fabian Socialist, Eder would become one of England's first psychoanalysts and translators of Freud and Jung; see Hynes, *Edwardian Turn of Mind*, 368.

28 Martin, New Age *under Orage*, 123.

29 C. H. Norman, "A Study in Jingoism," *New Age* 6 (6 Jan. 1910): 223.

30 C. R. Hennings, "Our German Cousins and the English Nation," *New Age* 6, Supplement (20 January 1910): 3.

31 See Hugh A. MacDougall, *Racial Myth in English History: Trojans, Teutons, and Anglo-Saxons* (Hanover: University Press of New England, 1982), 89–103; and Stuart Anderson, *Race and Rapprochement: Anglo-Saxonism and Anglo-American Relations, 1895–1904* (East Brunswick: Farleigh Dickinson University Press, 1981), 17–61.

32 For a typical Victorian expression of the view that the English, their institutions, and their love of freedom are "Teutonic" in origin, see Lord Acton, "Political Thoughts on the Church," *The History of Freedom and Other*

Essays, ed. J. Figgis, R. Laurence (London: Macmillan and Co., 1909), 204.

33 W. R. Titterton, "Why Not Surrender to Germany?" *New Age* 6 (14 April 1910): 562–63; further citations included in the text.

34 On the centrality of the qualities of "healing and absorption" to early twentieth-century English Liberalism and the Liberal state, see Robert Colls, "Englishness and the Political Culture," in *Englishness: Politics and Culture 1880–1920*, ed. Robert Colls and Philip Dodd (London: Croom Helm, 1986), 35–39.

35 E. J. Hobsbawm, *The Age of empire, 1875–1914* (New York: Random House, 1987), 86. For another period articulation of this view of Prussia, see S. Verdad [J. M. Kennedy], "Foreign Affairs," *New Age* 9 (28 September 1911): 510.

36 Colls, "Englishness and the Political Culture," 30–35.

37 On the Agadir Crisis, see Geoffrey Barraclough, *From Agadir to Armageddon: The Anatomy of a Crisis* (New York: Holmes and Meier, 1982), and Hobsbawm, *Age of empire*, 321.

38 Kennedy translated two volumes of the first complete English edition of Nietzsche's works – *On the Future of Our Educational Institutions; Homer and Classical Philology* (Edinburgh: T. N. Foulis, 1909) and *The Dawn of Day* (London: G. Allen & Unwin, 1911) – and two studies of the German philosopher by European authors – Leone Sera, *On the Tracks of Life: The Immorality of Morality* (London: J. Lane, 1909) and Henri Lichtenberger, *The Gospel of Superman: The Philosophy of Friedrich Nietzsche* (Edinburgh: T. N. Foulis, 1910). For discussion of the English Nietzsche movement before the Great War, see David S. Thatcher, *Nietzsche in England, 1890–1914: The Growth of a Reputation* (University of Toronto Press, 1970).

39 For Kennedy's view on the role of Rousseau and the Revolution in spreading Individualism and Liberalism to England, see "Tory Democracy. (9). Philosophy and Politics," *New Age* 9 (10 August 1911): 341. Kennedy, "The House of Lords," *New Age* 9 (31 August 1911), asserts that, "[t]he French revolutionists had a fanatical belief in the erroneous doctrine of the equality of man. It remained for other aristocracies to show that they possessed qualities which rendered them superior to their fellows" (417); on literary romanticism, Kennedy, *English Literature, 1880–1905* (London: Stephen Swift, 1912), contends that, "the slow poison of romanticism spread to England" from France via Lamartine, Hugo, Baudelaire and Verlaine (25).

40 [Kennedy] Verdad, "Foreign Affairs," *New Age* 9 (25 May 1911): 76.

41 Martin, New Age *Under Orage*, 123.

42 [Kennedy] Verdad, "Foreign Affairs," *New Age* 9 (13 July 1911): 243.

43 *Ibid.*

44 *Ibid.* (3 August 1911): 315.

45 *Ibid.*

46 *Ibid.*, (28 September 1911): 509

47 Kennedy, "Tory Democracy: (3) The Influence of Philosophers," *New Age* 9 (1 June 1911), praises Nietzsche for criticizing the "baser elements" of

"modern Democracy," namely "the stupidity and greed of the masses, their inability to appreciate great leaders, their romanticism and idealism, their innate and ineradicable contempt for what is noble, their aversion to art, their utter lack of will and self-control" (100).

3 ADVANCING ART AND EMPIRE

1 The Futurists and their work were called "anarchistic" in "The New Crazy 'Exploding' Pictures by 'Art Anarchists,' " *The Illustrated London News* (20 March 1912): n.p., rpt. *Futurism and Futurisms*, ed. Pontus Hulten, trans. various hands (New York: Abbeville, 1986), 572, and in "The Aims of Futurism," *Times* (21 March 1912): 2. They were called "nihilistic" by P. G. K[onody], "The Italian Futurists: Nightmare Exhibition at the Sackville Gallery," *Pall Mall Gazette* (1 March 1912): 5; Roger Fry, "Art: The Futurists," *Nation* (9 March 1912): 945; and Huntly Carter, "Blaspheming Creation," *New Freewoman* 1 (1 December 1913): 238. They were accused of being "morbid" in "The Aims of Futurism" (2), and "destructive" in "The Aims of Futurism," and by J. B. M[anson], "The Italian Futurists and the X-Rays in Art," *Outlook* (23 March 1912): 440. They were called "degenerate" by M[anson], 440; along the same lines, C. H. Collins Baker, "Futurist Academics," *Saturday Review* (9 March 1912) accused them of "low-development" (301). These articles are collected in J. B. Bullen, ed. *Post-Impressionists in England* (London: Routledge, 1988).

2 Walter Sickert, "The Futurist 'Devil-among-the-Tailors,'" *English Review* 10 (April 1912): 148.

3 Marinetti, "Initial Manifesto of Futurism" (20 Feb. 1909), *Exhibition of Works of the Italian Futurist Painters* (London: Sackville Gallery, 1912); rpt. in *Futurism*, ed. Joshua C. Taylor (New York: Museum of Modern Art, 1961), 124.

4 Sickert, "Futurist 'Devil-among-the-Tailors,' " 148.

5 Walter L. Adamson, *Avant-Garde Florence: From Modernism to Fascism* (Cambridge, Mass.: Harvard University Press, 1993), 143. Adamson's work recovers the Libyan war's impact on Florence's emerging avant-garde, in particular its role in intensifying nationalism among formerly internationalistic intellectuals and encouraging them to embrace Marinetti's Milan based Futurist movement (143–52). Andrew Hewitt, *Fascist Modernism: Aesthetics, Politics, and the Avant-Garde* (Stanford University Press, 1993), offers a more theoretical consideration of Futurist nationalism in the context of ideas of decadence (68–101). Other accounts that situate Futurism in the context of Italian politics include, James Joll, "F. T. Marinetti: Futurism and Fascism," *Three Intellectuals in Politics* (New York: Pantheon, 1960), 133–184; Robert Wohl, *The Generation of 1914* (Cambridge, Mass.: Harvard University Press, 1979), 160–202; George L. Mosse, "The Political Culture of Italian Futurism," *Confronting the Nation: Jewish and Western Nationalism* (Hanover: Brandeis University Press, 1993), 91–105; and Emilio Gentile, "The Conquest of Modernity: From Modernist Nationalism to Fascism,"

trans. Lawrence Rainey, *Modernism / Modernity* 1 (September 1994): 55–87.

6 The international crises before the Great War included the Austrian annexation of Bosnia-Herzegovina of 1908 and the Agadir Crisis in Morocco of summer 1911 (see chapter 2, above). See Geoffrey Barraclough, *From Agadir to Armageddon: The Anatomy of a Crisis* (New York: Holmes and Meier, 1982), and Eric Hobsbawm, *The Age of empire 1875–1914* (London and New York: Random House, 1987), 321–22.

7 Commenting on the Balkan crisis of fall 1912, S. Verdad [J. M. Kennedy], "Foreign Affairs," *New Age* 11 (3 October 1912), cautioned, "that the Turks, if they get Italy off their hands, wish to deal with Bulgaria in such a way that there need be no further trouble in that quarter for two or three generations to come" (533).

8 Over the past two decades much of value has been written on the English reception of the Futurist movement in the years before the Great War. Not surprisingly, literary and art historians from America and England in particular have studied the topics, establishing the neglected but defining influence of Futurism on England's emerging modernist art and literature, especially the Vorticist movement. Though these analyses generally acknowledge the efforts of Europe's avant-gardists to put "art into life," they tend to construe the English reception of Futurism rather narrowly, considering aesthetic influence and interpersonal relations, but downplaying the impact of national and international politics. See William C. Wees, *Vorticism and the English Avant-Garde* (University of Toronto Press, 1972), 86–179; Richard Cork, *Vorticism and Abstract Art in the First Machine Age*, 2 vols. (London: Gordon Fraser, 1976), 1: 214–38; Giovanni Cianci, "Futurism and the English Avant-Garde: The Early Pound Between Imagism and Vorticism," *Arbeiten aus Anglistik und Amerikanistik* 1 (1981): 17–27; Michael Levenson, *A Genealogy of Modernism: A Study of English Literary Doctrine 1908–1922* (Cambridge University Press, 1984), 120–36; Reed Way Dasenbrock, *The Literary Vorticism of Ezra Pound and Wyndham Lewis: Towards the Condition of Painting* (Baltimore and London: Johns Hopkins University Press, 1985), 13–61; Marjorie Perloff, *The Futurist Moment: Avant-Garde, Avant Guerre, and the Language of Rupture* (University of Chicago Press, 1986), 162–93; and Lawrence Rainey, "The Creation of the Avant-Garde: F. T. Marinetti and Ezra Pound," *Modernism / Modernity* 1 (September 1994): 195–219.

9 Charles Lapworth, *Tripoli and Young Italy* (London: S. Swift and Co., 1912); Francis McCullagh, *Italy's War for a Desert: Being Some Experiences of a War-Correspondent with the Italians in Tripoli* (London: Herbert and Daniel, 1912). Further citations to both works included in the text. For other examples of the pro-Italian response, see Romney, "Military Notes," *New Age* 11 (4 July 1912): 222 (an attack on McCullagh), and Sir Francis Vane, "Italian Patriotism and a Festa," *New Age* 12 (14 November 1912): 34–35; for another example of the anti-Italian view, see Ernest W. Bennett, *With the Turks in Tripoli* (London: Methuen, 1912).

10 Vane, "Italian Patriotism and a Festa," contends similarly that "this par-

ticular fight has moulded Italy into one whole . . . It has had the effect of widening the mind so that it has a patriotic outlook larger than the province, and now embraces Italy" (35).

11 Lapworth's book and Sickert's essay were published in March 1912. McCullagh was writing his Preface the same month, for *Italy's War for a Desert* describes a visit Marinetti and Boccioni paid McCullagh in early March to "fight a duel" because his articles had "criticise[d] the conduct" (xxiii) of the Italian "troops in Tripoli" (xxiv). Wees, *Vorticism and the English Avant-Garde*, cites McCullagh's account of this visit (94–95) to support his claim that Marinetti and Boccioni, "[n]ot content to let the exhibition, the catalogue, Marinetti's lecture, and the many articles in the press force Futurism upon the English consciousness . . . tried to bring Futurist violence directly into English life" (94), but makes little effort to contextualize this event in terms of Italian politics.

12 [Kennedy] Verdad, "Foreign Affairs," *New Age* 10 (25 April 1912) also evaluates Marinetti's views on war as political in nature and caught up with the Turko-Italian conflict, explaining that "Marinetti, the Italo-Egyptian leader of the Futurists, finds in war . . . the 'hygiene of the world' – he repeats the phrase in his latest brochure about Tripoli" (605). The translation McCullagh quotes is the one from the Sackville Gallery catalogue, further evidence for the simultaneity of the Turko-Italian war and the Futurists' arrival in England and the entwinement in English consciousness of Futurism and the war.

13 Marinetti, "Initial Manifesto of Futurism," 125.

14 *Ibid.*, 124.

15 *Ibid.*

16 M[anson], 440; "The Aims of Futurism," 2.

17 Christopher Seton-Watson, *Italy from Liberalism to Fascism 1870–1925* (London: Methuen, 1967), 349–65. Mosse, "The Political Culture of Italian Futurism," recovers the Futurists' invention of a modernist alternative to official nationalism's conventional self-presentation "as an immutable and unchanging force, the repository of eternal and unchanging truth," an alternative which incorporated modern technology into its nationalist system as "a vital national symbol" and placed the individual rather than the masses "at its center" (94).

18 Kennedy, "When a Poet Dies," *New Age* 10 (25 April 1912), an article on the Italian poet Giovanni Pascoli, notes that after "seven or eight months . . . the enthusiasm" in Italy for the war is "as great as ever, and this will not surprise anyone who has noted during the last few years the growing feeling of imperialism from Lombardy to Sicily" (609). Lapworth, *Tripoli and Young Italy*, tells us that Pascoli is an "elder poet whom the Tripoli campaign has furnished with youthful inspiration and ardour" (261).

19 The Turko-Italian war was a crucial event in the process of European destabilization in the years before the Great War. It encouraged the Bulgarians, Serbians, and Greeks to initiate a war with Turkey in October

1912, an event which further destabilized the Balkans, increased Serbian and Austria-Hungarian tensions, and thus helped bring about the Sarajevo assassination on 28 June 1914, which provoked the War. See Hobsbawm, *Age of empire*, 321.

20 The full text of this important political manifesto, "Tripoli Italiana," dated 11 October, 1911, runs:

> Noi futuristi che da più anni glorifichiamo tra i fischi dei Podagrosi e dei Paralitici, l'amore del pericolo e della violenza, il patriottismo e la guerra, sola igiene del mondo, siamo felici di vivere finalmente questa grande ora futurista d'Italia, mentre agonizza l'immonda genìa dei pacifisti, rintanata ormai nelle profonde cantine del loro risible palazzo dell' Aia.
>
> Abbiamo recentemente cazzottato con piacere nelle vie e nelle piazze i più febbricitanti avversari della guerra, gridando loro in faccia questi nostri saldi principii:
>
> 1. – Siano concesse all' individuo e al popolo tutte le libertà tranne quella di essere vigliacco.
>
> 2. – Sia proclamato che la parola ITALIA deve dominare sulla parola LIBERTA.
>
> 3. – Sia cancellato il fastidioso ricordo della grandezza romana, con una grandezza italiana cento volte maggiore.
>
> L'Italia ha oggi per noi la forma e la potenza di una bella "dreadnought" con la sua squadriglia d'isole torpediniere. Orgogliosi di sentire uguale al nostro il fervore bellicoso che anima tutto il paese, incitiamo il Governo italiano, diventuto finalmente futurista, ad ingigantire tutte le ambizioni nazionali, disprezzando le stupide accuse di pirateria e proclamando la nascita del Panitalianismo.
>
> We Futurists who for many years have glorified – among the hisses of the diseased and the paralytics – the love of danger and violence, patriotism and war, the only hygiene of the world, we are happy to live finally in this Italy's great Futurist hour, while in its death agonies the foul pack of pacifists, scurries back to the deep basements of the ridiculous palace at the Hague.
>
> We have recently fought with pleasure in the streets and piazzas the most feverish adversaries of the war, shouting in their faces these our firm principles:
>
> 1. Let all liberties be granted to the individual and to the people, except the freedom to be cowardly.
>
> 2. Let it be proclaimed that the word ITALY must dominate the word LIBERTY.
>
> 3. The fastidious memory of Roman grandeur must be erased by an Italian grandeur one hundred times greater.
>
> Italy has today for us the form and potency of a beautiful "dreadnought," with her squadrons of island torpedo boats. Proud to feel that the war-like fervor which animates the whole country equals our own, we incite the Italian government, finally become futurist, to magnify all national ambitions, scorning the stupid accusations of piracy and proclaiming the birth of Pan-Italianism. (my translation).

Original French version, rpt. under title, "Pour la guerre, seule hygiène du monde et seul morale éducatrice," in Marinetti, *La Bataille de Tripoli* (Milan: Edizioni Futuriste, 1912), [front matter]; original Italian version, rpt. in *Archivi del Futurismo*, Maria Drudi Gambillo and Teresa Fiori (eds.), 2 vols. (Rome: De Luca, 1958–62) 1:31–2. Joll, "Marinetti: Futurism and Fascism" (150–51), and Hewitt, *Fascist Modernism* (99), cite and discuss this manifesto.

21 H. Stuart Hughes, *Consciousness and Society: The Reorientation of European Social Thought, 1890–1930*, 2nd. edn. (1961; New York: Vintage, 1977), 33–66.

22 The exhibition opened at the Bernheim Gallery in Paris on 5 February 1912. From there it traveled to London, Berlin, Brussels, The Hague, Amsterdam, and Munich. When the show closed at the end of November, the Futurists had in a sense "conquered" Europe.

23 Marinetti, "Primo Manifesto Politico" (1909), had begun by identifying as the Futurists' "*sole* program pride, energy, and *national expansion*," [unico programma l'orgoglio, l'energia e l'espansione nazionale], *Archivi del Futurismo*, 1:31, emphasis added.

24 Lewis (ed.), *BLAST: Review of the Great English Vortex* (1914; Santa Barbara: Black Sparrow, 1981): 8; further citations included in the text.

25 Miriam Hansen, "T. E. Hulme, Mercenary of Modernism, or, Fragments of Avantgarde Sensibility in Pre-World War I Britain," *ELH* 47 (1980): 355–85, identifies the "defensive nationalism" the Vorticists "mustered . . . in their confrontation with F. T. Marinetti" (362), but does not pursue the point.

26 Marinetti and C. R. W. Nevinson, "Vital English Art," *Observer* 6 (7 June 1914). "Vital English Art" is both a Futurist attack on all forms of "passéism" in England and a blueprint for a new Futurist art and society in England. The polemic concludes by calling upon the "English public to support, defend, and glorify the genius of the great Futurist painters or pioneers and advance-forces of vital English Art," identifying as Futurists many of the soon-to-be Vorticists. "Vital English Art" is partially reprinted in Nevinson, *Paint and Prejudice* (New York: Harcourt Brace, 1938), 58–60; I am quoting it from Cork, *Vorticism and Abstract Art*, 1:228–30.

27 The Rebels' letter was published in *The New Weekly*, *The Observer*, and *The Egoist* (13, 14, 15 June); it is reprinted in Lewis, *The Letters of Wyndham Lewis*, ed. W. K. Rose (Norfolk, Conn.: New Directions, 1963), 62. Cork, *Vorticism and Abstract Art* (I: 227–34), and Dasenbrock, *Literary Vorticism of Ezra Pound and Wyndham Lewis* (22–23), discuss the letter's role in the formation of Vorticism.

28 Lewis, "Automobilism," *New Weekly* 2 (20 June 1914): 13; rpt. Lewis, *Creatures of Habit and Creatures of Change: Essays on Art, Literature and Society 1914–1956*, ed. Paul Edwards (Santa Rosa: Black Sparrow Press, 1989), 33–34; further citations included in the text, page references to the reprint.

29 *BLAST* was thus transformed from a review of "Cubism, Futurism, Imagisme and ALL Vital Forms of Modern Art" into a "Review of the Great English Vortex"; the first quotation is from the advertisement for *BLAST* on the final page of *The Egoist* for 1 and 15 April, 1914, the second is the subtitle from the opening page of *BLAST*.

30 For a sense of the international tenor of modern cultural doctrine in England around this time, see chapters 1 and 2 above, and Cork, *Vorticism and Abstract Art*, Samuel Hynes, *The Edwardian Turn of Mind* (1968; London: Pimlico, 1991), Wallace Martin, The New Age *under Orage: Chapters in English*

Cultural History (New York: Barnes & Noble, 1967), and Wees, *Vorticism and the English Avant-Garde.*

31 Matthew Arnold, "The Literary Influence of Academies," in *Essays in Criticism, First Series*, 2nd. edn., ed. Sister Thomas Marion Hoctor (1875; University of Chicago Press, 1968), esp. 41–52; also see chapter 1 above.

32 The fullest articulation of the view of *BLAST* as the greatest artwork of the English avant-garde is in Wees, *Vorticism and the English Avant-Garde* (181–92); Cork, *Vorticism and Abstract Art*, similarly deems it "an epoch-making publication, the first to launch the idea of a home-grown abstraction on a stagnant and philistine English art world!" (1: 266). The fullest effort to show the importance of Vorticist aesthetics for the later modernism of Pound and Lewis is Dasenbrock, *Literary Vorticism of Ezra Pound and Wyndham Lewis*; Perloff, *Futurist Moment*, too is illuminating in this regard, though somewhat more restrained (162–93).

33 For a discussion of the official nationalism of nineteenth-century Europe, see Benedict Anderson, *Imagined Communities: Reflections on the Origin and Spread of Nationalism* (London: Verso, 1983), 50–66. For a sense of Edwardian anxieties about national decline and "degeneration," see Hynes, *Edwardian Turn of Mind*, esp. 15–53, and Robert Colls, "Englishness and the Political Culture," in *Englishness: Politics and Culture 1880–1920*, ed. Colls and Philip Dodd (London: Croom Helm, 1986), esp. 46–48; for a sense of Edwardian efforts to counter that decline by vitalizing English life, see Jonathan Rose, *The Edwardian Temperament, 1895–1919* (Athens: University of Ohio Press, 1986), 74–116.

34 Lewis (ed.), *BLAST*, 7–43; further citations included in the text. As my argument makes clear, I cannot fully agree with Alan Munton, "Wyndham Lewis: War and Aggression," in *Wyndham Lewis and the Art of Modern War*, ed. David Peters Corbett (Cambridge University Press, 1998), that in *BLAST* 1 "[i]t was not [Lewis's] purpose to isolate and assess the official cultures of aggressive nation states and select 'the best.' Rather, he was concerned to synthesise what was creative and oppositional in them to form a complex cultural internationalism that ignored the crude oppositions of hegemonic nationalism" (30). While I agree with Muton that the Blast-Bless structure of Manifesto 1 shows both antagonism to and support of both France and England, and thus problematizes "the crude oppositions of hegemonic nationalism," I do not believe that the cumulative cultural aim of *BLAST*'s polemics is "a complex cultural internationalism." As I argue, *BLAST* propounds an avant-garde nationalism, that assails established cultural institutions and ideals of Englishness, even as it works to assert the superiority of English avant-garde art and support the British empire.

35 Aldington's name appears on the list of signatories that concludes the *BLAST* manifestos (43).

36 Robert von Hallberg, "Libertarian Imagism," *Modernism/Modernity* 2 (April 1995): 63–79; for more on Stirner, Marsden, and Egoism see, Levenson, *Genealogy of Modernism*, 63–8; Bruce Clark, *Dora Marsden and Early Modernism:*

Gender, Individualism, Science (Ann Arbor: University of Michigan Press, 1996).

37 Compare Stuart Hall and Bill Schwarz, "State and Society, 1880–1930," *The Hard Road to Renewal: Thatcherism and the Crisis of the Left* (London: Verso, 1988), 95–122, which explains that "rejection of Victorian liberalism was often sufficient, in its own right, to promote alliances between groupings which, according to the more familiar, standard political classifications of today, appear to have little in common" (113); I owe this citation to Janet Lyon, "Militant Discourse, Strange Bedfellows: Suffragettes and Vorticists before the War," *differences: A Journal of Feminist Cultural Studies* 4 (1992), 100–33.

38 Quoted in Alun Jones, *The Life and Opinions of T. E. Hulme* (Boston: Beacon Press, 1960), 144; I own this citation to Wees, *Vorticism and the English Avant-Garde*, 221.

39 Much of the information in these two paragraphs is from Wees, "Appendix B," *Vorticism and the English Avant-Garde*, 217–22.

40 As Hansen, "T. E. Hulme, Mercenary of Modernism," explains, "[b]eyond the more open display of violence and more unabashed calls to direct action, however, there was little common ground between, on the one hand, the politics of industrial revolt and, on the other, a movement of predominantly middle-class women fighting for the vote – even less between those two and the Protestant land-owning class of Ulster that organized, under the neo-feudal leadership of Sir Edward Carson and with tacit support of the Conservative Party, to sabotage Liberal Home Rule legislation for Ireland" (357). But as David Kadlec, "Pound, *BLAST*, and Syndicalism," *ELH* 60 (1993), points out, "[t]he urgency of economic struggle and the glamour of class war were lures for artists and intellectuals who lacked the hard lines of opposition that shaped and strengthened such current social movements as labor reform, woman suffrage, and Irish nationalism" (1016).

41 Lyon, "Militant Discourse, Strange Bedfellows," not only recovers the "interdependencies between the militant women's movement and the English avant-garde" (101–02), but also argues convincingly that "the actions of the militant Suffragettes were making literal (and in fact mapping out) to an astonishing degree the metaphors and metalepses of iconoclasm used by the English avant-garde" (120). Lyon, "Women Demonstrating Modernism," *Discourse* 17.2 (Winter 1994–95): 6–25, makes her points even more strongly, terming the militant Suffragettes "performers" and "symbols" of the avant-garde (8), explaining that when "suffragettes attacked art galleries and museums – in an impulse characteristic (one might say constitutive) of the rhetoric of the contemporary artistic avant-garde – they secured an important intersection of political and artistic avant-gardes with the linchpin of gender" (17), and contending that "traditional historians of modernism" have obscured "the kind of avant-garde experimentation with anti-institutional performativity and spectacle that drove suffragette activism" (18).

42 Lyon, "Militant Discourse, Strange Bedfellows," identifies this "strain of radical conservative imperialism" (117) in both *BLAST*'s anti-liberal art polemics and Christabel Pankhurst's anti-liberal Suffragette tract *The Great*

Scourge and How to End It (1913), rpt. in *Suffrage and the Pankhursts*, ed. Jane Marcus (London: Routledge, 1987), 187–240.

43 Anderson, *Imagined Communities*, 87.

44 On Victorian "Anglo-Saxonism," see Stuart Anderson, *Race and Rapprochement: Anglo-Saxonism and Anglo-American Relations, 1895–1904* (East Brunswick: Farleigh Dickinson University Press, 1981) and Hugh A. MacDougall, *Racial Myth in English History: Trojans, Teutons, and Anglo-Saxons* (Hanover: University Press of New England, 1982).

45 Tom Nairn, *The Break-up of Britain: Crisis and Neo-Nationalism* (London: New Left Books, 1977), argues that A. E. Housman and the Georgians popularized this "romantic nationalism" (262) through the "sentimental reveries and sighing dramas" (260) that "go on in the rustic English limbo" of their poetry (261); John Stevenson, *The Pelican Social History of Britain: British Society 1914–1945* (New York: Penguin, 1984), explains that early twentieth-century Britain's "culture, folk memory and 'myth of itself' was still bound up with a rural past – a past which was, by the nature of things, increasingly far removed from direct experience" (29–30); and John Ferguson, *The Arts in Britain in World War I* (London: Stainer & Bell, 1980), points out that even after the Great War began, Academy painters were as likely to portray "knights in armour . . . as contemporary battles" (27). I owe these citations to Mark Morrisson.

46 Robert Bridges, "Dunstone Hill," *Poetical Works of Robert Bridges* (London: H. Milford, 1914), 354; Bridges was appointed poet laureate in 1913. Peter Brooker and Peter Widdowson, "A Literature for England," in *Englishness: Politics and Culture*, 116–163, trace the ways in which Bridges, Housman, Walter de la Mare, and other English poets contributed to the "formation of a myth of rural England" (118) by "forging" a poetry based in the "sentimental love of the mother-country, particularly when traced to recollections of youth and perceptions of rural England" (117).

47 Ford, "Literary Portraits – XLIII: Mr. Wyndham Lewis and 'Blast,'" *Outlook* 34 (4 July 1914): 16.

48 Richard Aldington, "Blast," *Egoist* 1 (15 July 1914): 272.

49 *Ibid.*

50 Solomon Eagle [J. C. Squire], "Books in General," *New Statesman* 3 (4 July 1914): 406.

51 [Review of *BLAST*], *The Morning Post*, rpt. *BLAST* 2 (London, 1915): 104; Stephen Phillips, "Views and Reviews," *Poetry Review* 5 (July 1914): 48.

52 Later, in his first autobiography, *Blasting and Bombardiering* (1937; New York: Riverrun, 1982), Lewis wrote of *BLAST*'s reception that "[e]veryone by way of being fashionably interested in art . . . wanted to look at this new oddity, thrown up by that amusing spook, the Zeitgeist. So the luncheon and dinner-tables of Mayfair were turned into showbooths. For a few months I was on constant exhibition . . . The editor of *Blast* must at all costs be viewed; and its immense puce cover was the standing joke in the fashionable drawing-room, from Waterloo Place to the border-line in Belgravia" (46–47).

53 David Graver, "Vorticist Performance and Aesthetic Turbulence in *Enemy of the Stars*," *PMLA* 107 (May 1992): 482, 483.

54 *Ibid.*, 484.

55 Perloff, *Futurist Moment*, identifies Marinetti's balancing act of "creat[ing] . . . essentially a new literary genre [the art manifesto] . . . that might meet the needs of a mass audience even as, paradoxically, it insisted on the avant-garde, the esoteric, the antibourgeois" (81).

56 Rupert Brooke, "Peace," *The Collected Poems of Rupert Brooke: With a Memoir* (London: Sidgwick & Jackson, 1918), 5.

57 Anderson, *Imagined Communities*, 82, 84–89.

58 Renato Poggioli, *The Theory of the Avant-Garde*, trans. Gerald Fitzgerald (1962; Cambridge, Mass.: Harvard University Press, 1968), 94–101.

59 On Pound's prewar attraction for anarchism, see von Hallberg, "Libertarian Imagism"; on the links between syndicalism and Pound's Vorticist aesthetics and politics, see Kadlec, "Pound, *BLAST*, and Syndicalism"; on Marinetti's interest in Sorel's radical syndicalism and in Mussolini's revolutionary socialism, see Joll, "Marinetti: Futurism and Fascism," 133–39.

60 As Poggioli, *Theory of the Avant-Garde*, somewhat dramatically puts it, "[a] totalitarian order opposes avant-garde art not only by official and concrete acts . . . but also by, first of all, creating, almost unwillingly, a cultural and spiritual atmosphere which makes the flowing of that art, even when restricted to marginal and private forms, unthinkable even more than materially impossible" (100).

4 "SURROUNDED BY A MULTITUDE OF OTHER BLASTS"

1 Paul Fussell, *The Great War and Modern Memory* (1975; Oxford University Press, 1979), does not mention *The War Number* (though it does briefly quote the first issue of *BLAST* [106]). Even a more recent account, Allyson Booth, *Postcards from the Trenches: Negotiating the Space between Modernism and the First World War* (Oxford University Press, 1996), overlooks the second issue of the Vorticist journal.

2 Studies that contribute to this account include, William C. Wees, *Vorticism and the English Avant-Garde* (University of Toronto Press, 1972), 197, 202–6; Richard Cork, *Vorticism and Abstract Art in the First Machine Age*, 2 vols. (London: Gordon Fraser, 1976), I: 281–96; David Ayers, *Wyndham Lewis and Western Man* (New York: Macmillan, 1992), 61–2; Tom Normand, *Wyndham Lewis the Artist: Holding the Mirror up to Politics* (Cambridge University Press, 1992), 80–83. And while Normand's more recent, "Wyndham Lewis, the Anti-War War Artist," in *Wyndham Lewis and the Art of Modern War*, ed. David Peters Corbett (Cambridge University Press, 1998), 38–57, is closely focused on Lewis's wartime artistic production, because it aims to articulate the complexity of Lewis's anti-war aesthetics as they developed after he had experienced the realities of war, it neglects the more pro-war art and polemics that dominate *BLAST* II.

3 Samuel Hynes, *A War Imagined: The First World War and English Culture* (New York: Macmillan, 1990), 65–67.

4 Lewis, "Editorial," *BLAST* II: War Number (July 1915; Santa Barbara: Black Sparrow, 1981), 5; further citations to *BLAST* 2 included in the text.

5 For a discussion of Masterman's career, see Hynes, *The Edwardian Turn of Mind* (1968; London: Pimlico, 1991), 54–72.

6 The quotation is from the journal of Thomas Hardy, who attended the meeting, as quoted in Florence Emily Hardy, *The Later Years of Thomas Hardy* (London: Macmillan, 1930), 163; I am quoting it from Hynes, *A War Imagined*, 26.

7 "Britain's Destiny and Duty: Declaration by Authors, A Righteous War," *Times* (18 September 1914): 3. For a discussion of Masterman's Department of Information and the role of the arts in supporting the war effort, see Hynes, *A War Imagined*, 25–56.

8 Robert Bridges, "A Holy War," letter to the editor, *Times* (2 September 1914): 10.

9 H. G. Wells, *The War That Will End War* (New York: Duffield & Co., 1914), 11.

10 Germany began the siege of Antwerp on 26 September 1914; the city fell on 9 October (*The Chronology of the Great War*, ed. Edward Gleichen [1918–20; London: Greenhill Books, 1988], 57).

11 Cork, *A Bitter Truth: Avant-Garde Art and the Great War* (New Haven: Yale University Press, 1994), also notes the relation of Lewis's cover to Sickert's painting (76).

12 Sickert's *Soldiers* is admired in "New English Art Club. Three Remarkable Works," *Morning Post* (2 December 1914), where the reviewer speculates that Sickert "might well become the first great military painter in England" (3); quoted in Hynes, *A War Imagined*, 35.

13 Lewis, "A Later Arm than Barbarity," 298.

14 Hynes, *A War Imagined*, 58–67.

15 George Morrow, "How a Cubist . . .," *Punch, Or The London Charivari* 147 (14 Oct. 1914): 325; rpt. in Paul Edwards, *Wyndham Lewis: Art and War* (London: Lund Humphries, 1992), 28. Edwards suggests interestingly that Morrow's "Cubist" is actually based on a contemporaneous caricature of Lewis by E. X. Kapp, which is reproduced in Cork, *Vorticism and Abstract Art*, 1:160.

16 For a discussion of the role of visual types in the propaganda posters used by and against the Suffragette movement, see Lisa Tickner, *The Spectacle of Women: Imagery of the Suffrage Campaign 1907–14* (University of Chicago Press, 1988), 167–226; for an example of the common typological representation of the lunatic, see a pro-suffrage poster titled 'Convicts and Lunatics" by Emily Harding Andrews (c. 1908), plate 4 in Tickner; for an example of the typological representation of the Jew, see a pro-Suffrage postcard titled "This is Allowed to Vote" by Edwyn Llewellyn (1907), which Tickner reproduces (fig. 19) and explains "contrasts the political status of the educated, middle-class white woman with that of immigrants [including Jews] . . . and the newly enfranchised American Negro" (37). For more

general discussions of period representations of Jews, see Sander Gilman, *Difference and Pathology: Stereotypes of Sexuality, Race and Madness* (Ithaca: Cornell University Press, 1985) and Bryan Cheyette, *Constructions of "the Jew" in English Literature and Society: Racial Representations, 1875–1945* (Cambridge University Press, 1993). For a discussion of the significance of typological conceptions for modernist race thinking before the Great War, see my "Thinking Race in the *Avant Guerre*: Typological Negotiations in Ford and Stein," *Yale Journal of Criticism* 10.2 (1997): 371–95.

17 "Junkerism in Art: The London Group at the Goupil Gallery," *Times* (10 March 1915): 8.

18 Modris Eksteins, *Rites of Spring: The Great War and the Birth of the Modern Age* (New York: Doubleday, 1989), 76; Eric Hobsbawm, *The Age of empire 1875–1914* (New York: Random House, 1987), 46–47; 317–21.

19 Eksteins, *Rites of Spring*, 87.

20 Hynes, *A War Imagined*, 52–56. The first-published of these texts, compiled by the well-known patriot and author of adventure tales, William Le Queux, is titled *German Atrocities: A Record of Shameless Deeds* (London: G. Newnes, 1914). It gathers together newspaper reports, quotations from government officials, and interviews with soldiers and civilians in order to substantiate the assertion that accounts of German brutality, no matter how outrageous, are true: "[t]his fearful and disgraceful record of a Nation's shame and of an Emperor's complicity in atrocious crimes against God and man is no work of fiction, but a plain and unvarnished statement of the grim and terrible work of the Kaiser's Huns of Attila" (5).

21 George Bernard Shaw, "Common Sense About the War," War Supplement, *New Statesman* 4 (14 November 1914), rpt. Shaw, *What I Really Wrote About the War*, vol. 21, *The Collected Works of Bernard Shaw*, 30 vols. (New York: William. H. Wise & Co., 1930–32), 90.

22 *Ibid.*, 102.

23 Hynes, *A War Imagined*, 81–87.

24 Clive Bell, *Peace at Once* (Manchester and London: National Labour Press [1915]), 38–9.

25 Compare Giovanni Cianci, "A Man at War: Lewis's Vital Geometries," in *Volcanic Heaven: Essays on Wyndham Lewis's Painting and Writing*, ed. Edwards (Santa Rosa: Black Sparrow, 1996), 21–22; C. J. Fox and Robert Edward Murray, "The War Fiction," in *Volcanic Heaven*, 68; and Normand, "Wyndham Lewis, the Anti-War War Artist," 41.

26 Ford Madox Ford, *When Blood is Their Argument: An Analysis of Prussian Culture* (London: Hodder and Stoughton, 1915), 164, 206; for a discussion of Ford's tract in the context of the homefront war against culture, see Hynes, *A War Imagined*, 71–2.

27 In the Ford archive at Cornell's Carl A. Kroch Library, there are letters to Masterman which show Ford's ambivalence as he was writing the tract, as declarations of national loyalty offset efforts to place responsibility for the work on Masterman's shoulders (21 October 1914; 15 January 1915).

28 Masterman rewarded Ford's loyalty by praising his polemic publicly; C. F.

G. M[asterman], "Reviews," *Nation* 16 (27 March 1915), explains that Ford has "brilliantly accomplished" (840) his "bitter and, at times, passionate indictment of Prussian 'Kultur' " (838).

29 See Arthur Kitson, "The War and the Prophets" [letter], *New Age* 15 (3 Sept. 1914): 429 and T. W. Rolleston, "Literature and Politics in Modern Germany," *Hibbert Journal* 13 (October 1914): 82–88, esp. 83.

30 For fuller account of Lewis's war fictions, see Fox and Murray, "The War Fiction," 65–85; and Christine Hardegen, "Wyndham Lewis's First World War Art and Literature," in *Wyndham Lewis and the Art of Modern War*, 58–77; however, neither Fox and Murray nor Hardegen provide an account of "The Crowd Master."

31 See Normand, *Wyndham Lewis the Artist*, 80–83; Ayers, *Wyndham Lewis and Western Man*, 61–2.

32 See Martin Conway, *The Crowd in Peace and War* (New York: Longmans, Green, 1915); William McDougall, *An Introduction to Social Psychology* (1908; Boston: J. W. Luce, 1911) and *Psychology: The Study of Behaviour* (London: Williams and Norgate, 1912); Wilfred Trotter, *Instincts of the Herd in Peace and War* (1916; London: T. Fisher Unwin, 1923); Graham Wallas, *Human Nature in Politics* (1908; Boston and New York: Houghton Mifflin, 1909). For further discussion of these writers and texts, see A. M. Quinton, "Social Thought in Britain," in *The Twentieth Century Mind: History, Ideas, and Literature in Britain*, 3 vols., ed. C. B. Cox and A. E. Dyson (Oxford University Press, 1972), I: 132–34; Reba N. Soffer, "New Elitism: Social Psychology in Prewar England," *The Journal of British Studies* 8.2 (May 1969): 111–30; Soffer, "The Revolution in English Social Thought, 1880–1914," *American Historical Review* 75.7 (December 1970): 1938–64; L. S. Hearnshaw, "Psychology," in *Twentieth Century Mind*, I: 226–43; Paul Crook, *Darwinism, War and History: The Debate over the Biology of War from the "Origin of Species" to the First World War* (Cambridge University Press, 1994), 146–51.

33 Eksteins, *Rites of Spring*, 55–56; Hobsbawm, *Age of Empire*, 324–26.

34 "London and the Coming of War: Impressive Midnight Scene," *Times* (5 August 1914): 9.

35 Edwards, *Wyndham Lewis: Art and War*, points out that "[l]ike most theorists of 'crowd-psychology', Lewis considered that to become part of a crowd is to merge one's individual will to life and survival within a larger collective" (28).

36 Wallas, *Human Nature in Politics*, 53–54.

37 Trotter, *Instincts of the Herd in Peace and War*, 30; further citations included in the text. Trotter's book reprints his two most important pieces, "Herd Instinct and its Bearing on the Psychology of Civilised Man," *Sociological Review* 1 (1908): 227–48 and "Sociological Applications of the Psychology of Herd Instinct," *Sociological Review* 2 (1909): 36–54. Lewis's sense that wars begin with the gathering of crowds also resembles Conway's work on the role of war-passion in national crowds; Conway, *The Crowd in Peace and War*, explains that "[g]usts of passion are the most frequent cause of actual war," because war-passion spreads through national crowds by "contagion"

(269–70). I owe this citation to Crook, *Darwinism, War and History*, 147. Interestingly, Lewis may have encountered Conway at the Slade School of Art in 1901; Lewis was a student there from 1898–1901, Conway was Slade professor of fine art from 1901–04. On Lewis's time at Slade, see Jeffrey Meyers, *The Enemy: A Biography of Wyndham Lewis* (1980; Boston: Routledge & Kegan Paul, 1982), 9–11; on Conway's career, see Crook, *Darwinism, War and History*, 147.

38 See Klaus Theweleit, *Male Fantasies*, vol. 2, *Male Bodies: Psychoanalyzing the White Terror*, trans. Erica Carter, Chris Turner, and Stephen Conway (Minneapolis: University of Minnesota Press, 1989); Andreas Huyssen, *After the Great Divide: Modernism, Mass Culture*, Postmodernism (Bloomington: University of Indiana Press, 1986), 44–64.

39 Benedict Anderson, *Imagined Communities: Reflections on the Origin and Spread of Nationalism* (London: Verso, 1983), argues that it is the sense of "fraternity" generated by the imagined community of the nation which has made "it possible, over the past two centuries, for so many millions of people, not so much to kill, as willingly to die for such limited imaginings" (16).

40 For Lewis's retrospective account of his time in north Britain and the declaration of war, see *Blasting and Bombardiering* (1937; New York: Riverrun, 1982), 56–59.

41 Compare Cianci, "A Man at War," 20.

42 See Sapper [Herman Cyril McNeile], *Sergeant Michael Cassidy RE* (London: Hodder and Stoughton, 1915), and Ian Hay [Beith], *The First Hundred Thousand: Being the Unofficial Chronicle of a Unit of "K (1)"* (Boston: Houghton & Mifflin, [1915]). For an account of British novels of the early war, see Hynes, *A War Imagined*, 49–52; for a discussion of Beith's *First Hundred Thousand*, see Fussell, *Great War and Modern Memory*, 28–29.

43 Multum's "Crowd Master" seems, from the description Blenner gives, a parody of *BLAST* 1's manifestos by a nationalistic American avant-gardist instead of a nationalistic English one. Like Lewis's earlier polemics, Multum's oppose the " 'soft-conservatisms' of England" and contain an "ingenious tirade against hair" (100); compare *BLAST* 1: *Review of the Great English Vortex*, ed. Lewis (1914; Santa Barbara: Black Sparrow, 1981): 11–28, esp. 25, where Lewis blesses the "HAIRDRESSER" for waging "systematic mercenary war on th[e] WILDNESS" of hair.

44 See Martin Hardie and Arthur K. Sabin, *War Posters Issued by Belligerent and Neutral Nations 1914–1919* (London: A. & C. Black, 1920); Joseph Darracott, *The First World War in Posters: From the Imperial War Museum, London* (New York: Dover, 1974).

45 John Turner, "British Politics and the Great War," in *Britain and the First World War*, ed. Turner (London: Unwin Hyman, 1988), 121–24.

46 On Partridge, see Darracott, *First World War in Posters*, xxii.

47 On Brangwyn, see *Ibid.*, xvii and Cork, *A Bitter Truth*, 291–93.

48 The poster is reproduced in Hardie and Sabin, *War Posters*, plate 5.

49 See, for example, Cork, *Vorticism and Abstract Art*, 1: 286.

50 The socialist intelligentsia's skepticism about alliance with Russia is cap-

tured in Marmaduke Pickthall, "Teuton and Slav: A Word in Season," *New Age* 15 (20 August 1914), which explains that "Imperial Germany must be stopped in her design to dominate the world by force of arms," but warns that 'to crush Germany as our allies, I fear, may wish to crush her, would be simply to bestow on Russia the hegemony of Europe – Russia, much less civilised than Germany, yet inspired with the same dream of universal conquest" (367).

51 Shaw, "Common Sense About the War," 86.

52 The conventional wisdom concerning the poetry of *BLAST* 2 is that only Pound's "Dogmatic Statement on the Game and Play of Chess" and Eliot's two early pieces, "Rhapsody on a Windy Night" and "Preludes," are worthy of attention. See Wees, *Vorticism and the English Avant-Garde*, 205; Cork, *Vorticism and Abstract Art*, 1: 292–94.

53 Alun Howkins, "The Discovery of Rural England," in *Englishness: Politics and Culture 1880–1920*, ed. Robert Colls and Philip Dodd (London: Croom Helm, 1986), 79–80; Peter Brooker and Peter Widdowson, "A Literature for England," in *Englishness: Politics and Culture*, explains that as the "poet-soldier," Brooke "combined the ruling-class values with which Britain entered the war, giving expression to both the sense of pastoral England as 'Home' and the readiness for self-sacrifice in the service of a nation at war" (121).

54 Rupert Brooke, "The Soldier," *The Collected Poems of Rupert Brooke: With a Memoir* (London: Sidgwick & Jackson, 1918), 9.

55 Brooker and Widdowson, "A Literature for England," identify Brooke (with Kipling) as "the nation's bedfellows," who "openly propagandised for empire" and "glorified war and are remembered still for doing so" (116).

56 Hynes, *A War Imagined*, 28–33.

57 Barry Pain, "The Kaiser and God," *Times* (28 August 1914): 9. Georgian poet and editor of *Poetry and Drama*, Harold Monro, in "Varia," *Poetry and Drama* 2 (September 1914), an editorial lamenting the quality of most war poetry as "rhymed leading articles" (250), regretfully notes that "Barry Pain's jingle, 'The Kaiser and God'" has become "generally popular" (251).

58 Ford, "On Impressionism," *Poetry and Drama* 2 (June 1914): 169; further citations included in the text.

59 To my knowledge, the only extended study of Saunders's work is Brigid Peppin, *Helen Saunders 1885–1963* (Oxford: Ashmolean Museum/Graves Art Gallery, 1996). Though Peppin's monograph is primarily interested to discuss Saunders as a visual artist, it does briefly describe "A Vision of Mud" as a poem that "uses images relating to front-line battle to describe the survival of individual consciousness amid suffocating mud and blood" (15). Tickner, "Men's Work? Masculinity and Modernism," *differences: A Journal of Feminist Cultural Studies* 4.3 (1992) not only points out that in her *Female Figures Imprisoned* (1913; reproduced in Tickner, 'Men's Work," 21), "Saunders probably comes closer than anyone else in the prewar avant-garde to producing an overtly feminist painting," but also calls the literary

contributions of Saunders and Jessica Dismorr to *BLAST* II "remarkable for the attempt to harness elements of Vorticist enthusiasm and vocabulary to 'feminist' themes" (22), and even terms "A Vision of Mud," "extraordinary" (31). My understanding of Saunders's poem has also benefited from discussions with David Thompson.

60 *The Chronology of the Great War*, ed. Gleichen, 211.

61 R. H. C. [Alfred Orage], "Readers and Writers," *New Age* 15 (10 September 1914): 449.

62 R. H. C. [Orage], "Readers and Writers," *New Age* 15 (8 October 1914): 549.

63 George L. Mosse, "Two World Wars and the Myth of the War Experience," *Journal of Contemporary History* 21 (1986): 491–513; compare Mosse, *Fallen Soldiers: Reshaping the Memory of the World Wars* (New York: Oxford University Press, 1990).

64 Robert Wohl, *The Generation of 1914* (Cambridge, Mass.: Harvard University Press, 1979), 83–92.

65 Winston Churchill [Valediction for Brooke], *Times* (26 April, 1915); quoted in Edward Marsh, "Memoir," in Brooke, *Collected Poems*, clix.

66 Brooke, "Peace," *Collected Poems*, 5.

67 Wohl, *Generation of 1914*, 91.

68 Theweleit, *Male Bodies.*

69 Julian Symons, "Friends of the Enemy: Reassessing the uncomfortable art of Wyndham Lewis," *TLS* (10 July 1992): 16–17, comments briefly that "Lewis was ready for the War . . . it expressed the meaning of Vorticism" (16).

70 Such accounts follow Peter Bürger, *Theory of the Avant-Garde*, trans. Michael Shaw (1974; Minneapolis: University of Minnesota Press, 1984).

71 Renato Poggioli, *Theory of the Avant-Garde*, trans. Gerald Fitzgerald (1962; Cambridge, Mass.: Harvard University Press, 1968), 94–101.

5 ANTI-INDIVIDUALISM AND FICTIONS OF NATIONAL CHARACTER IN LEWIS'S '*TARR*'

1 Rebecca West, "Tarr," *Nation* 23 (10 August 1918): 506–508; rpt. *Agenda* 7/8 (Autumn-Winter, 1969): 69, 68.

2 *Ibid.*, 68.

3 Geoffrey Wagner, *Wyndham Lewis: A Portrait of the Artist as the Enemy* (New Haven: Yale University Press, 1957), 237.

4 Fredric Jameson, *Fables of Aggression: Wyndham Lewis, the Modernist as Fascist* (Berkeley: University of California Press, 1979), 87–104. Jameson argues that "the objective preconditions of the narrative structures that inform Lewis' imagination, far from being familial or archaic, are rather to be sought in a very different space, namely in the objective configurations of the political history of pre-1914 Europe" (11). While I find this statement compelling and useful, Jameson's psycho-Marxist study is astonishingly *un*interested in the specific characteristics of those "objective configurations." Jameson does

not consider Lewis's prewar works, and in his analysis of *Tarr*, the only point at which he addresses the "political history of pre-1914 Europe," he depends on the revised edition of the novel (published in 1928) rather than the first edition, completed in the war's opening year. Thus Jameson anachronistically can project onto Lewis's chaotic German artist, Kreisler, a post-war view of Germany as what he calls, "the pariah of European politics and the victim of Versailles" (89). The history that Jameson evokes is, in fact, a sketchy, cliché-prone history that, he admits, only recognizes as "objective configurations," "the great new emergent and transnational forces of Communism and Fascism" (11). So Jameson's complicated analysis, which insists on the complexity of Lewis's literary achievement, nonetheless reduces that work, finding as its "repress[ed] . . . structural center," Lewis's "implacable lifelong opposition to Marxism itself" (18), an account which fails to account for *Tarr* as Lewis originally wrote it. For a related critique of Jameson's "historicism," see David Peters Corbett, "Introduction: 'the Subject of Modern War,'" in *Wyndham Lewis and the Art of Modern War*, ed. Corbett (Cambridge University Press, 1998), 3–4.

5 Jameson, *Fables of Aggression*, 90.

6 *Ibid.*, 6.

7 Michael Levenson, *Modernism and the Fate of Individuality: Character and Novelistic Form from Conrad to Woolf* (Cambridge University Press, 1991), 121–44.

8 *Ibid.*, xiii.

9 *Ibid.*

10 For an illuminating discussion of Joyce's involvement with Marsden, *The Egoist*, and the complexities of philosophical egoism, see Jean-Michel Rabaté, "Joyce the Egoist," *Modernism/Modernity* 4.3 (September 1997): 45–65.

11 Andrew Thacker, "Dora Marsden and *The Egoist*: 'Our War is With Words,'" *English Literature in Transition, 1880–1920* 36:2 (1993), notes that Joyce's novel, "ur-text of male self-creation, sits comfortably alongside" Marsden's Individualist editorials (182).

12 Paul O'Keeffe's "Afterword" to Wyndham Lewis, *Tarr: The 1918 Version*, ed. O'Keeffe (Santa Barbara: Black Sparrow, 1990), provides a comprehensive account of *Tarr*'s complex composition and publication history (361–77).

13 Scott W. Klein, *The Fictions of James Joyce and Wyndham Lewis: Monsters of Nature and Design* (Cambridge University Press, 1994), argues that "Lewis's most important fictions" – *The Childermass* (London: Methuen & Co., 1928) and *The Apes of God* (1930; Santa Barbara: Black Sparrow, 1984) in Klein's account – "are in large part parodic responses to Joyce" (8). But Klein does not think, as I do, that Lewis's first published novel (certainly one of his most "important fictions") is also a "parodic response" to Joyce; he contends that the evident "parallels" between *Portrait* and *Tarr* (i.e., both are "autobiographically based novels about young artists" serialized in *The Egoist*) are "coincidental" (7–8). As I show, however, Lewis began to style his fictional project as a satiric rewriting of Joyce's modernism with *Tarr*.

14 Paul Edwards, "Lewis's Myth of the Artist: from Bohemia to the Underground," in *Volcanic Heaven: Essays on Wyndham Lewis's Painting and Writing*, ed.

Edwards (Santa Rosa: Black Sparrow, 1996), argues similarly regarding Kreisler "that what Lewis is saying through this character is that all attempts to live the myth of the totally authentic life (and in his 1913–14 play *Enemy of the Stars* he traces these back to Max Stirner's *The Ego and Its Own*) lead by way of some form of transgression to nihilism, violence and death" (32).

15 Reed Way Dasenbrock, in an unpublished paper presented at the 108th MLA Convention, "Anatomies of Internationalism in *Tarr* and *Howards End*" (28 December 1992), recognizes these competing conceptions of nationality in *Tarr*. I disagree with Dasenbrock's view, however, that those competing conceptions result primarily from *Tarr*'s palimpsestic composition. O'Keeffe, "Afterword," esp. 370–82, makes the strongest case that *Tarr* is not a unified work but an incoherent literary palimpsest.

16 Miriam Hansen, "T. E. Hulme, Mercenary of Modernism, or, Fragments of Avantgarde Sensibility in Pre-World War I Britain," *ELH* 47 (1980): 355–85, is to my knowledge the earliest study to note the influence of Stirner among English modernists (384 n. 68). See also Levenson, *A Genealogy of Modernism: A Study of English Literary Doctrine 1908–1922* (Cambridge University Press, 1984); Andrew Thacker, "'Our War is With Words'"; Robert von Hallberg, "Libertarian Imagism," *Modernism/Modernity* 2 (April 1993): 63–79; Mark Morrisson, "Marketing British Modernism: *The Egoist* and Counter-Public Spheres," *Twentieth Century Literature* 43.4 (Winter 1997); Bruce Clark, *Dora Marsden and Early Modernism: Gender, Individualism, Science* (Ann Arbor: University of Michigan Press, 1996).

17 Max Stirner, *The Ego and his Own: The Case of the Individual Against Authority*, trans. Steven T. Byington (1844; New York: Benjamin R. Tucker, 1907), 83; further citations included in the text.

18 On the differences in emphasis between the American translation of Stirner's book and the original version, see Rabaté, "Joyce the Egoist," 49–52.

19 Dora Marsden, "Views and Comments," *New Freewoman* 1 (15 December 1913): 244. Originally a dissenting feminist journal, Marsden's *New Freewoman* was renamed *The Egoist* at the start of 1914 to reflect the increasingly Stirnerian concerns of its editor and contributors.

20 Marsden, "Views and Comments," *Egoist* 1 (2 March 1914): 84.

21 *Ibid.*, 84–85.

22 Huntly Carter, "The Curve of Individualism," *Egoist* 1 (1 April 1915): 60. For a discussion of Carter's role as contributor to Marsden's journal, see Clark, *Dora Marsden and Early Modernism*, 141–46.

23 George W. Stocking, Jr., *Race, Culture, and Evolution: Essays in the History of Anthropology*, 2nd. edn. (1968; University of Chicago Press, 1982), 251; Reba Soffer, "The Revolution in English Social Thought, 1880–1914," *American Historical Review* 75.7 (December 1970): 1958; Jonathan Rose, *The Edwardian Temperament 1895–1919* (Athens: Ohio University Press, 1986), 136–7.

24 Sir Francis Galton, "Hereditary Talent and Character," *MacMillan's Magazine* 12 (August 1865): 318–27; rpt. in *Images of Race*, ed. Michael D. Biddiss (New York: Holmes and Meier, 1979), 61. Galtonian eugenics arose in

response to turn-of-the-century English anxieties of decline and "degeneration," which it both aggravated (by identifying, in Galton's words, the tendency of "civilization" to "diminish the rigour of the application of the laws of natural selection" and thus "preserve . . . weakly lives"[69]) and sought to address (through "selective breeding"). Thus while Galton's eugenics texts, especially *Hereditary Genius* (1869; New York: Horizon Press, 1952), strive to maintain a posture of scientific disinterestedness, concerned with the condition of the "human race," his worries about the detrimental effects of "civilisation" reveal his motives to be strongly nationalistic: the "race" he really wants to "improve" is the English. Robert Colls, "Englishness and the Political Culture," in *Englishness: Politics and Culture 1880–1920*, ed. Colls and Philip Dodd (London: Croom Helm, 1986), points out that the nationalist motives behind English eugenics are made especially clear in the work of Galton's protégé, the eugenicist-sexologist-man-of-letters, Havelock Ellis, whose *Study of British Genius* (London: Hurst & Blackett, 1904), applies Galton's statistical methods to the recently published *Dictionary of National Biography*, and concludes that the greatest share of "eminent persons" in the United Kingdom has been produced by "the most anciently civilized" English counties of the southern and south midland shires; Ellis's findings, as Colls explains, correspond "perfectly to the hegemony of the English 'south country' over the United Kingdom" (39). For an account of the role of Darwinian and Galtonian concepts in the elitist thinking of Ellis, H. G. Wells, and Alfred Orage, see Tom Gibbons, "Modernism and Reactionary Politics," *Journal of Modern Literature* 3.5 (July 1974): 1140–57.

25 Marsden, "Quid Pro Quo," *Egoist* 1 (15 August 1914): 302.

26 Leigh Henry, "Liberations: Studies of Individuality in Contemporary Music. 1 Balilla Pratella and Futurist Music," *Egoist* 1 (15 April 1914): 147.

27 John Cournos, "Gaudier-Brzeska's Art," *Egoist* 2 (1 September 1915): 137.

28 In 1914, *The Egoist*'s first year of publication, it featured poetry by the Imagist poets F. S. Flint, Richard Aldington, H. D., John Gould Fletcher, Amy Lowell, and John Rodker; reviewed and reproduced photographs of art works by the Vorticist sculptor Gaudier-Brzeska; and included favorable articles on the Vorticist painters Lewis and Edward Wadsworth.

29 Rabaté, "Joyce the Egoist," maintains it "was more than mere coincidence" that Joyce's work should have found its way into the pages of Marsden's journal"; as a young man, Joyce "distinguished himself early by a Stirnerian attitude" (52).

30 James Joyce, *A Portrait of the Artist as a Young Man* (1916; New York: Penguin, 1976), 246; further citations included in the text.

31 Rabaté, "Joyce the Egoist," explains that "when Joyce was offered the possibility of serializing his novel describing how a young Irish man refuses the traps that are his family's values, the dominant Catholicism that had triumphed over Parnell, and even a well-meaning but stumbling Irish nationalism, he could recognize not only that he had found a kindred spirit in Dora Marsden, but also that his struggle against several varieties of

imperialism (British and Roman, at least) could be promoted by her reasonably militant journal" (56).

32 Compare the ending of another individualistic *Bildungsroman* of the *avant guerre*, D. H. Lawrence's *Sons and Lovers*, ed. Julian Moynahan (1913; New York: Penguin, 1968); in the novel's last moments, Lawrence's artist-hero, Paul Morel, overcomes his dependent attachment to his deceased mother and determinedly embraces his future:

> She was the only thing that held him up . . . He wanted her to touch him, have him alongside with her.
>
> But no, he would not give in. Turning sharply, he walked towards the city's gold phosphorescence. His fists were shut, his mouth set fast. He would not take that direction, to the darkness, to follow her. He walked quickly towards the faintly humming, glowing town, quickly. (420)

33 Weldon Thornton, *The Antimodernism of Joyce's* Portrait of the Artist as a Young Man (Syracuse University Press, 1994), provides the fullest case for the critical distance between Joyce and Stephen.

34 Lewis (ed.), *BLAST* 1: Review of the Great English Vortex (1914; Santa Barbara: Black Sparrow, 1981): 7–8.

35 *Ibid.*, 11–20.

36 O'Keeffe, "Afterword," 361–65; West, "Tarr," is probably the earliest critical acknowledgment of the Dostoyevskian qualities of *Tarr*, explaining that like the work of Dostoyevsky, "it too is inquisitive about the soul" and asserting that Otto Kreisler "is worthy to stand beside Stavrogin" (67) .

37 Thacker, "'Our War is With Words'" and von Hallberg, "Libertarian Imagism" argue that Imagist poetry was another literary form in which Individualist ideals were articulated.

38 Dennis Brown, *Intertextual Dynamics within the Literary Group – Joyce, Lewis, Pound, and Eliot: The Men of 1914* (London: Macmillan, 1990), explains that beside *Tarr*, "Joyce's *Portrait* appears narcissistic and marginal" (69).

39 Lewis, *Tarr: The 1918 Version*, 23; further citations included in the text.

40 Given Tarr's aggressive masculinism, it may seem ironic that his words recall those of militant suffragette polemic; Christabel Pankhurst, *The Great Scourge and How to End it* (1913), rpt., *Suffrage and the Pankhursts*, ed. Jane Marcus (London: Routledge, 1987), 187–240, in its defense of the WSPU's goal of "Votes for Women and Chastity for Men," affirms that "Art is creative. Sexual excess is a waste of man's creative energy" (231). But as Janet Lyon, "Militant Discourse, Strange Bedfellows: Suffragettes and Vorticists before the War," *differences: A Journal of Feminist Cultural Studies* 4.2 (1992), points out, Pankhurst's association "between sexual restraint and artistic creation" was also made by the London avant-garde (115).

41 Lawrence, *Sons and Lovers*, 418.

42 The "Kreisleriana" are a sequence of short works focused on the fictional musician-composer, first-published in small German literary and music journals between 1810 and 1814 and collected in E. T. A. Hoffmann, *Fantasy Pieces in Callot's Manner: Pages from the Diary of a Traveling Romantic*, trans.

Joseph M. Hayse (1814–15; Schenectady: Union College Press, 1996), 15–53. The first two volumes of Hoffmann's great unfinished novel, *Lebens-Ansichten des Katers Murr nebst fragmentarischer Biographie des Kapellmeisters Johannes Kreisler in zufälligen Makulaturblättern*, were published in 1820 and 1821, respectively; the final volume was never completed. This novel is available in English as *The Life and Opinions of Kater Murr, with the Fragmentary Biography of Kapellmeister Johannes Kreisler on Random Sheets of Scrap Paper*, vol. 2 of *Selected Writings of E. T. A. Hoffmann*, ed. and trans. Leonard J. Kent and Elizabeth C. Knight (University of Chicago Press, 1969).

43 Lewis, "Futurism, Magic and Life," *BLAST* I, jestingly affirms that the "Futurist theoretician should be a Professor of Hoffman [*sic.*] Romance, and attempt the manufacture of a perfect being" (132); Lewis, "The Art of the Great Race," *BLAST* II: *War Number*, ed. Lewis (July 1915; Santa Barbara: Black Sparrow, 1981), alluding to Goethe, *The Sorrows of Young Werther*, *Novels and Tales*, trans. R. D. Boylan (London: George Bell & Sons, 1901), argues that "Goethe, with a book, set free the welt-schmerzen of the Suicidal Teuton. The razors flashed all over the Teuton world. The pistol-smoke went up from every village" (70).

44 Robert Currie was the first to establish the influence of Hoffmann's *Murr* on Lewis's *Tarr*, in his *Genius: An Ideology of Literature* (New York: Shocken Books, 1974), 117–18, and especially in his, "Wyndham Lewis, E. T. A. Hoffmann, and *Tarr*," *Review of English Studies* 30.118 (1979): 169–81. My understanding of the relations between the works of Hoffmann and Lewis has also benefited from the comments of Loren Kruger.

45 For discussion of the role of money in Lewis's novel and its critique of Bohemian society, see Currie, "Wyndham Lewis, E. T. A. Hoffmann, and *Tarr*," 169; and Edwards, "Lewis's Myth of the Artist: from Bohemia to the Underground," 32–33.

46 Brown, *Intertextual Dynamics*, explains that "Kreisler is the artist as psychopath – the adult rogue male, at large, in a middle class order driven by machinery out of control. He is a bourgeois nightmare – lazy, rapistic, suicidal, parasitical, murderous, a creature of whim without any self-wisdom" (68).

47 Ian Duncan, "Towards a Modernist Poetic: Wyndham Lewis's Early Fiction," in *Wyndham Lewis: Letteratura/Pittura*, ed. Giovanni Cianci (Palermo: Sellerio, 1982), makes a similar argument about the rendering of identity in Lewis's early, posthumously published novel *Mrs Dukes' Million* (*c.* 1908–09): "[t]he original, authentic identity, certified by a narrative realm of moral absolutes, does not exist at all, is no more than the product of social convention and custom" (73). Compare Christine Hardegen, "Wyndham Lewis's First World War Art and Literature," in *Wyndham Lewis and the Art of Modern War*, ed. David Peters Corbett (Cambridge University Press, 1998), 68.

48 My formulation here has benefited from comments on an earlier version of this chapter in Mark Conroy, "'Wyndham Lewis' Authoritarian Tempta-

tion," *Southern Humanities Review* 30.1 (Winter 1996): 32–33 (n. 20).

49 Brown, *Intertextual Dynamics*, contends that "*Tarr* suggested to those alert to such things, a way of writing about maleness – and especially the experience of war" that "was neither stream-of-consciousness nor Lawrentian empathy but satiric distance and stylistic *grotesquerie*" (72). Toby Avard Foshay, *Wyndham Lewis and the Avant-Garde: The Politics of the Intellect* (Montreal: McGill Queen's, 1992) 44–78, provides an analysis of Lewis's complex satiric stance in *Tarr* and concurs that the "ending of *Tarr* . . . is clearly satirical, with Tarr pretending to an attainment and a liberation which he very clearly has not achieved" (64). David A. Wragg, "Aggression, Aesthetics, Modernity: Wyndham Lewis and the Fate of Art," in *Wyndham Lewis and the Art of Modern War*, also recognizes Tarr's failure to realize his ideals (207–08). Michael Nath, "Wyndham Lewis: A Review of the Thersitean Mode," *Wyndham Lewis Annual 1994*, ed. Edwards (Bath: Wyndham Lewis Society / Bath College of Higher Education, 1994): 10–14, gives, in my view, the most sophisticated account of the theoretical and aesthetic *aporias* of Lewis's satire in *Tarr*, focused especially on the relationship between Tarr and his creator. For a more general assessment of Lewis's objectifying satiric method, see Alan Munton, "Wyndham Lewis: War and Aggression," in *Wyndham Lewis and the Art of Modern War*, 18–20.

50 That Rose Fawcett shares the surname of Millicent Fawcett, president of the moderate National Union of Women's Suffrage Societies, may hint at a lurking sexism behind Lewis's name choice here: in this context, Fawcett carries associations of Englishness, bourgeois class status, and gradualist feminist reform.

51 Lewis was not the only English writer of the period to use fiction to probe and question stereotypes of Germanness, of course; E. M. Forster, *Howards End* (London: E. Arnold, 1910), for instance, had also attempted to move beyond these stereotypes.

52 My account of these conceptions of German character is informed by Modris Eksteins, *Rites of Spring: The Great War and the Birth of the Modern Age* (New York: Anchor, 1989), 55–94.

53 Currie, "Wyndham Lewis, E. T. A. Hoffmann, and *Tarr*," points out that "Lewisian Germans characteristically *conflated* these motifs" of Germanness (171).

54 O'Keeffe, "Afterword," 377.

55 Thanks to Ian Duncan for helping me clarify this point.

56 Ann L. Ardis, "Reading 'as a Modernist' / Denaturalizing Modernist Reading Protocols: Wyndham Lewis's *Tarr*," in *Rereading Modernism: New Directions in Feminist Criticism*, ed. Lisa Rado (New York: Garland, 1994), presents a provocative analysis of the formal innovations and ideological implications of Kreisler's rape of Bertha, which tracks the "tension generated and sustained" in the scene "by the juxtaposition of two different reading protocols" (384): on one hand, a "realist" protocol which prompts readers to object to the "violent content" the scene portrays; on the other, a

"modernist" protocol, "which invites readers to jettison whatever ethical objections they might have in order to admire the narratological brilliance of Lewis's stylized presentation of the rape" (385). I am less convinced than Ardis, however, that Lewis's "modernist" formal innovations in *Tarr* necessitate the "jettisoning" of ethical objections. Bonnie Kime Scott, *Refiguring Modernism*, 2 vols., vol. 2: *The Women of 1928* (Bloomington: Indiana University Press, 1995), also provides a feminist reading of *Tarr* which emphasizes Kreisler's rape of Bertha (104–07), though her account is briefer and, to my mind, less compelling than Ardis's. Brown, *Intertextual Dynamics*, contends, contra feminist readings of Lewis as an, at best, thoughtless, at worst, pathological sexist, that "*Tarr* is about twentieth-century male sexism, with all its anarchic lust, scorn and ultimate self-contempt" (69); it is a novel which anatomizes the dynamics and dangers inherent in that masculinist ideology: "[t]his is an all-male world in which the aggression of all the main figures is directly related to the patriarchal order and the gender roles it has constructed. Attempts to subvert that order only result in heightened aggression and a caricatural heightening of negative male qualities. The connection to war is implicit. This is the bourgeois order as Lewis sees it, and the events encode the implications of its fearful structure" (70–71).

57 Hugh Kenner, *Wyndham Lewis* (Norfolk, Conn.: New Directions, 1954).

58 Peter Bürger, "Dissolution of the Subject and the Hardened Self: Modernity and the Avant-Garde in Wyndham Lewis's Novel *Tarr*," in *The Decline of Modernism*, trans. Nicholas Walker (Cambridge: Polity Press, 1992), 127.

59 Bürger, "Dissolution of the Subject and the Hardened Self," defends this conventional chronology of Lewis's turn against modernism. In his attempt to account for *Tarr*'s persistent exclusion from the canon, Bürger explains that "Lewis's later leanings towards fascism have probably been less decisive in this connection (for as we know similar attitudes have not prevented the canonization of Pound's work) than the fact that with his essay collection *Time and Western Man* [1927; Santa Rosa: Black Sparrow, 1993] he appeared on the scene as an engaged, not to say enraged, critic of literary modernism" (127). Levenson, *Modernism and the Fate of Individuality*, also opposes this prevailing view.

60 Bürger, "Dissolution of the Subject and the Hardened Self," 128. Brown, *Intertextual Dynamics*, asserts, similarly, that "[d]uring the war and, indeed, almost until the publication of *Ulysses* and *The Waste Land* (1922), Wyndham Lewis remained master of the Modernist game" (67). Obviously, I do not agree with O'Keeffe, "Afterword," that Lewis achieved the "fragmentation of meaning that occurs in such key Modernist texts as *The Waste Land* and *The Cantos* . . . by default . . . as a result of the novel's compositional timespan" (382).

61 Jameson, *Fables of Aggression*, calls Tarr "the first and last fully positive figure in Lewis' work" (98), while Bürger, "Dissolution of the Subject and the Hardened Self," explains that Lewis's novel, "[i]n so far as [it] is concerned with Tarr . . . narrates the production of the artist himself" (128), a project

he believes Tarr eventually "accomplishe[s]" (129); Conroy, "Wyndham Lewis' Authoritarian Temptation," makes the point with a bit more restraint (26–27).

62 As far as I know, only Levenson, in *Modernism and the Fate of Individuality*, has recognized the breadth of Lewis's critical attack.

63 I have made this argument in an earlier version of this essay, "Anti-Individualism and the Fictions of National Character in Wyndham Lewis's *Tarr*," *Twentieth Century Literature* 40 (Summer 1994): 226–55, esp. 252.

Bibliography

WORKS PUBLISHED BEFORE 1920

Acton, Lord. "Political Thoughts on the Church," *The History of Freedom and Other Essays*, ed. J. Figgis and R. Laurence (London: Macmillan, 1909).

"The Aims of Futurism," *The Times* (21 March 1912): 2.

Aldington, Richard. "Blast," *Egoist* 1 (15 July 1914): 272–73.

Allen, J. W. "The Back of Beyond," *English Review* 1 (March 1909): 618–24.

Arnold, Matthew. *Culture and Anarchy* (1869; Cambridge University Press, 1990).

"The Function of Criticism at the Present Time," in *Essays in Criticism*, First Series, ed. Sister Thomas Marion Hoctor (1875; University of Chicago Press, 1968), 8–30.

"The Literary Influence of Academies," in *Essays in Criticism, First Series*, ed. Sister Thomas Marion Hoctor (1875; University of Chicago Press, 1968), 31–52.

Baden-Powell, Robert Stephenson Smyth. *Scouting for Boys: A Handbook for Instruction in Good Citizenship* (London: Horace Cox, 1908).

Bagman, Holbein. "Englishmen and Aesthetic Sensibility," *New Age* 6 (18 November 1909): 59.

Bax, E. Belfort. "Bergson," *New Age* 9 (20 July 1911): 280–81.

[Beith, Ian Hay] Hay, Ian. *The First Hundred Thousand: Being the Unofficial Chronicle of a Unit of "K (1)"* (Boston: Houghton & Mifflin, [1915]).

Bell, Clive. *Peace at Once* (Manchester: National Labour Press, [1915]).

[Bennett, Arnold] Tonson, Jacob. "Books and Persons," *New Age* 8 (8 December 1910): 135.

Bennett, Ernest W. *With the Turks in Tripoli* (London: Methuen, 1912).

Boccioni, Umberto, and Carlo D. Carrà, Luigi Russolo, Giacomo Balla, Gino Severini. "Futurist Painting: Technical Manifesto" (11 April 1910), *Exhibition of Works of the Italian Futurist Painters* (London: Sackville Gallery, 1912); rpt. in *Futurism*, ed. Joshua C. Taylor (New York: Museum of Modern Art, 1961), 125–27.

Booth, Charles. *Life and Labour of the People of London* (1880–1903; London: Macmillan, 1902–03).

Bridges, Robert. "A Holy War" [letter], *The Times* (2 September 1914): 10.

"Dunstone Hill," *Poetical Works of Robert Bridges* (London: H. Milford, 1914), 354–55.
"Britain's Destiny and Duty: Declaration by Authors, A Righteous War," *The Times* (18 September 1914): 3.
Brooke, Rupert. "Peace," *The Collected Poems of Rupert Brooke: With a Memoir* (London: Sidgwick & Jackson, 1918), 5.
"The Soldier," *The Collected Poems of Rupert Brooke: With a Memoir* (London: Sidgwick & Jackson, 1918), 9.
Carter, Huntly. "Blaspheming Creation," *New Freewoman* 1 (1 December 1913): 238.
"The 'Blue Bird' and Bergson in Paris," *New Age* 9 (11 May 1911): 43–45.
"The Curve of Individualism," *Egoist* 1 (1 April 1915): 59–60.
"The Independants and the New Intuition in Paris," *New Age* 9 (25 May 1911): 82–83.
"Letters from Abroad: The New Idea of Dramatic Action. I," *New Age* 9 (20 July 1911): 271–72.
"Letters from Abroad: The Post-Expressionists," *New Age* 9 (26 October 1911): 617.
Churchill, Winston [Valediction for Brooke]. *The Times* (26 April 1915); rpt. in Edward Marsh, "Memoir," in Brooke, *The Collected Poems of Rupert Brooke: With a Memoir* (London: Sidgwick & Jackson, 1918), clviii–clix.
Collins Baker, C. H. "Futurist Academics," *Saturday Review* (9 March 1912): 300–01.
Conway, Martin. *The Crowd in Peace and War* (New York: Longmans, Green, 1915).
Cook, E. Wake. [Letter], *New Age* 10 (30 November 1911): 119.
Cournos, John. "Gaudier-Brzeska's Art," *Egoist* 2 (1 September 1915): 137–38.
Davies, W. H. "How It Feels to Be Out of Work," *English Review* 1 (December 1908): 168–70.
Dilke, Charles W. "Foreign Affairs," *English Review* 3 (October 1909): 495–500.
Dostoyevsky, Fyodor. "An Honest Thief," trans. Constance Garnett, *English Review* 2 (May 1909): 215–30.
Douglas, Norman. "The Island of Typhoëus," *English Review* 1 (February 1909): 398–419.
Eder, M. D. "On German Spies," *New Age* 6 (20 January 1910): 271–72.
Ellis, Havelock. *Study of British Genius* (London: Hurst & Blackett, 1904).
Ford, Ford Madox. "Literary Portraits–XLIII: Mr. Wyndham Lewis and 'Blast,'" *Outlook* 34 (4 July 1914): 15–16.
The Critical Attitude (London: Duckworth, 1911).
"The Old Houses of Flanders," *BLAST* II: *War Number*, ed. Wyndham Lewis (1915; Santa Barbara: Black Sparrow, 1981): 37.
"On a Notice of "BLAST," *Outlook* 36 (31 July 1915): 143–44.
"On Impressionism," *Poetry and Drama* 2 (2 June 1914): 167–75.
"On Impressionism (Second Article)," *Poetry and Drama* 2 (December 1914): 323–34.

The Spirit of the People: an Analysis of the English Mind (London: Alston Rivers, 1907).
When Blood is Their Argument: An Analysis of Prussian Culture (London: Hodder and Stoughton, 1915).
[Ford, Ford Madox]. "The Critical Attitude: Blue Water and the Thin Red Line," *English Review* 2 (April 1909): 135–44.
"The Critical Attitude: On the Objection to the Critical Attitude," *English Review* 4 (February 1910): 531–42.
"The Functions of the Arts in the Republic. IV. The Plastic Arts" *English Review* 1 (March 1909): 795–98.
"The Functions of the Arts in the Republic. I. Literature," *English Review* 1 (December 1908): 157–60.
"Political and Diplomatic: The Unemployed," *English Review* 1 (December 1908): 161–64.
"The Work of W. H. Hudson," *English Review* 2 (April 1909): 157–64.
Forster, E. M. *Howards End* (London: E. Arnold, 1910).
Fry, Roger. "Art: The Futurists," *Nation* (9 March 1912): 945–46.
Galton, Francis. *Hereditary Genius* (1869; New York: Horizon Press, 1952).
"Hereditary Talent and Character," *MacMillan's Magazine* 12 (London, 1865): 318–27; rpt. in *Images of Race*, ed. Michael D. Biddiss (New York: Holmes and Meier, 1979), 57–71.
Gaudier-Brzeska, Henri. "Vortex Gaudier-Brzeska (Written from the Trenches)," *BLAST* II: *War Number*, ed. Wyndham Lewis (1915; Santa Barbara: Black Sparrow, 1981): 33–34.
Gleichen, Edward, ed. *The Chronology of the Great War* (1918–20; London: Greenhill Books, 1988).
Goethe, Johann Wolfgang von. *Novels and Tales*, trans. R. D. Boylan (London: George Bell & Sons, 1901).
Graham, R. B. Cunninghame. "Andorra," *English Review* 1 (January 1909): 205–22.
"Aspects of the Social Question," *English Review* 1 (December 1908): 165–68.
"Spain's Future is in Spain," *English Review* 3 (September 1909): 335–42.
Hennings, C. R. "Our German Cousins and the English Nation," *New Age* 6, Supplement (20 January 1910): 3.
Henry, Leigh. "Liberations: Studies of Individuality in Contemporary Music. II. Balilla Pratella and Futurist Music," *Egoist* 1 (15 April 1914): 147–49.
Hobson, J. A. "The Extension of Liberalism," *English Review* 3 (November 1909): 673–86.
Hoffmann, E. T. A. "Kreisleriana," in *Fantasy Pieces in Callot's Manner: Pages from the Diary of a Traveling Romantic*, trans. Joseph M. Hayse (1814–15; Schenectady: Union College Press, 1996), 15–53.
The Life and Opinions of Kater Murr, with the fragmentary biography of Kapellmeister Johannes Kreisler on Random Sheets of Scrap Paper (1820–21), vol. 2 of Hoffmann, *Selected Writings of E. T. A. Hoffmann*, 2. vols., ed. and trans., Leonard J. Kent and Elizabeth C. Knight (University of Chicago Press, 1969).

Hudson, W. H. "Goldfinches at Ryme Instrinsica," *English Review* 2 (May 1909): 246–54.

"Stonehenge," *English Review* 1 (December 1908): 60–68.

Hulme, T. E. "Notes on Bergson 1," *New Age* 9 (19 October 1911): 587–88; rpt. Hulme, *Further Speculations*, ed. Samuel Hynes (Minneapolis: University of Minnesota Press, 1955), 28–30.

Joyce, James. *A Portrait of the Artist as a Young Man* (1916; New York: Penguin, 1976).

"Junkerism in Art: The London Group at the Goupil Gallery," *The Times* (10 March 1915): 8.

Kennedy, J[ohn]. M[cFarland]. *English Literature, 1880–1905* (London: S. Swift and Co., 1912).

"The House of Lords," *New Age* 9 (31 August 1911): 417.

The Quintessence of Nietzsche (London: T. W. Laurie, 1909).

"Tory Democracy: Philosophy and Politics," *New Age* 9 (10 August 1911): 341.

"Tory Democracy: The Influence of Philosophers," *New Age* 9 (1 June 1911): 100.

"When a Poet Dies," *New Age* 10 (25 April 1912): 609–10.

[Kennedy, J. M.] Verdad, S. "Foreign Affairs," *New Age* 9 (25 May 1911): 76.

"Foreign Affairs," *New Age* 9 (13 July 1911): 243.

"Foreign Affairs," *New Age* 9 (3 August 1911): 315.

"Foreign Affairs," *New Age* 9 (28 September 1911): 509–10.

"Foreign Affairs," *New Age* 10 (25 April 1912): 605.

"Foreign Affairs," *New Age* 11 (3 October 1912): 533.

Kitson, Arthur. "The War and the Prophets" [letter], *New Age* 15 (3 September 1914): 428–29.

K[onody]., P. G. "The Italian Futurists: Nightmare Exhibition at the Sackville Gallery," *Pall Mall Gazette* (1 March 1912): 5.

Kruchenykh, Alexei [Aleksander]. "New Ways of the Word (the Language of the Future, Death of Symbolism)" (1913), rpt. in *Russian Futurism through its Manifestos, 1912–1928*, ed. Anna Lawton, trans. Lawton and Herbert Eagle (Ithaca: Cornell University Press, 1988), 69–77.

Lapworth, Charles. *Tripoli and Young Italy: Being Some Experiences of a War-Correspondent with the Italians in Tripoli* (London: S. Swift and Co., 1912).

Lawrence, D. H. *Sons and Lovers* (1913; New York: Penguin, 1968).

Le Queux, William. *German Atrocities: A Record of Shameless Deeds* (London: G. Newnes, 1914).

The Invasion of 1910 (London: Eveleigh Nash, 1906).

Lewis, Wyndham. "Automobilism," *New Weekly* 2 (20 June 1914): 13; rpt. Lewis, *Creatures of Habit and Creatures of Change: Essays on Art, Literature and Society 1914–1956*, ed. Paul Edwards (Santa Rosa: Black Sparrow, 1989), 33–4.

"Constantinople Our Star," *BLAST* II: *War Number*, ed. Lewis (1915; Santa Barbara: Black Sparrow, 1981): 11.

"Enemy of the Stars," *BLAST* I: *Review of the Great English Vortex*, ed. Lewis (1914; Santa Barbara: Black Sparrow, 1981): 51–85.

"Futurism, Magic and Life," *BLAST* I: Review of the Great English Vortex, ed. Lewis (1914; Santa Barbara: Black Sparrow, 1981): 132–35.
"A Later Arm than Barbarity," *Outlook* 34 (5 September 1914): 298–99.
"Les Saltimbanques," *English Review* 3 (Aug. 1909): 76–87, rpt. Lewis, *The Complete Wild Body*, ed. Bernard Lafourcade (Santa Barbara: Black Sparrow, 1982), 237–47.
"A Man of the Week: Marinetti," *New Weekly* 1 (30 May 1914), 328–29; rpt. Lewis, *Creatures of Habit and Creatures of Change: Essays on Art, Literature and Society 1914–1956*, ed. Paul Edwards (Santa Rosa: Black Sparrow, 1989), 29–32.
"Modern Caricature and Impressionism," *BLAST* II: *War Number*, ed. Lewis (1915; Santa Barbara: Black Sparrow, 1981): 79.
"Our Wild Body," *New Age* 2 (5 May 1910): 8–10; rpt. Lewis, *The Complete Wild Body*, ed. Bernard Lafourcade (Santa Barbara: Black Sparrow, 1982), 251–56.
"Some Innkeepers and Bestre," *English Review* 2 (June 1909): 471–84, rpt. Lewis, *The Complete Wild Body*, ed. Bernard Lafourcade (Santa Barbara: Black Sparrow, 1982), 221–33.
Tarr: The 1918 Version, ed. Paul O'Keeffe (Santa Barbara: Black Sparrow, 1990).
"The Art of the Great Race," *BLAST* II: *War Number*, ed. Lewis (1915; Santa Barbara: Black Sparrow, 1981): 70–72.
"The Crowd Master," *BLAST* II: *War Number*, ed. Lewis (1915; Santa Barbara: Black Sparrow, 1981): 94–102.
"The European War and Great Communities," *BLAST* II: *War Number*, ed. Lewis (1915; Santa Barbara: Black Sparrow, 1981): 15–16.
"The Exploitation of Blood," *BLAST* II: *War Number*, ed. Lewis (1915; Santa Barbara: Black Sparrow, 1981): 24.
"The God of Sport and Blood," *BLAST* II: *War Number*, ed. Lewis (1915; Santa Barbara: Black Sparrow, 1981): 9–10.
"The London Group," *BLAST* II: *War Number*, ed. Lewis (1915; Santa Barbara: Black Sparrow, 1981): 77–79.
"The 'Pole,'" *English Review* 2 (May 1909): 255–65, rpt. Lewis, *The Complete Wild Body*, ed. Bernard Lafourcade (Santa Barbara: Black Sparrow, 1982), 209–18.
[Lewis, Wyndham]. "Editorial," *BLAST* II: *War Number*, ed. Lewis (1915; Santa Barbara: Black Sparrow, 1981): 5–6.
"Long Live the Vortex!," *BLAST* I: *Review of the Great English Vortex*, ed. Lewis (1914; Santa Barbara: Black Sparrow, 1981): 7–8.
"Manifesto" [I], *BLAST* I: *Review of the Great English Vortex*, ed. Lewis (1914; Santa Barbara: Black Sparrow, 1981): 9–28.
"Manifesto" [II], *BLAST* I: *Review of the Great English Vortex*, ed. Lewis (1914; Santa Barbara: Black Sparrow, 1981): 30–43
Lewis, Wyndham, ed. *BLAST* I: *Review of the Great English Vortex* (1914; Santa Barbara: Black Sparrow, 1981).

BLAST II: *War Number* (1915; Santa Barbara: Black Sparrow, 1981).

Lewis, Wyndham, *et al.* "Futurism" [letter], *Observer* (14 July 1914), rpt. in Lewis, *The Letters of Wyndham Lewis*, ed. W. K. Rose (Norfolk, Conn.: New Directions, 1963), 62.

Lichtenberger, Henri. *The Gospel of Superman: The Philosophy of Friedrich Nietzsche*, trans. J. M. Kennedy (Edinburgh: T. N. Foulis, 1910).

"London and the Coming of War: Impressive Midnight Scene," *The Times* (5 August 1914): 9.

M[anson], J. B. "The Italian Futurists and the X-Rays in Art," *Outlook* (23 March 1912): 439–40.

Marinetti, F. T. *La Bataille de Tripoli* (Milan: Edizioni Futuriste, 1912).

"Initial Manifesto of Futurism" (20 February 1909), *Exhibition of Works of the Italian Futurist Painters* (London: Sackville Gallery, 1912), rpt. in *Futurism*, ed. Joshua C. Taylor (New York: Museum of Modern Art, 1961), 124–25.

"Italian Tripoli" [Secondo Manifesto Politico] (11 October 1911), rpt. in *Archivi del Futurismo*, ed. Maria Drudi Gambillo and Teresa Fiori, 2 vols. (Rome: De Luca, 1958–62), I:31–32.

"Primo Manifesto Politico" (1909), rpt. in *Archivi del Futurismo*, ed. Maria Drudi Gambillo and Teresa Fiori, 2 vols. (Rome: De Luca, 1958–62), I:31.

"Speech at the Lyceum Club for Women in London," rpt. *Marinetti: Selected Writings*, ed. R.W. Flint, trans. Flint and Arthur A. Coppotelli (New York: Farrar, Straus and Giroux, 1972), 59–65.

Marinetti and C. R. W. Nevinson, "Vital English Art," *Observer* 6 (7 June 1914).

Marsden, Dora. "Quid Pro Quo," *Egoist* I (15 August 1914): 301–3.

"Views and Comments," *Egoist* I (2 March 1914): 83–85.

"Views and Comments," *New Freewoman* I (15 Dec. 1913): 244–45.

Marsh, Edward. "Memoir," in Brooke, *The Collected Poems of Rupert Brooke: With a Memoir* (London: Sidgwick & Jackson, 1918), xi–clix.

M[arwood]., A[rthur]. "British India," *English Review* I (Feb. 1909): 569–75.

"A Complete Actuarial Scheme for Insuring John Doe Against All the Vicissitudes of Life," *English Review* I (December 1908): 171–75.

M[asterman]., C. F. G. "Reviews," *Nation* 16 (27 March 1915): 838–40.

McCullagh, Francis. *Italy's War for a Desert* (London: Herbert and Daniel, 1912).

McDougall, William. *An Introduction to Social Psychology* (1908; Boston: J. W. Luce, 1911).

Psychology: The Study of Behaviour (London: Williams and Norgate, 1912).

[McNeile, Herman Cyril] Sapper. *Sergeant Michael Cassidy RE* (London: Hodder and Stoughton, 1915).

Money, L. G. Chiozza. *Riches and Poverty* (1905; London: Methuen, 1906).

Monro, Harold. "Varia," *Poetry and Drama* 2 (September 1914): 250–53.

Murry, John Middleton. "Bergson in Paris" [letter], *New Age* 9 (1 June 1911): 115–16.

Nevinson, Henry W. "Notes on the Balkans, with a Table," *English Review* I (December 1908): 182–87.

"Women's Vote and Men," *English Review* 3 (November, 1909): 687–96.

"The New Crazy 'Exploding' Pictures by 'Art Anarchists,'" *The Illustrated London News* (20 March 1912): n.p., rpt. *Futurism and Futurisms*, ed. Pontus Hulten, trans. various hands (New York: Abbeville, 1986), 572.
"New English Art Club. Three Remarkable Works," *Morning Post* (2 Dec. 1914): 3.
Nietzsche, Friedrich. *The Dawn of Day*, trans. J. M. Kennedy (London: G. Allen & Unwin, 1911).
On the Future of Our Educational Institutions; Homer and Classical Philology, trans. J. M. Kennedy (Edinburgh: T. N. Foulis, 1909).
Norman, C. H. "A Study in Jingoism," *New Age* 6 (6 January 1910): 223.
[Orage, Alfred] C., R. H. "Readers and Writers," *New Age* 15 (10 September 1914): 449.
"Readers and Writers," *New Age* 15 (8 October 1914): 548–49.
O'Sullivan, Vincent. "Paris as a Pleasure Resort," *New Age* 9 (15 June 1911): 161–63.
Pain, Barry. "The Kaiser and God," *The Times* (28 Aug. 1914): 9.
Pankhurst, Christabel. *The Great Scourge and How to End It* (1913) rpt. in *Suffrage and the Pankhursts*, ed. Jane Marcus (London: Routledge, 1987), 187–240.
Phillips, Stephen. "Views and Reviews," *Poetry Review* 5 (July 1914): 48.
Pickthall, Marmaduke. "Teuton and Slav: A Word in Season," *New Age* 15 (20 August 1914): 366–67.
Pound, Ezra. "Affirmations II. Vorticism," *New Age* 16 (14 January 1915): 277–78.
"Et Faim Sallir Le Loup Des Boys," *BLAST* II: *War Number*, ed. Wyndham Lewis (1915; Santa Barbara: Black Sparrow, 1981): 22.
"Present Day Criticism," *New Age* 10 (14 December 1911): 158.
Reason, Will. *Poverty* (London: Headley Brothers, 1909).
"Review [of *BLAST*]", *The Morning Post*, rpt. *BLAST* II: *War Number*, ed. Wyndham Lewis (1915; Santa Barbara: Black Sparrow, 1981): 104.
Reynolds, Stephen. *A Poor Man's House* (1908; London: John Cape, 1928).
Richmond, W. B. "Post-Impressionists" [letter], *Morning Post* (16 November 1910): 5.
Rolleston, T. W. "Literature and Politics in Modern Germany," *Hibbert Journal* 13 (Oct. 1914): 82–88.
Romney. "Military Notes," *New Age* 11 (4 July 1912): 222.
Rowntree, B. Seebohm. *Poverty: A Study of Town Life* (1901; London: Macmillan, 1902).
Sa[u]nders, Helen. "A Vision of Mud," *BLAST* II: *War Number*, ed. Wyndham Lewis (1915; Santa Barbara: Black Sparrow, 1981): 73–74.
Sera, Leone. *On the Tracks of Life: The Immorality of Morality*, trans. J. M. Kennedy and Oscar Levy (London: J. Lane, 1909).
Shaw, George Bernard. "Common Sense About the War," War Supplement, *New Statesman* 4 (14 November 1914), rpt. in Shaw, *What I Really Wrote about the War*, vol. 21, *The Collected Works of Bernard Shaw*, 30 vols. (New York: Wm. H. Wise & Co., 1930–32), 23–115.
Sickert, Walter. "The Futurist 'Devil-among-the-Tailors,'" *English Review* 10

(April 1912): 147–51.
[Squire, J. C.] Eagle, Solomon. "Books in General," *New Statesman* 3 (4 July 1914): 406.
Stirner, Max. *The Ego and his Own: The Case of the Individual Against Authority*, trans. Steven T. Byington (1844; New York: Benjamin R. Tucker, 1907)
Titterton, W. R. "Why Not Surrender to Germany?" *New Age* 6 (14 April 1910): 562–63.
Tolstoi, Leo. "The Raid (A Volunteer's Story. 1852)," trans. Constance Garnett, *English Review* 1 (December 1908): 69–80; (January 1909): 248–60.
Trotter, Wilfred. "Herd Instinct and its Bearing on the Psychology of Civilised Man," *Sociological Review* 1 (1908): 227–48.
Instincts of the Herd in Peace and War (1916; London: T. Fisher Unwin, 1923).
"Sociological Applications of the Psychology of Herd Instinct," *Sociological Review* 2 (1909): 36–54.
Vane, Sir Francis. "Italian Patriotism and a Festa," *New Age* 12 (14 November 1912): 34–35.
Wallas, Graham. *Human Nature in Politics* (1908; Boston: Houghton & Mifflin, 1909).
Webb, Sydney. "The Economic Aspects of Poor Law Reform," *English Review* 3 (October 1909): 501–16.
Wells, H. G. *Tono-Bongay* (1909; London: Collins, 1953).
"Why Britain Went to War," in *The War That Will End War* (New York: Duffield & Co., 1914), 9–15.
West, Rebecca. "Tarr," *Nation* 23 (10 August 1918): 506–8; rpt. in *Agenda* 7/8 (Autumn-Winter, 1969): 67–69.

WORKS PUBLISHED 1920 AND AFTER

Adamson, Walter. *Avant-Garde Florence: From Modernism to Fascism* (Cambridge Mass.: Harvard University Press, 1993).
Anderson, Benedict. *Imagined Communities: Reflections on the Origin and Spread of Nationalism* (London: Verso, 1983).
Anderson, Stuart. *Race and Rapprochement: Anglo-Saxonism and Anglo-American Relations, 1895–1904* (East Brunswick: Farleigh Dickinson University Press, 1981).
Ardis, Ann L. "Reading 'as a Modernist' / Denaturalizing Modernist Reading Protocols: Wyndham Lewis's *Tarr*," in *Rereading Modernism: New Directions in Feminist Criticism*, ed. Lisa Rado (New York: Garland, 1994), 373–90.
Ayers, David. *Wyndham Lewis and Western Man* (New York: St. Martins, 1992).
Balibar, Etienne and Immanuel Wallerstein. *Race, Nation, Class: Ambiguous Identities.*, trans. Chris Turner (1988; London: Verso, 1991).
Barraclough, Geoffrey. *From Agadir to Armageddon: The Anatomy of a Crisis* (New York: Holmes and Meier, 1982)
Bhabha, Homi, ed. *Nation and Narration* (London: Routledge, 1990).
Biddiss, Michael D., ed. *Images of Race* (New York: Holmes and Meier, 1979).

Blum, Cinzia Sartini. *The Other Modernism: F. T. Marinetti's Futurist Fiction of Power* (Berkeley: University of California Press, 1996).
Booth, Allyson. *Postcards from the Trenches: Negotiating the Space between Modernism and the First World War* (Oxford University Press, 1996).
Brantlinger, Patrick. "*Heart of Darkness:* Anti-Imperialism, Racism or Impressionism?," *Criticism*,. 4 (Fall 1985): 363–85
Brooker, Peter and Peter Widdowson. "A Literature for England," *Englishness: Politics and Culture 1880–1920.*, ed. Robert Colls and Philip Dodd (London: Croom Helm, 1986), 116–63.
Brown, Dennis. *Intertextual Dynamics within the Literary Group–Joyce, Lewis, Pound, and Eliot: The Men of 1914* (London: Macmillan, 1990).
Bullen, J. B., ed. *Post-Impressionists in England* (London: Routledge, 1988).
Bürger, Peter. "Dissolution of the Subject and the Hardened Self: Modernity and the Avant-Garde in Wyndham Lewis's Novel *Tarr,*" in *The Decline of Modernism*, trans. Nicholas Walker (Cambridge: Polity Press, 1992), 127–36.
The Theory of the Avant-Garde, trans. Michael Shaw (1974; Minneapolis: University of Minnesota Press, 1987).
Casillo, Robert. *The Genealogy of Demons: Anti-Semitism, Fascism, and the Myths of Ezra Pound* (Evanston: Northwestern University Press, 1988).
Cendrars, Blaise. *Inédits secrets*, ed. Miriam Cendrars, vol. 16, *Oeuvres complètes*, 16 vols., ed. Raymond Dumay and Nino Frank (Paris: Club français du livre, 1968–71).
Chase, William. *The Political Identities of Ezra Pound and T. S. Eliot* (Stanford University Press, 1973).
Cheyette, Bryan. *Constructions of "the Jew" in English Literature and Society: Racial Representations, 1875–1945* (Cambridge University Press, 1993).
Cianci, Giovanni. "Futurism and the English Avant-Garde: The Early Pound Between Imagism and Vorticism," *Arbeiten aus Anglistik und Amerikanistik* 1 (1981): 17–27.
"A Man at War: Lewis's Vital Geometries," in *Volcanic Heaven: Essays on Wyndham Lewis's Painting and Writing*, ed. Paul Edwards (Santa Rosa: Black Sparrow, 1996), 11–24.
ed. *Wyndham Lewis: Letteratura/Pittura* (Palermo: Sellerio, 1982).
Clark, Bruce. *Dora Marsden and Early Modernism: Gender, Individualism, Science* (Ann Arbor: University of Michigan Press, 1996).
Clifford, James. "On Ethnographic Self-Fashioning: Conrad and Malinowski," in *The Predicament of Culture: Twentieth-Century Ethnography, Literature, and Art* (Cambridge, Mass.: Harvard University Press, 1988), 92–113.
Colls, Robert. "Englishness and the Political Culture," in *Englishness: Politics and Culture 1880–1920*, ed. Robert Colls and Philip Dodd (London: Croom Helm, 1986), 29–61.
and Philip Dodd, eds. *Englishness: Politics and Culture 1880–1920* (London: Croom Helm, 1986).
Conroy, Mark. "Wyndham Lewis' Authoritarian Temptation," *Southern Humanities Review* 30.1 (Winter 1996): 21–33.

Corbett, David Peters. "Introduction: 'the Subject of Modern War,'" in *Wyndham Lewis and the Art of Modern War*, ed. Corbett (Cambridge University Press, 1998), 1–13.

ed. *Wyndham Lewis and the Art of Modern War* (Cambridge University Press, 1998).

Cork, Richard. *A Bitter Truth: Avant-Garde Art and the Great War* (New Haven: Yale University Press, 1994).

Vorticism and Abstract Art in the First Machine Age, 2 vols. (London: Gordon Fraser, 1976).

Cox, C. B. and A. E. Dyson, eds. *The Twentieth Century Mind: History, Ideas, and Literature in Britain*, 3 vols., vol. 1, *1900–1918* (Oxford University Press, 1972).

Crawford, Robert. *Devolving English Literature* (Oxford University Press, 1992).

Crook, Paul. *Darwinism, War and History: The Debate over the Biology of War from the* Origin of Species *to the First World War* (Cambridge University Press, 1994).

Currie, Robert. *Genius: An Ideology of Literature* (New York: Shocken Books, 1974).

"Wyndham Lewis, E. T. A. Hoffmann, and *Tarr*," *Review of English Studies* 30.118 (1979): 169–91.

Dangerfield, George. *The Strange Death of Liberal England* (1935; New York: G. P. Putnam, 1980).

Darracott, Joseph. *The First World War in Posters: From the Imperial War Museum, London* (New York: Dover, 1974).

Dasenbrock, Reed Way. "Anatomies of Internationalism in *Tarr* and *Howards End*," typescript.

The Literary Vorticism of Ezra Pound and Wyndham Lewis: Towards the Condition of Painting (Baltimore: Johns Hopkins University Press, 1985).

DiBattista, Maria and Lucy McDiarmid, eds. *High and Low Moderns: Literature and Culture, 1889–1938* (Oxford University Press, 1996).

Dodd, Philip. "Englishness and the National Culture," in *Englishness: Politics and Culture 1880–1920*, ed. Robert Colls and Philip Dodd (London: Croom Helm, 1986), 1–28.

Duncan, Ian. "Towards a Modernist Poetic: Wyndham Lewis's Early Fiction," in *Wyndham Lewis: Letteratura/Pittura*, ed. Giovanni Cianci (Palermo: Sellerio, 1982), 67–85.

Eagleton, Terry. *The Ideology of the Aesthetic* (Oxford: Basil Blackwell, 1990).

Fredric Jameson, and Edward Said. *Nationalism, Colonialism, and Literature* (Minneapolis: University of Minnesota Press, 1990).

Edwards, Paul. "Lewis's Myth of the Artist: from Bohemia to the Underground," in *Volcanic Heaven: Essays on Wyndham Lewis's Painting and Writing*, ed. Edwards (Santa Rosa: Black Sparrow, 1996), 25–39.

"'The Strange Actor' and 'Semitic Discourse,'" *Wyndham Lewis Annual 1997*, ed. Edwards (Bath: Wyndham Lewis Society, 1997): 32–38.

Wyndham Lewis: Art and War (London: Lund Humphries, 1992).

ed. *Volcanic Heaven: Essays on Wyndham Lewis's Painting and Writing* (Santa Rosa: Black Sparrow, 1996).

Wyndham Lewis Annual 1994 (Bath: Wyndham Lewis Society / Bath College of

Higher Education).

Wyndham Lewis Annual 1997 (Bath: Wyndham Lewis Society, 1997).

Eksteins, Modris. *Rites of Spring: The Great War and the Birth of the Modern Age* (1989: New York: Doubleday, 1990).

Ferguson, John. *The Arts in Britain in World War I* (London: Stainer & Bell, 1980).

Ferrall, Charles. "'Melodramas of Modernity': The Interaction of Vorticism and Futurism before the Great War," *University of Toronto Quarterly* 63 (Winter 1993/94): 347–68.

"*The New Age* and the Emergence of Reactionary Modernism Before the Great War," *Modern Fiction Studies* 38 (Autumn 1992): 653–67.

Ford, Ford Madox. *Return to Yesterday* (New York: Horace Liveright, 1932).

Thus to Revisit (1921; New York: Octagon, 1966).

Foshay, Toby Avard. *Wyndham Lewis and the Avant-Garde: The Politics of the Intellect* (Montreal: McGill Queen's, 1992).

Fox, C. J. and Robert Edward Murray, "The War Fiction," in *Volcanic Heaven: Essays on Wyndham Lewis's Painting and Writing*, ed. Paul Edwards (Santa Rosa: Black Sparrow, 1996), 65–85.

Fussell, Paul. *The Great War and Modern Memory* (1975; Oxford University Press, 1979).

Gambillo, Maria Drudi, and Teresa Fiori, eds. *Archivi del Futurismo*, 2 vols. (Rome: De Luca, 1958–62).

Gellner, Ernest. *Nations and Nationalism* (Ithaca: Cornell University Press, 1983).

Gentile, Emilio. "The Conquest of Modernity: From Modernist Nationalism to Fascism," trans. Lawrence Rainey, *Modernism/Modernity* 1 (September 1994): 55–87.

Gibbons, Tom. "Modernism and Reactionary Politics," *Journal of Modern Literature* 3.5 (July 1974): 1140–57.

Gilbert, Geoff. "Shellshock, Anti-Semitism, and the Agency of the Avant-Garde," in *Wyndham Lewis and the Art of Modern War*, ed. David Peters Corbett (Cambridge University Press, 1998), 78–97.

Gilbert, Sandra M. and Susan Gubar. *No Man's Land: The Place of the Woman Writer in the Twentieth Century*, 3 vols. (New Haven: Yale University Press, 1988–1993).

Gilman, Sander. *Difference and Pathology: Stereotypes of Sexuality, Race and Madness* (Ithaca: Cornell University Press, 1985).

GoGwilt, Chris. "Broadcasting News from Nowhere: R. B. Cunninghame Graham and the Geography of Politics in the 1890s," in *High and Low Moderns: Literature and Culture, 1889–1938*, ed. Maria DiBattista and Lucy McDiarmid (Oxford University Press, 1996), 235–54.

Graver, David. "Vorticist Performance and Aesthetic Turbulence in *Enemy of the Stars*," *PMLA* 107 (May 1992): 482–96.

Guy, Josephine M. *The British Avant-Garde* (London: Harvester Wheatsheaf, 1991).

Hall, Stuart, and Bill Schwarz. "State and Society, 1880–1930," *The Hard Road to Renewal: Thatcherism and the Crisis of the Left* (London: Verso, 1988), 95–122.

Halperin, Joan Ungersma. *Félix Fénéon, Aesthete and Anarchist in Fin-de-Siècle Paris* (New Haven: Yale University Press, 1988).

Hansen, Miriam. "T. E. Hulme, Mercenary of Modernism, or, Fragments of Avantgarde Sensibility in Pre-World War I Britain," *ELH* 47 (1980): 355–85.

Hardegen, Christine. "Wyndham Lewis's First World War Art and Literature," in *Wyndham Lewis and the Art of Modern War*, ed. David Peters Corbett (Cambridge University Press, 1998), 58–77.

Hardie, Martin and Arthur K. Sabin. *War Posters Issued by Belligerent and Neutral Nations 1914–1919* (London: A. & C. Black, 1920).

Hardy, Florence Emily. *The Later Years of Thomas Hardy* (London: Macmillan, 1930).

Hearnshaw, L. S. "Psychology," in *The Twentieth Century Mind: History, Ideas, and Literature in Britain*, vol. 1, *1900–1918*, ed. C. B. Cox and A. E. Dyson (Oxford University Press, 1972), 225–47.

Hewitt, Andrew. *Fascist Modernism: Aesthetics, Politics, and the Avant-Garde* (Stanford University Press, 1993).

Hobsbawm, E. J. *The Age of Empire 1875–1914* (New York: Random House, 1987).

Hoffmann, E. T. A. *Fantasy Pieces in Callot's Manner: Pages from the Diary of A Traveling Romantic*, trans. Joseph M. Hayse (1814–15; Schenectady: Union College Press, 1996).

Selected Writings of E. T. A. Hoffmann, 2 vols., ed. and trans., Leonard J. Kent and Elizabeth C. Knight (University of Chicago Press, 1969).

Holton, Bob. *British Syndicalism: 1900–1914: Myths and Realities* (London: Pluto Press, 1976).

Howkins, Alun. "The Discovery of Rural England," in *Englishness: Politics and Culture 1880–1920*, ed. Robert Colls and Philip Dodd (London: Croom Helm, 1986), 62–88.

Hughes, H. Stuart. *Consciousness and Society: The Reorientation of European Social Thought, 1890–1930* (1961; New York: Vintage, 1977).

Hulme, T. E. *Further Speculations*, ed. Samuel Hynes (Minneapolis: University of Minnesota Press, 1955).

Hulten, Pontus, ed. *Futurism and Futurisms*, trans. various hands (New York: Abbeville, 1986).

Huyssen, Andreas. *After the Great Divide: Modernism, Mass Culture, Postmodernism* (Bloomington: Indiana University Press, 1986).

Hynes, Samuel. *The Edwardian Turn of Mind* (1968; London: Pimlico, 1991).

A War Imagined: The First World War and English Culture (New York: Macmillan, 1990).

Jameson, Fredric. *Fables of Aggression: Wyndham Lewis, the Modernist as Fascist* (Berkeley: University of California Press, 1979).

Joll, James. "F. T. Marinetti: Futurism and Fascism," *Three Intellectuals in Politics* (New York: Pantheon, 1960), 133–84.

Jones, Alun. *The Life and Opinions of T. E. Hulme* (Boston: Beacon Press, 1960).

Julius, Anthony. *T. S. Eliot, Anti-Semitism, and Literary Form* (Cambridge

University Press, 1995).
Kadlec, David. "Pound, *BLAST*, and Syndicalism," *ELH* 60 (Winter 1993): 1015–31.
Kenner, Hugh. *Wyndham Lewis* (Norfolk, Conn.: New Directions, 1954).
Klein, Scott W. *The Fictions of James Joyce and Wyndham Lewis: Monsters of Nature and Design* (Cambridge University Press, 1994).
Lawton, Anna, ed. *Russian Futurism through its Manifestos, 1912–1928*, trans. Lawton and Herbert Eagle (Ithaca: Cornell University Press, 1988).
Ledger, Sally, and Scott McCracken, eds. *Cultural Politics at the Fin de Siècle* (Cambridge University Press, 1995).
Leighten, Patricia. *Re-Ordering the Universe: Picasso and Anarchism, 1897–1914.* (Princeton University Press, 1989).
Levenson, Michael. *A Genealogy of Modernism: A Study of English Literary Doctrine 1908–1922* (Cambridge University Press, 1984).
Modernism and the Fate of Individuality: Character and Novelistic Form from Conrad to Woolf (Cambridge University Press, 1991).
Lewis, Wyndham. *The Apes of God* (1930; Santa Barbara: Black Sparrow, 1984).
Blasting and Bombardiering (1937; New York: Riverrun, 1982).
The Childermass (London: Methuen & Co, 1928).
The Complete Wild Body, ed. Bernard Lafourcade (Santa Barbara: Black Sparrow, 1982).
Creatures of Habit and Creatures of Change: Essays on Art, Literature and Society 1914–1956, ed. Paul Edwards (Santa Rosa: Black Sparrow, 1989).
Hitler (London: Chatto & Windus, 1931).
The Letters of Wyndham Lewis, ed. W. K. Rose (Norfolk, Conn.: New Directions, 1963).
"The Strange Actor," *The New Statesman* 22 (1 March 1924): 474–76; rpt. Lewis, *Creatures of Habit and Creatures of Change: Essays on Art, Literature and Society 1914–1956*, ed. Paul Edwards (Santa Rosa: Black Sparrow, 1989), 89–95.
Time and Western Man, ed. Paul Edwards (1927; Santa Rosa: Black Sparrow, 1993).
Loewenstein, Andrea Freud. "The Molten Column Within: Wyndham Lewis," in *Loathsome Jews and Engulfing Women: Metaphors of Projection in the Works of Wyndham Lewis, Charles Williams, and Graham Greene* (New York University Press, 1993), 119–87.
Lyon, Janet. "Militant Discourse, Strange Bedfellows: Suffragettes and Vorticists before the War," *differences: A Journal of Feminist Cultural Studies* 4 (1992): 100–33.
"Women Demonstrating Modernism," *Discourse* 17.2 (Winter 1994–1995): 6–25.
MacDougall, Hugh A. *Racial Myth in English History: Trojans, Teutons, and Anglo-Saxons* (Hanover: University Press of New England, 1982).
Mackay, Jane and Pat Thane. "The Englishwoman," in *Englishness: Politics and Culture 1880–1920*, ed. Robert Colls and Philip Dodd (London: Croom

Helm, 1986), 191–229.

Marcus, Jane, ed. *Suffrage and the Pankhursts* (London: Routledge, 1987).

Marinetti, F. T. Marinetti: *Selected Writings*, ed. R.W. Flint, trans. Flint and Arthur A. Coppotelli (New York: Farrar, Straus and Giroux, 1972).

Martin, Wallace. The New Age *Under Orage: Chapters in English Cultural History* (New York: Barnes & Noble, 1967).

Meyers, Jeffrey. *The Enemy: A Biography of Wyndham Lewis* (1980; Boston: Routledge & Kegan Paul, 1982).

Michel, Walter. "'Inferior Religions,' the Wild Bod(ies), and the Early Stories," *Wyndham Lewis Annual 1994*, ed. Paul Edwards (Bath: Wyndham Lewis Society / Bath College of Higher Education): 15–23.

Morrison, Paul. *The Poetics of Fascism: Ezra Pound, T. S. Eliot, Paul de Man* (Oxford University Press, 1996).

Morrisson, Mark. "Marketing British Modernism: *The Egoist* and Counter-Public Spheres," *Twentieth Century Literature* 43.4 (Winter 1997): 439–69.

"The Myth of the Whole: Ford's *English Review*, the *Mercure de France*, and Early British Modernism," *ELH* 63 (1996): 513–33.

Mosse, George. *Fallen Soldiers: Reshaping the Memory of the World Wars* (Oxford University Press, 1990).

The Image of Man: The Creation of Modern Masculinity (Oxford University Press, 1996).

Nationalism and Sexuality: Middle-Class Morality and Sexual Norms in Modern Europe (Madison: University of Wisconsin Press, 1985).

"The Political Culture of Italian Futurism," *Confronting the Nation: Jewish and Western Nationalism* (Hanover, NH: Brandeis University Press, 1993), 91–105.

"Two World Wars and the Myth of the War Experience," *Journal of Contemporary History* 21 (1986): 491–513.

Munton, Alan. "'Imputing Noxiousness': Aggression and Mutilation in Recent Lewis Criticism," *Wyndham Lewis Annual 1997*, ed. Paul Edwards (Bath: Wyndham Lewis Society, 1997): 5–20.

"Wyndham Lewis: War and Aggression," in *Wyndham Lewis and the Art of Modern War*, ed. David Peters Corbett (Cambridge University Press, 1998), 14–37.

Nairn, Tom. *The Break-up of Britain: Crisis and Neo-Nationalism* (London: Verso, 1977).

Nath, Michael. "Wyndham Lewis: A Review of the Thersitean Mode," *Wyndham Lewis Annual 1994*, ed. Paul Edwards (Bath: Wyndham Lewis Society / Bath College of Higher Education, 1994): 10–14.

Nevinson, Christopher. *Paint and Prejudice* (New York: Harcourt Brace, 1938).

Nolan, Emer. *James Joyce and Nationalism* (New York: Routledge, 1994).

Normand, Tom. "Wyndham Lewis, the Anti-War War Artist," in *Wyndham Lewis and the Art of Modern War*, ed. David Peters Corbett (Cambridge University Press, 1998), 38–57.

Wyndham Lewis the Artist: Holding the Mirror Up to Politics (Cambridge University

Press, 1992).
North, Michael. *The Political Aesthetic of Yeats, Eliot, and Pound* (Cambridge University Press, 1991).
O'Keeffe, Paul. "Afterword," in Lewis, *Tarr: The 1918 Version*, ed. O'Keeffe (Santa Barbara: Black Sparrow, 1990), 361–82.
Peppin, Brigid. *Helen Saunders 1885–1963* (Oxford: Ashmolean Museum/Graves Art Gallery, 1996).
Peppis, Paul. "Anti-Individualism and the Fictions of National Character in Wyndham Lewis's *Tarr*," *Twentieth Century Literature* 40 (Summer 1994): 226–55.
"Thinking Race in the *Avant Guerre: Typological Negotiations in Ford and Stein*," *Yale Journal of Criticism* 10.11 (1997): 371–95.
Perloff, Marjorie. *The Futurist Moment: Avant-Garde, Avant Guerre, and the Language of Rupture* (University of Chicago Press, 1986).
Phillips, Kathy. *Virginia Woolf against Empire* (Knoxville: University of Tennessee Press, 1994).
Poggioli, Renato. *Theory of the Avant-Garde*, trans. Gerald Fitzgerald (1962; Cambridge, Mass.: Harvard University Press, 1968).
Quinton, A. M. "Social Thought in Britain," in *The Twentieth Century Mind: History, Ideas, and Literature in Britain*, 3 vols. ed. C. B. Cox and A. E. Dyson (Oxford University Press, 1972), 1: 113–35.
Rabaté, Jean-Michel. "Joyce the Egoist," *Modernism/Modernity* 4.3 (September 1997): 45–65.
Rado, Lisa, ed. *Rereading Modernism: New Directions in Feminist Criticism* (New York: Garland, 1994).
Rainey, Lawrence. "The Creation of the Avant-Garde: F. T. Marinetti and Ezra Pound," *Modernism/Modernity* 1 (September 1994): 195–219.
Redman, Tim. *Ezra Pound and Italian Fascism* (Cambridge University Press, 1991).
Regan, Stephen. "W. B. Yeats and Irish Cultural Politics," in *Cultural Politics at the Fin de Siècle*, ed. Sally Ledger and Scott McCracken (Cambridge University Press, 1995), 66–84.
Robinson, Alan. *Symbol to Vortex: Poetry, Painting, Ideas, 1885–1914* (New York: St. Martins, 1985).
Rose, Jonathan. *The Edwardian Temperament, 1895–1919* (Athens: Ohio University Press, 1986).
Said, Edward W. *Culture and Imperialism* (New York: Knopf, 1994).
Schorske, Carl. *Fin-de-Siècle Vienna* (New York: Knopf, 1980).
Scott, Bonnie Kime. *Refiguring Modernism*, 2 vols., vol. 2, *The Women of 1928* (Bloomington: Indiana University Press, 1995).
Seton-Watson, Christopher. *Italy from Liberalism to Fascism 1870–1925* (London: Methuen, 1967).
Shannon, Richard. *The Crisis of Imperialism 1865–1915* (London: Paladin, 1974).
Shaw, George Bernard. *The Collected Works of Bernard Shaw*, 30 vols. (New York: Wm. H. Wise & Co., 1930–32).

Shell, Marc. *Children of the Earth: Literature, Politics, Nationhood* (Oxford University Press, 1993).

Sherry, Vincent. "Anatomy of Folly: Wyndham Lewis, the Body Politic, and Comedy," *Modernism/Modernity* 4.II (April 1997): 121–38.

Ezra Pound, Wyndham Lewis and Radical Modernism (Oxford University Press, 1993).

Smith, Dennis. "Englishness and the Liberal Inheritance After 1886," in *Englishness: Politics and Culture 1880–1920*, ed. Robert Colls and Philip Dodd (London: Croom Helm, 1986), 254–82.

Soffer, Reba N. "New Elitism: Social Psychology in Prewar England," *The Journal of British Studies* 8.II (May 1969): 111–30.

"The Revolution in English Social Thought, 1880–1914," *American Historical Review* 75.VII (December 1970): 1938–64.

Sonn, Richard. *Anarchism and Cultural Politics in Fin de Siècle France* (Lincoln: University of Nebraska Press, 1989)

Stevenson, John. *The Pelican Social History of Britain: British Society 1914–1945* (New York: Penguin, 1984).

Stocking, George W., Jr. *Race, Culture, and Evolution: Essays in the History of Anthropology*, 2nd. edn. (1968; University of Chicago Press, 1982).

"The Turn-of-the-Century Concept of Race," *Modernism/Modernity* 1 (January 1994): 4–16.

Symons, Julian. "Friends of the Enemy: Reassessing the Uncomfortable Art of Wyndham Lewis," *TLS* (10 July 1992): 16–17.

Taylor, Joshua C., ed. *Futurism* (New York: Museum of Modern Art, 1961).

Thacker, Andrew. "Dora Marsden and *The Egoist*: 'Our War Is With Words,'" *English Literature in Transition: 1880–1920* 36: II (1993): 179–96.

Thatcher, David S. *Nietzsche in England, 1890–1914: The Growth of a Reputation* (University of Toronto Press, 1970).

Theweleit, Klaus. *Male Fantasies*, vol. 2, *Male Bodies: Psychoanalyzing the White Terror*, trans. Erica Carter, Chris Turner, and Stephen Conway (Minneapolis: University of Minnesota Press, 1989).

Thompson, David M. "Calling in the Realists: The Reputation and Revision of Lawrence's *Sons and Lovers*," *Novel* (Spring 1994): 233–56.

Thornton, Weldon. *The Antimodernism of Joyce's* Portrait of the Artist as a Young Man (Syracuse University Press, 1994).

Tickner, Lisa. "Men's Work? Masculinity and Modernism," *differences: A Journal of Feminist Cultural Studies* 4.III (1992): 1–37.

The Spectacle of Women: Imagery of the Suffrage Campaign 1907–1914 (University of Chicago Press, 1988).

Torgovnick, Marianna. *Gone Primitive: Savage Intellects, Modern Lives* (University of Chicago Press, 1990).

Tratner, Michael. *Modernism and Mass Politics: Joyce, Woolf, Eliot, Yeats* (Stanford University Press, 1995).

Turner, John. "British Politics and the Great War," in *Britain and the First World War*, ed. Turner (London: Unwin Hyman, 1988), 121–24.

ed. *Britain and the First World War* (London: Unwin Hyman, 1988).
von Hallberg, Robert. "Libertarian Imagism," *Modernism/Modernity* 2 (April 1993): 63–79.
Wagner, Geoffrey. *Wyndham Lewis: A Portrait of the Artist as the Enemy* (New Haven: Yale University Press, 1957).
Webb, R. K. *Modern England From the Eighteenth Century to the Present* (New York: Harper & Row, 1968).
Wees, William C. *Vorticism and the English Avant-Garde* (University of Toronto Press, 1972).
Weir, David. *Anarchy and Culture: The Aesthetic Politics of Modernism* (Amherst: University of Massachusetts Press, 1997).
Williams, Raymond. *The Politics of Modernism* (London: Verso, 1989).
Wohl, Robert. *The Generation of 1914* (Cambridge Mass.: Harvard University Press, 1979).
Wragg, David A. "Aggression, Aesthetics, Modernity: Wyndham Lewis and the Fate of Art," in *Wyndham Lewis and the Art of Modern War*, ed. David Peters Corbett (Cambridge University Press, 1998), 181–210.

Index